The Search

THE SEARCH

Information Gathering for the Mass Media

Lauren Kessler
Duncan McDonald

School of Journalism
University of Oregon

Previously published in a first edition as
Uncovering the News:
A Journalist's Search for Information

Wadsworth Publishing Company
Belmont, California
A Division of Wadsworth, Inc.

Communications Editor: Kris Clerkin
Editorial Assistant: Nancy Spellman
Production Editor: Vicki Friedberg
Designer: Kaelin Chappell
Print Buyer: Randy Hurst
Permissions Editor: Jeanne Bosschart
Copy Editor: Tom Briggs
Compositor: G & S Typesetters, Inc.
Cover Design: Nancy Brescia
Printer: Malloy Lithographing

Figures 4.8 and 4.15 are from the *Legal Resource Index* and are reprinted with permission of 1991 Information Access Company.

Figure 4.16 is reprinted with permission of the American Psychological Association, publisher of *Psychological Abstracts* and the PsycINFO Database. Copyright © 1967–1991 by the American Psychological Association.

This book is printed on acid-free recycled paper that meets Environmental Protection Agency Standards.

1 2 3 4 5 6 7 8 9 10—96 95 94 93 92

Library of Congress Cataloging-in-Publication Data

Kessler, Lauren.
    The search : information gathering for the mass media / Lauren Kessler, Duncan McDonald.
      p. cm.
    Substantially rev. ed. of: Uncovering the news. c1987.
    Includes bibliographical references and index.
    ISBN 0-534-16278-9
    1. Mass media—Research—Methodology. 2. Mass media—Authorship.
I. McDonald, Duncan, 1945– . II. Kessler, Lauren. Uncovering the news. III. Title.
P91.3.K45 1992
028.7'08'8097—dc20   91-13843

To the memory of Barbara W. Tuchman,
who used her extraordinary information-gathering
skills to bring the past to life.

Contents

Preface

The search for information is a quest for meaning and understanding. It is a demanding, critical process that forms the foundation for all messages of the mass media. In preparing these messages, media professionals are both hunters and gatherers. They follow trails, evaluate clues, stalk the most promising material and collect their findings.

When their search is finished, serious writing can begin.

The Search is a guide and mentor for the information gatherer. It is an outgrowth of our first information-gathering book, *Uncovering the News*. In the five years since the publication of that work, we have been struck by the rapid development of college courses in research and information gathering by journalism, mass communications and English programs. It is compelling recognition that both the student and professional must have a solid understanding of search strategies and of information evaluation before any meaningful writing can take place. At the same time, we have realized that the first title of our work focused too narrowly on "the news" and all that implies. In fact, our focus has always been broader—and deeper. Our growing information society has indeed broken away from its "news-editorial" tether.

In building on the work of *Uncovering the News*, *The Search* operates on the assumption that depth, detail and context are achievable goals in any media task. Reference works, indexes, periodicals of all stripes, official documents and interviews form the basis for inquiry; that investigation, which corroborates information from identified sources, forms a natural outline for media writing, whether that be an in-depth magazine article or a public service advertising campaign.

Seasoned information gatherers are not often fooled. They understand the range of information sources and their relative worth. However, these professionals don't harbor illusions about the completeness of their information and writing. Pressures of time, space and competition all interfere with polished work. A well-crafted media message balances these pressures against the strength of its information foundation. *The Search* provides an examination and analysis of information-gathering strategies that will help the media writer go forward with confidence and resolve.

Readers of *Uncovering the News* will note some significant additions to *The Search*.

First, we have added two "master searches" that are developed, by chapter themes, throughout the book. These searches, using contemporary public policy topics, provide an in-depth look at how we really acquire and evaluate information. We have added a chapter on interviewing, a common information-gathering technique, as well as one on the beginning stages of writing—when we move from information organization to information presentation to a specified audience.

Finally, in this expanded text, we have compiled a glossary of sources that should be a quick reference for the information gatherer.

In preparing this book, we have benefited from the counsel and selfless help of these dedicated librarians at the University of Oregon: Sara Brownmiller, Rod Christensen, Paul Frantz, Dennis Hyatt, Ruth South and Tom Stave. It is altogether appropriate that these skilled professionals would be such valuable allies in producing a book to help the information gatherer. Our experience with them is a testimonial that librarians should be a primary source in any media project. We would also like to thank the following reviewers for their thoughtful comments: Karen Christy, Bowling Green State University; John Clogston, Michigan State University; Steve Greene, San Jose State University; Barbara Hartung, San Diego State University; and Don Shaw, University of North Carolina. Unfortunately it is impossible to list the many media professionals who have offered thoughts and direction for *The Search*. However, we are buoyed by their continuing desire to uncover a process that will lead them to truth and certainty.

We hope *The Search* will be a helpful source to you as well!

Lauren Kessler
Duncan McDonald
Eugene, Oregon

Mass Media Searchers

The media surround us.

We awaken to the clock radio, scan the morning newspaper over a cup of coffee, leaf through a magazine while waiting for an appointment, relax in front of the television set after a hard day and gaze at the movie screen on Saturday night. We seek and sample the media's diversity every day. With each form, with each medium, we try to satisfy a different need. Because the forms vary so widely—from a classified ad to an episode of "L.A. Law," from an eye-in-the-sky traffic report to "Friday, the 13th, Part 32"—it is easy to forget the one similarity that overwhelms all the differences: information.

Information is at the heart of all media messages. The newspaper reporter dogs its trail. The broadcast journalist pursues it. The magazine writer ferrets it out. The advertising copywriter and public relations specialist search for it. All need information before they can construct their messages, be they investigative stories or beer commercials. Of course, the messages differ; the forms and styles vary; the purposes are not the same. But at the core is information. And at the core of every media writer's job is information gathering.

The searchers

Newspaper, television and radio newswriters are constantly ravenous for information. They need it quickly to supply the daily, or sometimes hourly, demands of their medium. They need it to provide the "quick information fix" most of their audience is looking for: a few words, a few paragraphs that alert us to the important incidents of the day. These journalists exist on the front line, racing to the scene—from a fire around the corner to an uprising halfway around the world—to uncover information, mold it into the format their medium demands, and transmit it to a waiting public.

They ask: "What happened?" "When?" "Where?" "How?" In pursuit of the answers, they may dash to the scene or to the nearest reference book; they may call an expert or an electronic database. They are in a hurry, but they find that gathering the information generally takes at least twice as long as preparing it for presentation.

Some broadcast and print journalists specialize in analytical, in-depth work. They attempt to answer the "why" behind the story by delving into issues and exploring the meaning of events and actions. They want to put "quick information fix" news in context so the public can better understand it and learn from it.

These journalists are prodigious information gatherers. They make use of people, documents and institutions as they cast their net widely for all relevant material. They know the riches of the library and the virtually untapped wealth of government documents. They know how to locate experts who don't just have impressive-sounding titles but have solid, reliable information.

Other media writers, such as advertising copywriters and public relations specialists, aim to persuade us. Donate to a charity. Try a new shampoo. Practice safe sex. They offer words and images that attempt to shake us up, prod us out of old habits and help us establish new ones. To do this, they need information, for the more generally informed people are, the more information they expect when trying to come to a decision.

These persuaders need information about the product, service or cause they will represent. What is it? How does it work? What's new or different? What's the benefit to the consumer or others? To construct powerful messages, they need information about the competition. To construct targeted messages, they need information about us, the people to whom the messages will be directed.

They are information hounds, tapping into business and finance databases, studying census data and reviewing scientific studies. They are also active information creators, designing and carrying out their own studies, conducting target group interviews and commissioning surveys.

The tradition of information gathering

Information gathering takes up more of the media writer's time than any other activity. Whether attending meetings, reading reports, checking documents or interviewing experts, media writers are always on the trail of accurate information—and have been since the press's earliest days. Consider the long and rich tradition of journalistic information gathering in this country:

▶ Journalists have long acted as the public's *eyes and ears*, attending governmental sessions, committee hearings, conferences and events on the public's behalf. Today C-SPAN's cameras bring the proceedings of both the U.S. House and Senate into our homes. But the tradition began more than 175 years ago when one early newspaper, the *National Intelligencer*, gained prominence by specializing in congressional information gathering. Each day Congress was in session, the *National Intelligencer*'s two publisher-editors were in the gallery listening and taking notes. In those days before Minicams and tape recorders, the two newspapermen depended on the then-exotic skill of shorthand to capture debate and discussion. The result was accurate, sometimes verbatim accounts of legislative action that were quoted extensively in the young nation's other newspapers.

▶ Journalists have long specialized in *eyewitness* accounts, gathering information while it unfolded and communicating it with immediacy and drama. Long before the legendary Walter Cronkite covered the first thrilling NASA liftoffs, long before the equally legendary Edward R. Murrow reported the bombing of London during World War II, information-hungry journalists were on the scene telling audiences what they saw. Consider the account from this journalist, who covered a New York City fire in 1835:

Just came from the scene. From Wall Street to Hanover Square, and from the Merchant's Exchange to the East River, all on fire. About

300 stores burned, and burning down—probably five millions of property lost. About 1000 merchants ruined, and several Insurance Companies gone. . . .

Good God! in one night we have lost the whole amount for which the nation is ready to go to war with France!

▶ Journalists have long acted as *detectives*, digging up information that others would rather have kept hidden from public view. In 1990 a Washington, D.C., television reporter shocked the nation with a story about racially motivated inequities in reporting the results of drug tests for NFL athletes. A hundred years earlier, another young reporter shocked her readers with an exposé based on solid detective work. Elizabeth Cochrane ("Nelly Bly"), on assignment for the New York *World*, went undercover to report on the ghastly conditions at a state insane asylum. In the 1970s two young Washington, D.C., reporters helped change history by digging into events surrounding the break-in at the Watergate office complex. In the early years of this century, another detective-reporter, Upton Sinclair, also helped change history when he wrote about unsanitary conditions in the meat packing industry in his classic novel *The Jungle*.

▶ Journalists have a long tradition of acting as serious *researchers*, painstakingly documenting important stories by following paper trails, conducting solid interviews and piecing together evidence. A team of *Time* magazine reporters delved into America's toxic waste problem by studying government and corporate documents, commissioning opinion polls, conducting on-site inspections and interviewing hundreds of sources. In the 1970s and 1980s, the dogged investigator Seymour Hersh broke a number of significant stories—including the Vietnam War's My Lai massacre and former President Richard Nixon's fall from power—through exhaustive research. But these impressive modern-day information gatherers were merely following in the footsteps of journalistic researchers like Ida Tarbell, one of the original muckrakers for *McClure's*, a turn-of-the-century magazine. Tarbell's meticulous research exposed the unfair business practices of John D. Rockefeller and his Standard Oil Company.

▶ Media writers in the fields of advertising and public relations have long track records as *data hounds*, commissioning surveys, ordering studies, culling existing research, using government-generated statistics and supporting an array of pollsters and rating services. The wealth of information they have gathered— from the first unsophisticated Nielsen ratings and Gallup surveys of the 1950s to the refined demographic and psychographic data of the 1990s—has made it possible to pinpoint, understand and reach specific audiences with targeted messages.

Information gathering in the information age

We live in an information age in which more people than ever before are involved in creating, collecting, analyzing and disseminating information. The federal government alone employs more than 700,000 people whose primary job is to gather and evaluate information. Virtually every corporation, institution, agency, foundation, association, city and school district in the nation employs information specialists who create and help control the flow of information. The U.S. Government Printing Office, the largest publisher in the world, produces more than 50,000 informational books, brochures, pamphlets and documents each year.

We don't just live in an information age; we live amid an information glut. In a society so saturated with data, facts and opinions, the media writer's job is more challenging than ever. Information hunting is both easier and more difficult today than it has ever been before.

The sheer volume of data means today's media writer need never be at a loss for information and need never be dependent on a single source. Consider the controversy over the presence of the pesticide Alar in apples and apple products. Because of the volume of information generated by government and private groups, a public relations spokesperson for an apple growers' association or citizens' action group would not have to use exhaustive investigative techniques to locate information. The Department of Agriculture issued reports. Scientists at various research centers conducted experiments and issued reports. Powerful lobbying groups on both sides expressed opinions. Food industry representatives offered comments. Amid the riches of this information, the conscientious media writer could evaluate, question, probe and finally piece together a meaningful report based on numerous sources.

But the sheer volume of information also makes information gathering more difficult and more daunting. With so many documents to examine, people to interview, facts to evaluate and opinions to balance, the task of information gathering sometimes swells to herculean proportions. But it's not just the quantity of information that can be daunting; it's the problem of assessing its quality as well.

That's because the information age is also the age of specialization, in which few people understand the "big picture" and many know only minuscule parts. Those who know its parts are isolated from one another and reinforce their isolation by creating a special language, or jargon, that only they and their colleagues can understand. The media writer, often not truly an expert in anything, must attempt not only to understand the information generated by these legions of specialists but also to try to draw together the facts into a coherent whole. To deal with all these specialists and their reports, documents and opinions, the journalist must become a scrupulous researcher and a master translator.

This information age is also the age of digitization and computer storage of information, which brings with it both benefits and problems. As more and more information—from vital government documents to daily stock exchange reports—becomes available through electronic libraries (databases), media writers may find that they can gather information more quickly and efficiently. Without leaving their offices, they can tap into electronic storehouses of information and extract in minutes data that might otherwise have taken them hours, days or even weeks to gather. Those who work far from the country's few information capitals can research just as thoroughly as their big-city colleagues. Geography makes no difference in the era of computerized information.

But computerization of information may also make the media writer's job more difficult, for with the new technology comes additional costs. Tapping into databases takes both money and skill. Media organizations have to budget funds either for new hardware and software, on-site experts and staff training or for outside search experts.

There is also the nagging fear that computerized information is easier to hide from view, easier to tamper with and simpler to destroy than piles of papers and documents. If information can be obscured, altered or zapped out of existence by a keystroke or two, digitization can have its dark side.

For better *and* for worse, the information age presents a new, tougher set of challenges for those who work in the media. To meet these challenges, media writers need to appreciate the scope of available information and learn how to tap into its vastness. They need to know what's out there and how to get it—quickly, efficiently and confidently.

Welcome to *The Search*

Because information gathering is the skill basic to *all* varieties of mass communication, you are about to read an entire book devoted to its practice. Whether your career goals include print or broadcast reporting, advertising or publications, the strategies, skills and information presented in this book will be vital to your work.

In the next 11 chapters you will learn how the basic strategy of information gathering operates and how to apply that strategy to researching in general libraries, specialty libraries and electronic databases. You will learn how to find experts and how to conduct productive interviews with them; how to extract information from governments, institutions and businesses; how to locate and make use of alternative sources of information; how to judge the credibility of the information you have; and how to structure information to prepare for the writing process. You will also read about some of the legal and ethical questions that concern information gatherers.

To enable you to track the information-gathering process and actually see it work, we have created two "master searches" that we will return to at the end of each chapter. After you read the material in each chapter, you will immediately see it applied to these ongoing projects. For the searches, we've chosen a social concern with broad public policy implications—domestic violence—and a health concern with important cultural and psychological overtones—weight-loss fads. These subjects will be our entree into the vast world of public information.

When we delve into the question of domestic violence, we will be looking for information on child abuse and neglect, spousal abuse and marital rape. These are serious crimes about which much data have been gathered, many reports, documents and stories have been written, and countless experts have expressed opinions. As we follow the information trail, it may help for you to imagine yourself as the media writer you would someday like to be. Those with an interest in news reporting for print or broadcast can think of themselves as being in pursuit of a timely story; for example, the trial of a child or spouse abuser. Those who see themselves as in-depth analytical writers might imagine they are gathering information for a lengthy story, multipart series or documentary on why domestic violence is so prevalent in our society. Those considering careers in advertising might imagine that they have been hired by a social service agency (a battered spouse hot line or a treatment center for child abusers, for example) to increase awareness and use of the service. Those who someday see themselves as public relations practitioners might consider that they have been hired by a city, county or other municipality to produce a public service campaign on domestic violence, for example, how to recognize it and what to do about it.

Our second master search will focus on weight-loss fads and frauds, from stomach stapling, jaw wiring and liposuction to more mundane approaches like best-selling "Factor X" diet plans, over-the-counter pills and weight-loss clinics. Those with an interest in news reporting might cover the death of a local citizen for whom the "Last Chance Diet" actually was, or they might report on a local hospital that has just announced it will be entering the lucrative weight-loss market by offering a wide range of treatments and therapies. Those with an inclination toward in-depth analytical writing might imagine a series on our national obsession with slimness or a detailed investigation of the best way to lose weight. Those who envision careers as advertising copywriters or public relations writers might imagine being hired by the American Medical Association or American Dietetic Association. In this scenario their job might be to develop an information or public service campaign exploding diet myths and promoting lifelong eating habits that lead to health and permanent weight control.

Focusing on your special interest will help you remember that information gathering is the central skill for all media writers, regardless of the form or purpose of their message. Let's begin the search process with a look at the most fundamental technique of all—developing a search strategy.

2

Developing and Using Search Strategies

"Gather all information that could be remotely apropos."

—fortune cookie message

There you are, assignment in hand. Lurking close by are assorted demons who can thwart your information search: Time. Detail. Context. Newness. And of course, confusion. Energy and dedication will help you overcome these hurdles, but you will surely stumble if you don't have a plan. That's what this chapter is about—developing a search strategy and using it effectively.

Effective searches begin with properly targeted questions. The same questions can become important components of a strategy or plan. For example:

1. What do I *think* I want to know?
2. What are the expected issues in my search?
3. What are the expected results of my search?
4. What sources could contribute to my search?
5. Where do I find all this information?
6. How is the needed information cataloged, indexed or otherwise stored?

These are not casual questions. They form the foundation of any search, regardless of its complexity. Let's examine these questions as we create strategies for the two master searches discussed in Chapter 1.

What (and how much) do I need to know? Assessing your information needs

Very few searches are open-ended. You almost always have a goal in mind for your information pursuits, from a simple detail for a brief news story to a list of experts for a magazine feature proposal to statistics for the foundation of a public service advertising campaign. Assessing your needs—the goals of your search—will help you define the characteristics of that search.

The amount and depth of required information are directly related to the type of sources you will consult. For example, "quick-burst" sources such as encyclopedias, dictionaries, almanacs, directories and chronologies can provide immediate answers to focused questions. These sources can point you to brief summaries of facts, to bodies of statistics and also to people and institutions with answers. Let's turn to the domestic violence search and frame a narrow question that can be answered with a single source: Has the number of child abuse cases in the United States been increasing?

This question obviously seeks a number, which can be found quickly in a source that dispenses short summaries or statistics. Your strategy here would be to locate an up-to-date, well-indexed source that will provide a quick answer to your query. An almanac—a concise compilation of facts and figures—could be helpful.

For this quick response we would choose an almanac of statistics— the Census Bureau's annual *Statistical Abstract of the United States*. (At this point, you're no doubt asking, "How was I supposed to know that?" Well, this is part of learning about the information-gathering environment. You ask a specific question, narrow the focus of your source to a statistical compendium and then identify the appropriate almanac from a host of choices. To help you in this process, we have compiled annotated lists of useful reference sources in the Glossary of Sources, beginning on page 209. In addition, you'll soon see, especially after Chapter 3, "Discovering the Library," what your most common research sources are.) Using the *Statistical Abstract* is not that difficult, despite the fact that it contains thousands of tables of numbers, because it is so well-indexed. (We'll discuss how to use indexes later in this chapter.)

A search of the *Abstract*'s index takes us to this heading: *Child Abuse, neglect*. It reveals two tables of data that are shocking and tragic: Since 1978, the number of child abuse reports per 1,000 population has increased by an average of 10 percent annually. Those numbers become even more alarming in a dispassionate table of figures that breaks down the abuse, nationally and regionally, according to minor maltreatment, major injuries, emotional maltreatment and sexual abuse.

You found an answer to your question *within one minute* of picking up the appropriate "one-stop" reference.

Suppose, on the other hand, you are looking for a broad range of recent research and data on child abuse. Then you'll be engaging in a *multilevel search* for which your quick-fix search actually laid the foundation. The data you discovered in the *Statistical Abstract* listed a source in addition to the Census Bureau: the American Humane Association of Denver, which prepared a national report on child abuse. This demonstrates an important search axiom: Every topic has a home. That is, there are academic, governmental and associational hosts for most information. In the case of child abuse the academic disciplines that would be interested in the topic are sociology, psychology, education and law, to name a few. As a protector of individual and group welfare, the government is vitally interested in child abuse. At the state and local levels there may be variants of agencies like Children and Family Services; at the federal level many agencies and commissions are part of the Department of Health and Human Services. Numerous associations that provide research, clearinghouse and lobbying efforts have responded to the growing problem of child abuse and neglect. Tapping into these sources usually begins with the same type of consultation that answered one simple question in a brief search: In almost every case, directories and some type of encyclopedic reference work get you started.

In a multilevel search the move from a one-stop reference source usually takes this path:

▶ **Step 1:** "Tips" from directories, almanacs and the like point you to other sources. A brief search for a statistic on child abuse also yielded information about the American Humane Association. What other groups might help expand our field of inquiry? One basic directory—*The Encyclopedia of Associations*—leads you to Childhelp USA, which operates a National Child Abuse hot line (1-800-4-A-Child), and the National Center on Child Abuse, which operates the Clearinghouse on Child Abuse and Neglect and which has an electronic database of information available. That's a good start, and you can add to this part of the search later.

▶ **Step 2:** Next, you want to determine the *range of published material* (books, periodicals, special reports, etc.) that exists on your topic. This takes you to cataloged information, indexed and sometimes in abstract (summary) form. Book indexes today include the following forms: the venerable card catalog, microfiche, compact disc and even interactive database. Indexes also exist for a wide range of periodicals and government documents, from general to highly specialized. Learning what indexes exist, what they contain and when to use them is an important part of developing an effective search strategy. In the child abuse search, for example, you find that the *Social Science Index*, *Public Affairs Information Service Index* and *Sociological Abstracts*, along with the index to the federal *Monthly Catalog*, are good targets for your inquiry.

▶ **Step 3:** A third level of an extended search takes you to the bibliography, a published list of sources on a given topic. These bibliographies are sometimes annotated; that is, each source is briefly summarized and evaluated to help the information gatherer determine whether or not to pursue that source. This is usually a multidisciplinary contributor to your search, and it can be a valuable timesaver. As you are discovering, you can be led to many sources through directories and indexes; in this case a quick search of the *Bibliographic Index* would lead you to *Child Abuse and Neglect: An Annotated Bibliography* and *Violence in the Family: An Annotated Bibliography*. Although these bibliographies were created in an academic setting, governments and associations also provide effective lists or bibliographies on selected topics. For example, the U.S. Department of Education, through its Division of Adult Education and Literacy, offers a regularly revised bibliography on adult education and literacy resource materials. The *Bibliographic Index* and several federal government indexes (step 2) helped you track these sources.

▶ **Step 4:** Finding experts and appropriate spokespersons for background, commentary, opinion and detailed interviews is your next step. You have already surveyed the published field, and you are becoming more conversant with your topic. In the domestic violence search you have already become aware of associations and services that may have reliable people to help you with your topic.

After completing this process, you should be well-briefed on the scope of your topic and its relevant background. By evaluating what you already know about that topic, you can now identify issues that will help you increase your knowledge and broaden your perspective.

Focusing on issues and outcomes

Critical to the success of your search is setting boundaries for your topic and its associated questions. Let's turn to the weight-loss fad search to illustrate this. Let's assume that your search will attempt to target recent trends and the effects of such trends. This part of your strategy has you asking four questions:

1. What is the true focus of my search?
2. What are the key issues raised in this focus?
3. What specific questions might be answered during my search?
4. What categories of sources would be most helpful in addressing these issues and questions?

Setting your focus

If your search is too broad, chances are you won't even know where to begin, much less expect to meet your deadline! For example, you may wisely avoid tackling *all* types of weight-loss programs and their relative effectiveness and safety. Instead, you may want to investigate *why* the weight-loss industry is booming and *how* these services are being monitored and regulated. Rather than ending up with a lengthy listing of services, you now have a set boundary for your inquiry, which will provide vital context for an important physical, economic and cultural issue as well as a framework for your search. Setting a focus, then, helps you define not only what is really important for your search but what is manageable as well.

Defining key issues

If you focus on why great numbers of people are turning to weight-loss programs, you should be able to break down your search according to issues, or components. In this search our issues would be medical (dietary habits, current medical advice), cultural (social and psychological influences on how we "see" our bodies and the health effects of mass media images), and political (public policy response to this highly profitable industry and to health hazards). Obviously, selection of these issues guarantees you a more complicated, in-depth search; however, defining these issues and giving them a "home" also guarantees you a more complete organization of your findings.

Framing specific questions

These key issues now help you identify specific questions to answer. Here are some questions that are logically and directly connected to the focus you created for your search:

1. What are current dietary habits?
2. Are they significantly different from past habits?
3. Are we a more sedentary society today? If so, why?
4. What medical and cultural factors have been responsible for an increased use of weight-loss programs?
5. To what extent have our mass media influenced how we view our bodies and health?
6. How are people being protected (medically and financially) from unsafe and fraudulent practices?

This is not a complete list, of course. But at this point you should see the connection between your framework, issues and questions. We should point out, however, that focusing on issues and questions doesn't occur in an information vacuum. Focus does not result from guessing. You arrive at your focus after properly backgrounding yourself on your topic. That is part of the assessment of your information needs.

Identifying appropriate sources

Remembering the search axiom "Every topic has a home," you can now connect questions to potential sources: disciplines, institutions and people with serious interest in the issues we have framed. If the issue is nutrition and diet, you look to health-care sources. If the issue is lifestyles today, you could examine sociology, anthropology and leisure studies.

You review the research on why the nation's population is perceived as less physically fit than it was 40 years ago, or why households may operate under greater stress and with perhaps even less leisure time than they did 20 years ago. If you are concerned about media effects, examine sources that discuss the influence of media messages—advertising, news and entertainment—on how we perceive bodies and health and on how those media affect our perception of ourselves. You look, then, for sources dealing with media analysis and criticism.

Tapping into selected sources

As you'll discover in Chapter 3, most information is stored, cataloged and indexed in some fashion. As you begin your search to answer questions, you need to tap into the "access points" of your topic.

This begins with an investigation of indexes and citations that should lead you to a wide variety of sources—if you determine the proper keywords for your search. A keyword is a descriptive word (or words) that allows broader topics to be conveniently indexed; for example, as descriptors *violence* and *children* are too broad to help you quickly find sources dealing with child abuse. However, *abuse, child abuse, child neglect, family violence* and *crimes against children* are keywords that will help direct you to appropriate sources. In the weight-loss example good descriptors are *diet, reducing diets, diet therapy* and *nutrition*. Subtopics are *adverse effects, deception* and *misrepresentation*.

Keywords are not arbitrary and capricious labels meant to turn your "browsing" into a nightmarish journey through library catacombs. They are generally well-conceived access points to broader information. The selection of these access points is influenced by your ability to identify synonyms or related words. The early background research you do in setting boundaries for your topic always yields words and concepts that make your use of indexes more efficient. In addition, "brainstorming" related topics gives an added dimension to your search. A massive but helpful source of appropriate keywords is the *Library of Congress Subject Headings*, which has grown to three volumes and which adds 8,000 new headings annually. It's an excellent tool for reducing your search time and for narrowing your target.

Keywords are effective for any index. In addition, they are timesaving and moneysaving aids in computer searches, whether by interactive database or by passive compact disc technology.

Finding needed sources

All that remains now is the "simple" matter of tracking down the information you want to know. Consider sources as willing servants—all you have to do is learn how to summon them! Crucial to your development as an information gatherer is an ability to distinguish primary, or originating, sources from secondary ones. An in-depth article about the health hazards of some liquid diet plans in *Time* magazine may seem quite informative, but chances are most of its information is not primary—it's summarized and synthesized, borrowed from many original sources. Greater depth about specific hazards of three of the most popular liquid diets could be found, for example, in *The New England Journal of Medicine*. The entire research analysis that was the basis for the *Journal* article—funded through the National Institutes of Health—may be on file in the NIH and at various medical schools. The original report could be traced through various medical, scientific and governmental indexes as well.

Although we'll deal with sources in more depth in subsequent chapters, let's take a quick look at some categories and locations of sources. We will focus on the following:

- ▶ General, research and specialized libraries
- ▶ Governments
- ▶ Universities and research centers
- ▶ Associations
- ▶ Businesses
- ▶ Personal interviews

The library

Consider the library a warehouse, a repository that collects and catalogs information—but don't assume it is the *sole* holder of that information. A U.S. Senate hearing on fraudulent weight-loss schemes and on a lack of regulation by the Food and Drug Administration may well be in the library stacks (or on microfiche) in government document holdings, but the report of that hearing is also held by the superintendent of documents, federal government bookstores, several government agencies, researchers studying weight-loss fraud, and members of groups like the American Dietetic Association.

Nonetheless, a library—whether it is located in a university or in a hospital, a county courthouse or a state capitol—can be a treasure trove of reference materials, books, newspapers, magazines, specialized journals, microfilm, maps, records, videotapes and a host of documents. When you choose to work with libraries, you must master a strategy that quickly gets you to appropriate indexes and then to the published source itself. (Much more on this in Chapter 3.)

Government

Our federal government may be the world's most prolific publisher, but it is challenged by the output of regional, state and local governments. For example, the U.S. Department of Health and Human Services is the prime federal player in child abuse issues, but similar organizations exist at the state level (for example, Children's Services Division) and at the local level (for example, county welfare department). In the weight-loss fad/fraud search, you learn, through the use of a popular directory, that the U.S. Department of Agriculture operates a specialized library called the Food and Nutrition Information Center. You can be sure that smaller but similar organizations exist at lower government levels as well. Federal and state laws as well as local ordinances influence government enforcement agendas. To understand and evaluate the work and documents of these bodies, you first must comprehend their organization. Directories, almanacs, manuals and even organizational charts will help you. An important key here is to know your rights of access to public records and to meetings of government bodies. (We discuss this in the Appendix.)

Universities and research centers

Institutions of higher learning and of research in the sciences, social sciences and arts are rich resources for the information gatherer. The research output of university professors alone fills the pages of thousands of specialized journals annually, from the *Journal of Advertising Research* to the *Journal of Experimental Zoology*. When you have narrowed your search and set your focus, don't overlook the incredible range of expertise available at academic institutions. Free-standing research centers (institutes often separate from universities or a consortium of faculty from several universities) are generally productive sources as well. At least three excellent directories can point you toward a helpful source: *Research*

Centers Directory, Directory of Government Sponsored Research and *International Research Centers Directory.*

Associations

When you consider that the *Encyclopedia of Associations* lists more than 20,000 organizations, clubs and non-profit associations and that the *American Lobbyists Directory* lists almost 30,000 organizations represented by federal and state lobbyists, you begin to realize the battalion of information gatherers at your disposal. Add to that the thousands of other organizations represented in the *Directory of Newsletters,* and you have an army at your service. In the weight-loss search, for example, you find that the American Dietetic Association can provide reports, pamphlets, speeches, congressional testimony and newsletters about nutrition, diet, fads and frauds. Academics and researchers belong to associations as well. Perhaps the National Academy of Science and the Center for Science in the Public Interest would be helpful. (More on this in the discussion of experts in Chapter 8.)

Businesses

Whether large or small, businesses generate vast quantities of information and documents. Government takes an interest in some corporate activity, which in turn results in public reporting by many of these firms. Business is scrutinized by both the popular and the specialized press (one electronic database alone indexes and abstracts almost 1,000 business publications). Again, directories will tell you how businesses are organized, who runs them, what their product/service lines are and what their corporate affiliates are. Government agencies like the Securities and Exchange Commission (SEC), the Federal Trade Commission and state corporation commissions all maintain records on reports of business activity. A publicly held company (one that sells its stock to the public) must reveal its income, expenses, executive pay, pending lawsuits, financial problems and new discoveries that may affect the value of its stock. A company that sells a liquid diet formula, for example, must reveal any problems it is having with its product. Such information may not just be of interest to the SEC; it will also attract the attention of the Food and Drug Administration. As you can see, no source operates in an information vacuum.

Personal interviews

As you will see in Chapter 9, on the art and craft of the interview, people are often excellent sources of anecdotes, information and opinion. The effective searcher will use the interview in several ways: to quickly find other good sources of information; to verify information obtained from other sources; to give context to a complicated or controversial topic; and to reflect peoples' expertise and experiences in order to help understand their opinions and views. People can be the glue that binds the information you obtain from disparate sources; they can inject life and meaning into that information.

Keeping your strategies flexible

A search strategy should never be set in concrete. A search's direction and emphasis will change because of new information and leads that develop as that search progresses. To ignore new "clues" is shortsighted at best. Let's return to our example of the domestic violence search, focusing on the increase in child abuse cases nationwide. The initial strategy was to look at statistics and try to determine trends and causes. In this quick-burst strategy we find numbers. They tell us that such abuse is increasing at an alarming rate. We get curious (naturally—we're after information!) and we want to know *why* these numbers are soaring.

As we turn our attention to "why," our focus shifts from collectors and custodians of statistics to disciplines and institutions dealing with law, social work and psychology, among others. Having changed our focus, we now must set new boundaries for that inquiry and look for appropriate sources.

As you analyze your topic and try to determine the best strategy to discover needed information, remember that a helpful ally of a good plan is curiosity—lots of it. Good information gatherers constantly ask "Why?" and "What does this mean?" To that, you should add, "What is missing here?" Like the topics and questions you develop, curiosity can be focused. If you remain curious about an issue you believe you have defined well, that could be a signal that your work isn't finished yet.

What *more* needs to be uncovered?

Remain curious, but stay in focus!

A search checklist

If you can satisfactorily answer the following questions, it is a good indication that you have the foundation for an effective search plan. This is by no means an exhaustive list, but it's all you need to get started!

1. **Have I properly outlined what I want to know?**
   ▶ Does this outline suggest an order of importance for the information I am seeking?

2. **What issues are within the boundaries I've created for this search?**
   ▶ Are these issues consistent with the focus I have created?

3. **Is it possible at this early stage to identify possible results or outcomes of my search?**
   ▶ Do these outcomes suggest a particular hypothesis or focus?

4. **Am I ready to list specific questions that will address the issues I have raised?**
   ▶ Do any of my questions expand the original boundaries of my search?

5. **Are my issues and questions clear enough that I can identify appropriate sources?**
   ▶ Will the range of my sources give both breadth and depth to my search?

6. **Do I have a plan for finding the information I need?**
   ▶ Have I discovered the basic information and publication outlets for my sources?

3

Discovering the Library

I'm sort of a library nut," says Barry Mitzman, KCTS-TV (Seattle) public affairs programming director. "When I'm on a story, the library has traditionally been my first stop. I have never worked on a story that didn't involve good, solid time in the library."

"The library is full of phenomenal sources," says St. Paul (Minn.) *Pioneer Press* features editor Ken Doctor. "I go there to get story ideas, then background, then potential contacts."

Still, a disturbing number of media writers rarely cross the threshold of their public libraries. Why?

No time, they say. Deadline pressure, they insist. Too tedious, they contend. Sometimes they're right; most often they're not. The real problem is not time, pressure or tedium. The real problem is they don't know their way around a library.

In fact, going to a nearby library to research an issue may be a far more efficient and accurate way to gather information than sitting in the office making phone calls. Especially when time is tight, it makes sense to go straight to the reputable, documented, verifiable sources found in the library.

But some media professionals don't understand what a library has to offer. They think of it as an overheated mausoleum stacked high with outdated books and esoteric journals, a place useful to students and scholars but irrelevant to harried media writers.

Many media writers don't understand how to use a library. They've never learned how libraries are organized. With the exception of referring to the card catalog (or analogous online system) and leafing through the *Readers' Guide to Periodical Literature*, they don't know how to find information in the library. Because they know neither the system nor its guides, they see library research as tedious and time-consuming. In a way, they're right, for even the simplest search can become interminable when the researcher doesn't know where to go. But that's the researcher's fault, not the library's. Library research can be conducted quickly and efficiently if you understand what materials are housed in a library and how to find them.

What's in the library?

Not all libraries are created equal, but they all contain at least some of the same kinds of materials, and almost all depend on the same organizational system (the Library of Congress numbering system). A major university library may have 7 million volumes and the local branch of your city library barely 7,000, but they have much more in common than you might think. This chapter offers an introduction and general description of the library's riches. The Glossary of Sources, which begins on p. 209, lists and details numerous specific sources.

Common sources

Whether you're stalking the library at Harvard or at Humboldt State, you will find these categories of sources relevant to journalistic research:

Reference material

From multinational directories of corporations to the local phone book, reference materials can be invaluable to the researcher. So numerous that they could fill a modest library by themselves, reference books bring together facts from a vast number of sources and arrange them for quick and convenient use. Although they cover thousands of different topics, all reference books serve the information hunter in two basic ways: Either they answer questions directly—as with dictionaries, encyclopedias and almanacs—or they point to where the answers can be found—as with directories and indexes. Some reference tools do a little of both.

Published books

Media writers wanting background information, historical context, authoritative details or additional sources can turn to their library's collection of published books. Books can provide the depth and documentation needed for certain projects. Books can help generate questions as well as point the researcher toward experts in the field (for example, the author of the book and those cited by the author). But books do have their limits for mass media researchers. Unlike reference tools, they may require a hefty investment in time. The information they include may be too specialized or may be expressed in the often mind-boggling jargon of experts. Because most books take years to be written, an additional year to be published and another six months to find their way to library shelves, they don't contain recent information or breaking news. On the other hand, they often contain excellent bibliographies.

Magazines and journals

Periodicals are so numerous and so varied that few library collections do more than scratch the surface. Media writers can use magazines to provide relatively quick reference and background material and to help locate additional sources and other experts. Magazines are generally *secondary sources*; that is, they provide secondhand information on a subject. A *Time* magazine article might discuss studies conducted on fasting or stomach-stapling as ways to lose weight. But what you're getting is the *Time* magazine writer's secondhand version of what the research showed. To get at the *primary source*, you must look at the medical journal in which the study appeared (and, if necessary, talk to the researchers themselves).

Periodicals can be classified according to their intended audience. Consumer magazines are directed to general, non-expert readers; trade or business publications are published for those involved in specific occupations (from dentists to dog groomers); scholarly, academic or research journals are published by and for experts in a variety of disciplines in the humanities, social sciences and hard sciences.

Newspapers

Newspapers can be indispensable sources of both timely and historical information. Media writers who need to research a current issue, trace the origins of a problem or compile a list of potential sources will find newspapers helpful. University libraries carry local, regional, national and international newspapers. City libraries often have decent collections of regional papers. A newspaper's in-house library, sometimes called a *morgue* because it houses already published ("dead") stories, is also a source. Remember, like magazines, newspapers are almost always secondary sources and thus should be used for gathering background information and pinpointing primary sources, such as the documents and people cited in the article.

Government documents

The U.S. government is a major source of information for the researcher. Almost 1,400 special libraries across the country—many housed within major university libraries—select titles from more than 25,000 new publications issued annually by the government. Both the scope and depth of this information are awesome. Government-gathered statistical data—from the number of salmon caught commercially to the number of children inoculated against measles—can be vital to the media writer. Agency and department reports, congressional committee hearings, debate transcripts, and thousands of pamphlets, newsletters and journals all provide media writers with detailed, specialized information they probably could not find elsewhere. A host of special catalogs and indexes are available to help the researcher locate material (see Chapter 4).

Special collections

Many libraries, especially university libraries, contain special collections of material. The letters, notes and diaries of noteworthy people as well as the papers relating to particular businesses or organizations may be housed in a special collection. Maps and charts may constitute another special collection. Audiotapes (as in oral history collections) and videotapes (as in special collections of televised news coverage) are also common. These collections generally have their own catalogs and guides—and sometimes even their own librarians.

Common technologies

Not so long ago, everything housed in a library was made of paper. But bound volumes take up a great deal of shelf space, and paper, especially the kind used in today's books and magazines, deteriorates quickly (and taxes a natural resource that takes decades to replenish). With an eye toward libraries' diminishing space, information producers are taking increasing advantage of other technologies. In any moderately well-stocked library, you will encounter the following:

Paper

Most books and current magazines and journals exist in libraries as sheaves of paper bound between covers. Most reference works exist as paper (although some exist in other forms as well). But many other items that started out as paper—from the soon-to-be-anachronistic card catalog to bound volumes of newspapers and periodicals—are now being handled in other forms.

Microfilm

In a growing number of libraries, all but the most recent issues of many newspapers and periodicals are stored on microfilm. Researchers may bemoan having to place rolls of microfilm in special readers, twirl knobs and focus lenses, but microfilm is a reasonable solution to space and deterioration problems. In some cases microfilm may even be easier to use. Compare the quick access to the microfilmed *Magazine Index* with the much more time-consuming bound volumes of the *Readers' Guide to Periodical Literature*.

Microfiche

One sheet of microfiche, no bigger than a large index card, can preserve scores of pages in miniature form. This makes microfiche well-suited for storing large volumes like catalogs and indexes. Fiche is faster and easier to use than its older cousin, microfilm, and is a popular library technology. Some information services, like *Newsbank*, an extremely useful newspaper research tool, could not exist without microfiche.

CD/ROM

In case you're wondering, CD/ROM stands for compact disc/read-only memory. This recent technology allows for the storage of staggering sums of information—82,000 typewritten pages on a single disk—that can be called up quickly via computer terminal. You can't ask complex questions of the data or arrange it in fancy ways as you can when you use an interactive database, but you can get basic information very quickly. Because the technology is much less expensive than interactive databases, it is also much more common in today's libraries. With CD/ROM, it's no longer necessary to peruse the shelves for the right volume, leaf through it to find the right page and then scan the page. With a few keystrokes, you're there. The *Social Science Index* and *Public Affairs Information Service* are two of the major research tools now on CD/ROM.

Online computer databases

At some of the computer terminals that are slowly replacing study tables in today's libraries, you can access interactive databases that allow you (or a trained librarian) to search through vast stores of information with a few well-placed keystrokes. Imagine that you're looking for a book your home library doesn't own. A computer database can locate it almost anywhere in the country within seconds. Databases covering just about any information-generating human activity you can imagine can be accessed at most of today's larger libraries (see Chapter 5).

How to find facts fast

Library research for those on a strict deadline entails finding facts fast. Knowing what reference tools are out there is a big step toward becoming an intelligent, effective information gatherer. But there are so many tools that it helps to have a guide. Mary Barton and Marion Bell's *Reference Books: A Brief Guide* is an inexpensive paperback that should be on every media writer's shelf. Eugene P. Sheehy's *Guide to Reference Books*, with its recent supplements, is also helpful. Reference librarians, superior sources themselves, can direct you where you need to go. In a crunch they are often available by phone to help you find facts fast.

When looking for information on the run, you should keep two things in mind. First, *one-step* guides will be your fastest sources. These are reference works, such as dictionaries and almanacs, that themselves contain the answers to your questions. In contrast, *two-step* or *multistep* guides point toward the information, thus sending you on at least one more search before you find the answer.

Second, thinking like an indexer will speed your trip through all kinds of reference tools, both single-step and multistep. It is important to remember that *your* name for something may not be the same as the name used by the people who wrote and organized the reference tool. For example, you may run to an encyclopedia looking for an entry under *domestic violence*. You find nothing. Does that mean the encyclopedia contains no information on this important subject? Probably not. More likely, it means those who organized the encyclopedia are using a different subject heading—*family violence, household violence* or *conjugal violence*, for example.

How do you know this? A book called the *Library of Congress Subject Headings*, which we mentioned in Chapter 2, gives you insight into how librarians and indexers think. You look up your word for the topic to discover if it's also the word the Library of Congress system uses. If not, you will find a list of alternatives. Spending a minute or two with this book can save you hours of frustration.

What follows are descriptions of a number of *types* of reference books relevant to the journalistic researcher. Remember that descriptions of specific one-step reference titles can be found in the Glossary of Sources beginning on p. 209.

Encyclopedias

Encyclopedias contain brief, readable articles on a profusion of subjects. Many of the articles are written by specialists and contain illustrations and bibliographies. Although media writers must go far beyond these volumes for detailed, up-to-date *primary* information, they can gain a quick overview of the subject by reading an entry in one of the leading encyclopedias, such as *The Encyclopaedia Britannica* or the *Encyclopedia Americana*.

The most overlooked feature of encyclopedias is the index volume, the researcher's guide to the entries in the other books. Another underused volume is the yearbook, the encyclopedia's annual update.

Almanacs

Imagine you're researching a story on violence and American politics, and you want to know which U.S. elected officials have been assassinated since 1865. Or suppose you're working on a public service advertising campaign to curb high-school dropout rates in your state. For context you want to know what the compulsory school attendance law is for each state.

You can get answers to these and countless other questions—from who won last year's pingpong championships to who heads the Republic of Vanuatu—in those wonderful compendia of important and trivial facts known as almanacs. *The World Almanac* and *Information Please Almanac* are both highly readable. *Statistical Abstracts of the United States* is a gold mine. Organized by subject with excellent indexes, these and other almanacs can be referred to quickly and easily.

Dictionaries

All good writers know how important dictionaries are to achieving precise, accurate use of the language. This is one reference tool they keep handy and use often. But few writers know of the existence of a wide range of specialty dictionaries that can help them decipher the "foreign languages," or jargon, used in various unfamiliar fields, from architecture to zoology.

Atlases

Maps can answer questions no other reference tool can; for example, what highway connects two towns? Where is the county line? They can present complex ideas in simple, graphic terms; for example, how do the countries of the world compare according to the average caloric intake of their population? Atlases are compilations of maps with related explanatory material, perhaps the most beautiful and revered of which is *The Times Atlas of the World*.

Biographical dictionaries and indexes

There are countless reasons why a media writer might need accurate biographical information quickly. Fortunately, biographical sources abound, from the general—*Current Biography*—to the specific—*American Men and Women of Science*. In fact, there are so many that they have their own guide, *Biographical Dictionaries and Related Work*, which lists nearly 5,000 works. With this kind of coverage, the person you're looking for need hardly be a household word.

Directories

Everyone knows the phone book is an excellent guide to the people and businesses of a community. It is the single most-used reference tool by professional and amateur information gatherers alike. But how many know of the thousands of other useful directories housed in the library? So many guides to businesses, industries, associations and professions are published that they have their own guide, *Directories in Print*.

Books of miscellany

Sometimes a writer just has to know when the first plastic license plate was made or who holds the rope-skipping record or which state celebrates Mecklenberg Day. These and other odd questions can be answered by referring to specialty books of curious facts, like the famous *Guinness Book of World Records*.

How to find books and articles

Finding a book or an article is a simple research task for those who understand indexes. Information hunters gain easy access to the wealth of information in the library and elsewhere by using these guides. There's no mystery to an index, but there are two tricks to using these tools efficiently. The first seems so obvious that it's amazing how many novice researchers forget it: Know what the index indexes. Two hours spent poring over the *Readers' Guide to Periodical Literature* trying to locate a listing for an article published in a research journal is two hours wasted. The *Readers' Guide* indexes general and consumer publications, not research journals. Every index contains a master list of what it indexes, almost always located in the front of the volume. Check it first.

The second trick is one you already know: Think like an indexer. Remember that your keyword may not be the index's keyword. Make a habit of checking the *Library of Congress Subject Headings* before you use an unfamiliar index.

What follows are brief descriptions of some of the major indexes commonly used by journalistic information gatherers.

Books

Depending on the size and technological advancement of your library, the familiar card catalog, the more modern microfiche or the increasingly popular online catalog will guide you to all the books housed in that library. Whether you're looking for a particular book by its title or author or just hunting for anything on a given subject, these are your primary guides. Each listing offers basic information about the book (title, author, publisher, number of pages, etc.) and the shelf number assigned to that book.

Suppose you consult the catalog and find that your library doesn't have many (or any) books on the subject you are researching. You know there must be books out there—books you can borrow through interlibrary loan—but you don't know titles or authors. What can you do?

The first place to look is the OCLC (Online Computer Library Center), a network of public, university and government libraries that have agreed to share resources. All books owned by all 6,000-plus participating libraries are in a central database that you can access through your library's computer. If the book is anywhere in the system, it can be found quickly and, in most cases, borrowed. The OCLC computer is simple to use and is generally accessible to library patrons.

Another place to look is the yearly three-volume reference set *Books in Print*. The author, title and subject volumes list almost all books in print in the United States. A final place to look for information about a book not in your home library is *The National Union Catalog* (*NUC*). This is a massive index of all the books housed in the nation's premier depository, the Library of Congress. Because there are more than 80 million books listed in the *NUC*, the number of volumes is daunting. But if you have a fair idea of when the book was published, the *NUC*, with its five-year cumulative indexes, is not difficult to use.

Newspapers

Many newspapers have their own indexes. Major papers like the New York *Times* have professionally compiled, frequently updated indexes that are easy to use. Other newspapers—perhaps your hometown paper is an example—are haphazardly and inconsistently indexed. These guides are generally available only at the libraries in or close to the city of publication. The *National Newspaper Index*, on microfilm and available at most libraries, offers a helpful combined index for the New York *Times*, *Wall Street Journal*, *Christian Science Monitor*, Los Angeles *Times* and Washington *Post*. Ultimately, however, the usefulness of any of these indexes depends on whether your library subscribes to the papers indexed. If it does, you will undoubtedly find them in microfilm form, and not in newsprint editions.

Newsbank, a monthly service that both indexes (in book form) and provides articles (on microfiche) from more than 100 of the nation's larger dailies and some 300 other newspapers, is an extremely useful tool. *Newsbank*'s indexers look for articles covering particular subject areas like education, employment, environment and business. The index, a popular one in libraries, points the researcher to the location of the article on a microfiche card.

Periodicals

Periodicals are well-served by an array of indexes, from those covering broad, general-interest magazines to those devoted to highly specialized journals. The best place to look for references to consumer magazines—from the familiar *Time* and *Newsweek* to the more exotic *Archery World*—is *Magazine Index*, a subject and author guide that indexes more than 400 consumer magazines. Magazines reflecting all varieties of opinions, interests and demographic groups are included. The *Magazine Index* exists in three forms. Microfilm, already set up on its own machine, contains the cumulative index for the most current three- to four-years' worth of magazines and is wonderfully simple to use. Microfiche, which covers a number of years prior to the microfilm index, is also available at many libraries. Online, the *Magazine Index* is available as a computer database, covering 1959–1970 and 1973–present.

Consumer magazines are also indexed in the venerable *Readers' Guide to Periodical Literature*, which used to be the mainstay of general periodical research. But, because the *Magazine Index* indexes every publication covered by the *Readers' Guide*—plus hundreds more—and is, in its cumulative forms, much easier to use, the *Readers' Guide* should not be the researcher's first choice. For historical research the *Readers' Guide* goes back to 1900 while *Poole's Index to Periodical Literature* indexes periodicals published from 1802–1908.

Specialty indexes abound. Whatever you're researching—from postmodern architecture to postnasal drip—specialty indexes, dictionaries and encyclopedias will guide the way. Some are one-step tools, like *Thomas' Register of American Manufacturers*, which allows you to track down the manufacturer of most any U.S. product. Others are two-step guides, like the *Public Affairs and Information Service Bulletin*, which directs you to periodicals, pamphlets and documents related to public policy and social issues. Specialty sources, arranged by subject, are listed in the Glossary of Sources beginning on p. 209.

The search

Reading about the riches of the library is one thing; making use of them is another. Good researchers not only know what's available, they also work from a search strategy to help them use the library's resources efficiently. We discussed search strategy in the previous chapter. When applying it to your work in the library, remember these two key elements:

► The search goes from the general to the specific, using reference guides such as encyclopedias and almanacs to build a basic core of knowledge, then moving to more detailed, specialized sources to deepen knowledge.

► The search is based on specific questions formulated at the start of the search and throughout the process as new information is discovered. These questions help break the search into its component parts and guide the researcher to specialized, primary material.

Now let's put these strategies to work and see how some of the sources discussed in this chapter can contribute to gathering information for our two master searches.

Domestic violence

Because you first want an overview, a general essay that lays the groundwork and explains concepts, an encyclopedia is a good first step. But before you peruse the index volume, make a quick stop at the *Library of Congress Subject Headings.* There you will find that *family violence, household violence, abused parents, child abuse* and *conjugal violence* are all possible listings for this broad subject.

The index volume of *Encyclopedia Americana,* for example, has no listing under *domestic violence,* but under *child abuse* you find three references, two of which contain just the kind of overview material you are looking for. In the first essay two medical doctors define child abuse, offer statistics, discuss types of abuse and abusers and detail current treatment options. This is good background information. It also points you to other sources: the two doctors, who are national experts in the field, and the several books they recommend at the end of the essay. In the second essay an attorney summarizes U.S. statutes concerning cruelty to children and in domestic relations. This legal overview may turn out to be important. And you now have the name of a national legal expert, the lawyer who wrote the article.

Another kind of background is purely statistical. Perhaps *Statistical Abstracts of the United States* can help you understand the current extent of domestic violence and assess whether it has increased over the years. One by one, you look up all the Library of Congress headings in the index. Only one pans out, *child abuse,* but here you've struck gold with two important and disturbing tables of figures. The first, which documents child abuse and neglect cases by region for the past eight years, tells you that cases have more than doubled during this time. A second table details all reported child maltreatment cases by type of maltreatment (sexual, emotional, physical, etc.) and by the age of the child, the caretaker and the abuser, respectively. The same table also gives you information about some of the characteristics of the families involved in these cases.

You're getting some good material on the child abuse question, but at the same time you're starting to worry about the lack of information regarding other aspects of the domestic violence issue. It's time to check books and periodicals. Here the *family violence* heading begins to pan out. In the library's catalog system you find more than two dozen entries under this heading, from a book on the history of family violence in 18th-century France to several recent psychological works with promising titles like *The Many Faces of Family Violence*. Under *child abuse* you find 88 books, including three bibliographies that will point you to an even greater diversity of sources. Under *conjugal violence* you find a dozen entries, including bibliographies on *domestic violence* and *spouse abuse*.

In the *Magazine Index*, *family violence* again yields promising results. Here you find references to scores of articles in popular magazines, from an article on battered women in *American Health* to a feature on violent couples published in *Vogue*. You find citations for articles dealing with the causes, history, legal aspects and prevention of domestic violence as well as a variety of personal narratives. These secondary sources will provide good background, as well as pointing you toward primary sources (the experts themselves, the abused or their abusers). In the *National Newspaper Index* you discover that the nation's top five dailies have published dozens of articles on family violence, child abuse, wife abuse and abused parents. *Newsbank* enlarges your newspaper search to include more than 400 U.S. newspapers. Here you find a variety of listings for articles on family violence and child abuse, ranging from stories about individual court cases to broad social and political analyses.

Now is the time to delve into specialty sources. Reasoning that domestic violence is both a social and a psychological issue, you decide to refer to both pertinent indexes: *Sociological Abstracts* and *Psychological Abstracts*. In *Sociological Abstracts* under *family violence*, you find many listings, including studies of marital violence and sibling violence (a category you hadn't come across before), interviews with persons in domestic violence shelters and reports from domestic violence treatment programs. Reading the abstracts, you discover a reference to a periodical called the *Journal of Family Violence*. You will want to check to see if your library subscribes to this publication. Thumbing through back issues to look both for relevant studies and for experts to interview may be quite useful. In *Psychological Abstracts* you find hundreds of listings under the broad category of *family relations*. You see by their titles that a number of them deal directly with domestic violence.

You're now ready to find the books and the magazine and journal articles you've identified and begin your serious reading on the subject of domestic violence. But before you disappear into the stacks, you check one last source, the *Encyclopedia of Associations*. Here, under *domestic violence*, you find 12 listings for organizations specializing in this issue, from Batterers Anonymous to the National Coalition Against Domestic Violence. The reference book gives you the address and phone number of the organization along with the director's name, a list of publications put out by the group and other helpful information. You add this information to your growing list of experts to contact.

Diet fads and frauds

Because this is such a diverse topic, including everything from grapefruit binges to complex surgical procedures, a stop at the *Library of Congress Subject Headings* is again a must before you venture forth. *Diet fads* gets you nowhere as a subject heading; neither does *dietary fads*. These phrases are probably too value-laden. You cast your net more broadly with *diets*. There will be relevant material here, but the category is quite broad, directing you to all manner of healthful nutritional plans, particularly those related to curing or ameliorating diseases. You narrow the category by looking under *reducing diets*. This seems a good place to find information about various eating plans—low-fat, low-sugar, high-carbohydrate—but it will not lead you to material on nondietary schemes. You brainstorm the problem and come up with *reducing, weight loss* and *weight control* as headings. You find that any of these will work.

Given the scope of the subject, you reason that it is unlikely you will find a general essay in an encyclopedia. You're right. Instead, you use your various subject headings to search through the library's book collection. Here you find more than 100 entries, ranging from books that themselves appear to promote diet fads (e.g., *The Key to Lasting Slimness*) to serious treatises on the psychology and psychobiology of weight loss. A few minutes with the *Magazine Index* nets you a wealth of material. Amid the harrowing personal narratives ("How a Fat Cookie King Lost 100 lbs. Eating Popcorn"), you also find references to articles on stomach bubble devices, mouth guards and behavior therapy from reputable journals like *FDA Consumer* and *Mayo Clinic Nutrition Letter*.

Checking through the *National Newspaper Index* under *reducing diets*, you find references to articles on weight-reducing preparations, camps and clinics. One particular story catches your eye, "The Risks of Rapid Weight Loss Programs," published in the Washington *Post*. You jot down the reference, knowing that your library subscribes to the *Post* on microfilm. You're surprised to find a special listing just for articles published on one kind of diet, the liquid protein diet. The headlines of the articles reveal that this reducing scheme sometimes has fatal results. This looks like something you will want to pursue further. You note the citations.

In *Newsbank*, under the heading *weight loss*, you find a variety of stories related to both specific diet plans—Opti-fast, liquid protein, T-factor—and more general approaches like hypnosis and the use of thyroid hormones. (Remember, you can read these stories immediately by using *Newsbank*'s accompanying microfiche holdings.) You note a number of stories under the subheading *fraud allegations*. You will want to read these carefully; they may suggest that you expand your research into legal issues.

Moving to the specialty sources, you know that obsession with thinness and the fad dieting that often results has broad societal implications. Perhaps *Social Sciences Citation Index*, an international, multidisciplinary index to more than 1,000 social science journals, can help. Using the subject index, you try various keywords, including *weight loss* and *reducing*, and find references to a few promising studies in psychiatric and behavioral journals. In *Sociological Abstracts*, under *diet*, you find a reference to what might be a relevant social psychological study, "Weight Satisfaction and Dieting Behavior of College Students." You will want to pursue the psychological angle to dieting in *Psychological Abstracts* as well. And, before you leave the reference section of the library to find the books and periodicals you've noted, you check the *Encyclopedia of Associations* for leads. Here, under *weight*, *diet* and *overeaters* headings, you find 15 organizations, several of which (Diet Research Center, American Dietetic Association, Eating Disorders Research and Treatment Program) may be able to provide you with materials to read and experts to question.

The search is on!

4

Specialty Libraries

The conscientious and curmudgeonly editor I. F. Stone of *I. F. Stone's Weekly* always seemed to sniff out the tough stories other journalists missed: political duplicity, bureaucratic waste, military adventurism, racial inequities. From 1953 to 1971 he regularly exposed and documented government malfeasance in his renowned Washington, D.C., newsletter. Was he a supersleuth with inside connections? A dogged muckraker who spent the wee hours in dark alleys listening to the whispers of secret informants?

No. In fact, Stone didn't even consider himself an investigative reporter. Neither did he have a special pipeline to the government. Where did his consistently provocative material—material his contemporaries at the New York *Times* and Washington *Post* never seemed to have—come from? Government documents.

Because he had hearing difficulties, Stone developed the habit of reading transcripts of congressional hearings and committee meetings rather than attending them. He combed the *Congressional Record* daily and spent hours perusing other documents. One of his basic operating principles was: "A government always reveals a good deal, if you take the trouble to find out what it says." Stone took the trouble—and proved his principle week after week.

Stone didn't have to go to great lengths to get this revelatory information, for the documents he used (plus literally millions more) are easily accessible to any informed researcher. They are housed in more than a thousand special government documents libraries throughout the nation. This chapter will focus on what to expect from and how to use a government documents library as well as two other specialty libraries of particular interest to the journalistic researcher: the law library and the health sciences library.

The government documents library

These special libraries are excellent sources of information not only about the government itself, as I. F. Stone found, but also about the nation, its people and their numerous activities. What is perhaps most important to remember about federal government documents is their relevance to *local* and *regional* concerns. Our national government, through its many and far-flung agencies, gathers detailed information about the economic and political life of states and municipalities as well as sophisticated data about everything from crimes committed to bushels of corn grown. You need not be on the trail of a major political scandal or involved in a nationwide public information campaign to benefit from a brush with government documents.

Consider why government documents are such a vital source for the media writer:

▶ They are written, tangible evidence upon which a writer can base a story or a campaign—and defend it.

▶ They contain details that no single person could possibly know or remember.

▶ They cover a scope of activities far greater than the knowledge of any single person.

▶ They can contain such a variety of information from such a vast array of sources that it would take a researcher months to gather the same data.

▶ They sometimes contain verbatim accounts that could not be obtained unless the information gatherer was physically present.

▶ They may be issued at regular intervals, making historical comparisons possible without trusting to sometimes faulty memory.

For all their advantages, however, government documents are hardly neutral sources of information. They are compiled and written by people—people whose careers, egos, and political and economic aspirations may affect the character of a report. For example, when the chief of the Federal Aviation Administration (FAA) issued a public report concluding that "near midair collisions decreased by 50 percent over the past four and a half years," he made his agency (and himself) look good. But on the same day, consumer advocate Ralph Nader released a series of documents obtained through the Freedom of Information Act contradicting that claim. Reports from three of nine regions showed that more than 100 midair near misses were not counted in the FAA chief's report, because they were categorized under other headings, such as *operations errors.*

Bureaucrats, administrators and officials want to look good and need to justify their own existence. Committees, bureaus, divisions, agencies and departments want to look efficient and productive. Everyone likes to report progress. Everyone would like to report that problems don't exist, aren't as bad as we thought or are almost solved. Information gatherers need to develop and nourish a healthy skepticism that allows them to see the possible pitfalls of depending on information obtained through any single source, including government documents. Just because something is published and has the imprimatur of the U.S. government doesn't guarantee its complete accuracy. On the other hand, history has proved I. F. Stone right. The government does reveal much about itself, the nation and its people (even when it doesn't want or intend to) through its documents.

What are federal government documents?

Anything published by any agency of any branch of the federal government in whatever form for whatever purpose is considered a government document. Some documents, like a White House manual on how to efficiently manage office personnel, are designed for internal use but might be available to the public on request. Others, like the technical specifications for the Stealth Bomber, are classified "top secret" and are available only to those with high-level security clearance. (In 1989 more than 5 million government documents were so classified.) Still others, like a Department of Agriculture bulletin on backyard gardening, are created specifically for public distribution. Many documents don't fall into any of these categories but instead constitute an ongoing record of the activities of various arms of the government. Although not created specifically for the public, these documents are nonetheless readily available and are often of great public interest. Transcripts of congressional hearings and committee reports are examples.

With such an all-encompassing definition of what constitutes a government document, it is little wonder that the U.S. government is considered the world's largest publisher. Its yearly output includes books, magazines, newsletters, manuals, maps, charts, reports, studies, speeches, circulars, proceedings, proclamations, hearings, decisions, bills and laws—so many and so varied that no one really knows how many exist.

Where to find government documents

In the early 1800s, with an eye toward opening up the government's business to its citizens, Congress mandated that various documents be printed and distributed to institutions outside the federal establishment. By the 1850s this mandate had been translated into the Federal Depository Library Program, a national network of designated government documents storehouses. Today the network includes 50 regional depository libraries, which house every unclassified government publication received by the Government Printing Office and deemed of interest to the public. More than 1,300 other depository libraries, many of which are associated with universities or colleges, choose from among 25,000 new publications each year.

A depository library is the most convenient place to locate government documents. (Figure 4.1 lists all 50 regional depositories.) To locate other depositories in your area, call the regional library nearest you or refer to the *Directory of Government Documents Collections and Libraries*, a reference guide available at your local library that lists all libraries with significant government documents. The book includes thousands of private, corporate, public and academic libraries, briefly describing the documents collection held by each.

Suppose your nearby government documents library doesn't include the material you need. What do you do? It depends on why the material isn't there. If the document has been publicly disseminated but just doesn't happen to be part of your local library's collection, you can probably locate it through the regional depository. Ask your local documents librarian for assistance. If the document is unclassified but has not been routinely distributed within the depository system, you have these options:

1. Mail-order it from the Office of the Superintendent of Documents, U.S. Government Printing Office. Ask your documents librarian for assistance.

2. Buy it directly from the issuing agency.

3. Contact your congressional representative and ask him or her to send the document to you.

4. Locate the document using the Freedom of Information Act (see the Appendix).

Regardless of where the document resides, the first step is to identify it. Knowing its name and publication information is essential. But with literally millions of publications in existence, the task seems impossible. Fortunately, a number of excellent indexes come to the rescue.

How to find government documents

Because of their bulk, indexes to government documents may look intimidating. Actually, they are easy to use if you remember two things: what kinds of documents the particular index covers and what system it uses. Several of the common indexes are two-step tools. When you look up (or keypunch in) the subject you're after, you're presented with a list of relevant documents that you can then locate at the library. Other indexes involve three steps. The index gives you a number that refers to listings in a separate abstracts volume; then the abstracts volume lists the publication information you need to locate the document as well as a summary of the document itself. Three steps would seem more cumbersome than two, but in fact, the addition of the abstracts volume is a time-saver. With the help of the information contained in the abstract, you won't waste your time searching for a document that, while it may have sounded promising, does not deliver the information you need. Here are brief explanations of the 10 indexes most important to journalistic information gatherers. When you become familiar with these guides, the vast world of government documents will be open to you.

Figure 4.1.　*Federal Depository Library Program*

The Federal Depository Library Program provides government publications to designated libraries throughout the United States. The regional depository libraries listed below receive and retain at least one copy of nearly every federal government publication, either in printed or microfilm form, for use by the general public. These libraries provide reference services and interlibrary loans; however, they are *not* sales outlets. You may wish to ask your local library to contact a regional depository to help you locate specific publications, or you may contact the regional depository yourself. Remember that there are more than 1,300 other, smaller depository libraries.

Arkansas State Library
One Capitol Mall
Little Rock, AR 72201
(501) 371–2326

Auburn Univ. at
Montgomery Library
Documents Department
Montgomery, AL 36193
(205) 279–9110, ext. 253

Univ. of Alabama Library
Documents Dept.—Box S
University, AL 35486
(205) 348–7369

Dept. of Library, Archives
and Public Records
Third Floor—State Cap.
1700 West Washington
Phoenix, AZ 85007
(602) 255–4121

University of Arizona Lib.
Government Documents
Dept.
Tucson, AZ 85721
(602) 626–5233

California State Library
Govt. Publications Section
P.O. Box 2037
Sacramento, CA 95809
(916) 322–4572

Univ. of Colorado Lib.
Government Pub. Division
Campus Box 184
Boulder, CO 80309
(303) 492–8834

Denver Public Library
Govt. Pub. Department
1357 Broadway
Denver, CO 80203
(303) 571–2131

Connecticut State Library
Government Documents Unit
231 Capitol Avenue
Hartford, CT 06106
(203) 566–4971

Univ. of Florida Libraries
Library West
Documents Department
Gainesville, FL 32611
(904) 392–0367

Univ. of Georgia Libraries
Government Reference Dept.
Athens, GA 30602
(404) 542–8951

Univ. of Hawaii Library
Govt. Documents Collection
2550 The Mall
Honolulu, HI 96822
(808) 948–8230

Univ. of Idaho Library
Documents Section
Moscow, ID 83843
(208) 885–6344

Illinois State Library
Information Services Branch
Centennial Building
Springfield, IL 62706
(217) 782–5185

Indiana State Library
Serials Documents Section
140 North Senate Avenue
Indianapolis, IN 46204
(317) 232–3686

Univ. of Iowa Libraries
Govt. Documents
Department
Iowa City, IA 52242
(319) 353–3318

University of Kansas
Doc. Collect.—Spencer Lib.
Lawrence, KS 66045
(913) 864–4662

Univ. of Kentucky
Libraries
Govt. Pub. Department
Lexington, KY 40506
(606) 257–3139

Louisiana State
University
Middleton Library
Govt. Docs. Dept.
Baton Rouge, LA 70803
(504) 388–2570

Louisiana Technical Univ.
Library
Documents Department
Ruston, LA 71272
(318) 257–4962

University of Maine
Raymond H. Fogler Library
Tri-State Regional
Documents Depository
Orono, ME 04469
(207) 581–1680

University of Maryland
McKeldin Lib.—Doc. Div.
College Park, MD 20742
(301) 454–3034

Boston Public Library
Government Docs. Dept.
Boston, MA 02117
(617) 536–5400 ext. 226

Detroit Public Library
Sociology Department
5201 Woodward Avenue
Detroit, MI 48202
(313) 833–1409

Michigan State Library
P.O. Box 30007
Lansing, MI 48909
(517) 373-0640

University of Minnesota
Government Pubs. Division
409 Wilson Library
309 19th Avenue South
Minneapolis, MN 55455
(612) 373-7813

Univ. of Mississippi Lib.
Documents Department
University, MS 38677
(601) 232-5857

Univ. of Montana
Mansfield Library
Documents Division
Missoula, MT 59812
(406) 243-6700

Nebraska Library Comm.
Federal Documents
1420 P Street
Lincoln, NE 68508
(402) 471-2045
*(In cooperation with
University of Nebraska-
Lincoln)*

University of Nevada Lib.
Govt. Pub. Department
Reno, NV 89557
(702) 784-6579

Newark Public Library
5 Washington Street
Newark, NJ 07101
(201) 733-7812

**University of New
Mexico**
Zimmerman Library
Government Pub. Dept.
Albuquerque, NM 87131
(505) 277-5441

**New Mexico State
Library**
Reference Department
325 Don Gaspar Avenue
Santa Fe, NM 87501
(505) 827-2033, ext. 22

New York State Library
Empire State Plaza
Albany, NY 12230
(518) 474-5563

**University of North
  Carolina at Chapel Hill**
Wilson Library
BA/SS Documents Division
Chapel Hill, NC 27515
(919) 962-1321

**University of North
  Dakota**
Chester Fritz Library
Documents Department
Grand Forks, ND 58202
(701) 777-2617, ext. 27
*(In cooperation with North
Dakota State Univ.
Library)*

State Library of Ohio
Documents Department
65 South Front Street
Columbus, OH 43215
(614) 462-7051

**Oklahoma Dept. of
  Libraries**
Government Documents
200 NE 18th Street
Oklahoma City, OK 73105
(405) 521-2502

Oklahoma State Univ. Lib.
Documents Department
Stillwater, OK 74078
(405) 624-6546

Portland State Univ. Lib.
Documents Department
P.O. Box 1151
Portland, OR 97207
(503) 229-3673

State Library of Penn.
Government Pub. Section
P.O. Box 1601
Harrisburg, PA 17105
(717) 787-3752

Texas State Library
Public Services Department
P.O. Box 12927 —Cap. Sta.
Austin, TX 78753
(512) 471-2996

Texas Tech. Univ. Library
Govt. Documents
  Department
Lubbock, TX 79409
(806) 742-2268

Utah State University
Merrill Library, U.M.C. 30
Logan, UT 84322
(801) 750-2682

University of Virginia
Alderman Lib.—Public Doc.
Charlottesville, VA 22901
(804) 924-3133

Washington State Library
Documents Section
Olympia, WA 98504
(206) 753-4027

West Virginia Univ. Lib.
Documents Department
Morgantown, WV 26506
(304) 293-3640

**Milwaukee Public
  Library**
814 West Wisconsin
  Avenue
Milwaukee, WI 53233
(414) 278-3000

**St. Hist. Lib. of
  Wisconsin**
Government Pub. Section
816 State Street
Madison, WI 53706
(608) 262-4347

Wyoming State Library
Supreme Ct. & Library Bldg.
Cheyenne, WY 82002
(307) 777-6344

Monthly Catalog of U.S. Government Publications

First issued in 1895, later revamped in 1976 and now available both on CD/ROM and as an online database, the *Monthly Catalog* is the federal government's official index to all its publications. The only index that attempts (although unsuccessfully) to be inclusive, it covers documents issued by all three branches of the government.

The CD/ROM version, which covers 1976–present, is wonderfully easy to use. (But it is relatively expensive, so expect only larger libraries to have it.) Although you can search the *Monthly Catalog* using the title, report number, or author or classification number of the document you're after, most journalistic researchers will use a keyword as an access point. Remember the importance of the *Library of Congress Subject Headings* here. The government documents librarian can custom-tailor your search by helping you develop a strategy that allows the computer to use overlapping categories. Using the online database version of the *Monthly Catalog* (also from 1976 to present) involves the same procedures with one very important difference: It costs money (see Chapter 5).

The procedure for locating government documents prior to 1976 is more cumbersome because the book version of the *Monthly Catalog* exists in two parts. The first part consists of seven indexes (author, keyword, title, subject, report number, stock number, classification number) published monthly and cumulated annually. (Two cumulative subject indexes covering 1895–1899 and 1900–1971 can help you with historical research.) Most journalistic researchers will use the subject index. In the index each document is named but identified only by a number. That number will guide you to the second part of this research tool, the *Monthly Catalog* itself. Organized numerically and arranged sequentially, the *Monthly Catalog* entry for that number includes all the information you need about the document to either find it on the shelves or order it from the government.

Congressional Information Service Index

Compiled by a private firm with a reputation for excellence, the *CIS/Index* indexes and abstracts most documents generated by Congress, including House and Senate reports, special publications, executive reports and committee hearings. The index is issued monthly and cumulates first quarterly, then yearly, then every four or five years. The outstanding feature of the CIS system is that every document listed in the index is available on microfiche from the CIS. Libraries routinely order many of these documents; all others are available on request.

The *CIS/Index* is organized somewhat like the book version of the *Monthly Catalog*, with an alphabetically arranged index volume that references you to a listing in a numerically arranged abstracts volume. But the CIS indexing system is much broader and more sophisticated in its scope, permitting you to look for a document according to the subject of the document or hearings, the subject discussed by individual witnesses, names of authors, names of subcommittees, and official and popular names of bills and laws.

American Statistics Index

The *ASI* is the most comprehensive guide to statistical material from the federal government, including that amazing compendium, the census. (For international data the best place to look is the *Index to International Statistics*, a publication of the United Nations.) Published by CIS, it identifies, indexes and abstracts statistical publications from the executive and legislative branches and from other federal entities. More than 800 periodicals are included; some are available in depository libraries while others can be ordered through ASI Microfiche Library or CIS Periodicals on Microfiche. The *ASI* is published monthly and cumulates both quarterly and yearly. It is also available as an online database.

Like the *CIS/Index* or the book-version *Monthly Catalog*, the *ASI* has an alphabetically arranged index volume where the researcher can look up a document by its subject, name, category or title. (A report number index is numerically arranged.) Once again, the subject index is probably the handiest. The index listing identifies the document by name and gives it a number. The number guides you to a listing in the numerically arranged abstracts volume, where you can get the information you need to find the document in the library or to order it.

Index to U.S. Government Periodicals

Although this commercially produced reference tool indexes fewer than 200 of the government's thousands of periodicals, it is nonetheless a helpful guide because of its unusual scope. The choice of periodicals is eclectic, ranging from highly technical journals like *Cancer Treatment Reports* to non-technical magazines for specialized audiences like *Black*

News Digest. The publications are selected, writes the publisher, because they contain substantive articles of lasting research or reference value.

All publications indexed are listed on the inside cover of each volume, and those available in depository libraries are identified with large dots. Periodicals not in a library's collection may be available from the issuing agency or through Microfilming Corporation of America. Ordering information appears in the beginning pages of each volume.

Using this index is simple because it has no accompanying abstracts volume. The alphabetically arranged author and subject index is issued in quarterly volumes and annual accumulations (sometimes slow in coming). The researcher need only look up the subject or author to find a full citation for the article.

Government Reports, Announcements and Index

In 1970 the National Technical Information Service (NTIS) was established to simplify public access to scientific and technical reports produced by federal agencies and their contractors. An agency within the Department of Commerce, the NTIS is the central source for reports about U.S.-government-sponsored research in both the physical and social sciences. The NTIS currently has close to a million and a half titles, all of which are available for sale. Unlike many other government documents they are not distributed for free to depository libraries because the NTIS is obligated by law to recover its costs from users. The index to the NTIS's considerable holdings is the *GRA&I*.

Issued semimonthly, the *GRA&I* consists of both index and abstracts volumes. The index itself comes in four parts: subject/keyword (a two-volume set), contract/grant number (two volumes), personal author and corporate author. Using the *GRA&I* involves the familiar index-to-abstracts process. But in the *GRA&I* the item listed in the index is followed by not one but three sets of numbers. The first set of numbers is needed if you intend to order the document from the NTIS. The middle set guides you to the abstracts volume. The final set is a price code. The NTIS citations are also searchable online and using CD/ROM.

CIS U.S. Serial Set Index

The *Serial Set* is an excellent historical source for journalists interested in tracing the evolution of congressional action. A grab bag of documents from the House, Senate and various executive branch agencies, it contains more than 325,000 individual titles spanning 1789–1969. (The *Serial Set* is an ongoing publications series. After 1969 the *CIS/Index* or the *Monthly Catalog* will be your guides.) The congressional reports, manuals and directories, as well as annual reports from federal executive agencies, are bound into more than 14,000 separate *Serial Set* volumes. The key that unlocks these volumes is the *CIS U.S. Serial Set Index*.

The *Serial Set* is divided into 12 historical periods (covering as few as 10 or as many as 60 years), and each part contains a subject list index (two volumes) and a numerical list of documents. The items listed in the index are followed by a code that tells you where to locate the document in one of the *Serial Set* volumes.

Congressional Record Index

The *Congressional Record* (*CR*), issued daily when Congress is in session, is not, as many may think, a verbatim account of what is said on the floor of the House or Senate. In fact, one study found that 70 percent of what is in the *CR* was never uttered in Congress. Instead the *CR* reprints articles, editorials, book reviews, tributes and assorted trivia submitted by members of Congress—some of which can be both informative and revealing. The 30 percent that does represent congressional speeches, debate and discussion may or may not be published verbatim. By law, members of Congress are allowed to edit their remarks—presumably for grammar and construction, not substance—before they reach the *CR*.

The *CR* has four sections: the proceedings of the House, the proceedings of the Senate, extensions of remarks and a daily digest including highlights of the legislative day, summaries of each chamber's action and a schedule for the next day. Each of the four sections—identified by the letters *H*(ouse), *S*(enate), *E*(xtensions) and *D*(igest)—is paged continuously and separately during each session of Congress. This daily record has a fortnightly index, the *Congressional Record Index*. The hardbound volume of the *CR*, normally two to three sessions behind in publication, is accompanied by its own master index.

The fortnightly index comes in two parts: a subject/name index to proceedings and debates and a history of bills/resolutions index arranged by chamber and according to bill or resolution number. The index listing will give you a letter—*H*, *S*, *E* or *D*—to guide you to one of the *CR*'s four parts and a number indicating the page containing the item you want.

CIS Federal Register Index

The *Federal Register* (*FR*) is a key information source for those concerned with government regulatory activities and programs. Issued every working day, it consists of the rules, proposed rules, notices and announcements emanating from all federal regulatory agencies. These documents provide public notice of actions, meetings, reports and decisions for all areas of regulatory concern. Cumulatively, the *FR* documents both the substance of and the reasoning behind regulatory actions. (Evidence of the reasoning behind the regulations has been required only since the Carter administration.) In 1984 the CIS began publishing the *CIS Federal Register Index*, your guide to the *FR*.

The index, issued weekly and cumulated both quarterly and semiannually, has four sections: a subject/name index, an index using the U.S. code of Federal Regulations number, an index using the federal agency docket number and a chronological listing by agency. Chances are good that you will be using the subject/name index. Each listing gives you all the information you need to find the document in the appropriate *FR* volume.

Weekly Compilation of Presidential Documents and Public Papers of the Presidents of the United States

For those who want comprehensive documentation of presidential actions and activities without setting foot in Washington, D.C., there are no better sources than the *Weekly Compilation* and the *Public Papers*. Issued weekly since 1965, the *Weekly Compilation* includes the texts of proclamations, executive orders, addresses, remarks, communications to Congress, letters, messages, telegrams and transcripts of news conferences. Acts approved by the president, nominations submitted to the Senate and a checklist of White House press releases are included as supplemental materials. These are all *public* documents. Presidents often donate their *private* papers to specific libraries, or they may establish libraries of their own. Since the Carter administration the *Public Papers* has been a cumulative, permanently bound republication of the *Weekly Compilation*. Before 1977 it was an edited version of this material.

The indexes to both these sources are easy to use. In the back of each issue of the *Weekly Compilation* are subject and name cumulative indexes to that issue and previous issues up to the end of the quarter. Quarterly, semiannual and annual indexes are issued separately. The index gives you the *Weekly Compilation* volume and page number, making short work of your research. The index for the *Public Papers* is in the back of each volume and is arranged either by subject or by category. Like the index in the back of any book, it cites the page within that volume where material can be found.

International documents

Although many U.S. federal documents deal with international concerns, a journalistic researcher might also want to delve into the wealth of documents produced by the United Nations and its 18 specialized agencies (UNESCO and WHO, who example). *UNDOC*, dating back to 1979 and cumulated annually on microfiche, is the most comprehensive list of documents and publications produced by the main U.N. agencies and the regional commissions. The *UNESCO List of Documents and Publications* will guide you to reports, proceedings, publications and articles in periodicals put out by or under the sponsorship of UNESCO. As previously mentioned, the *Index to International Statistics* provides a master guide to English-language statistical publications of major international intergovernmental organizations like the United Nations and the Organization of American States. (For additional information on government sources, see the listings in the Glossary of Sources beginning on p. 209.)

The law library

You could think of a law library as a special type of government documents library, for more than 50 percent of its holdings are documents produced by the judicial, legislative and executive branches of government. These documents—including court reports, statutes and administrative regulations—are a reflection of that government activity we think of as "the law."

Law libraries are a central part of all of the nation's more than 170 American Bar Association–accredited public and private law schools. They also exist, in vastly scaled-down versions, in the offices of major law firms across the country. Courthouses and state libraries also have law holdings. And, thanks to interactive computer technology, a vast law library exists as a full-text database called LEXIS (see Chapter 5). You are, therefore, never far from this important information resource.

The law, with its Latin phrases and its tortured syntax, is pretty intimidating stuff. And law libraries, with their endless shelves of seemingly mysteriously catalogued material, likewise can be daunting. But so many stories or information campaigns involve legal components that, as a journalistic information gatherer, you will at some point find yourself (sweaty-palmed) about to enter a law library. What can you do to prepare for that inevitable day?

1. Gain basic understanding about what a law library contains.
2. Learn about the major access points for legal research.
3. Understand the function of the law librarian.

What's in a law library?

Put most simply, you will find both the law itself and writings about the law in the library. "The law" includes three major categories. First is *case law* derived from the decisions made by various courts. This exists in a law library as court reports—the published decisions, opinions and dissenting opinions of several levels of state, district and federal courts. Most states do not publish the decisions of lower trial courts (New York and California are major exceptions), but rather wait until a case has reached an appeals court, where the point of law rather than the intricacies of the case will be the focal point. Most states publish their court of appeals and state supreme court decisions, and most academic law libraries carry these court reports for all 50 states. Decisions reached by circuit, district and federal courts and, of course, the U.S. Supreme Court are all vital elements of case law and are all available at academic law libraries.

Second is *statutory law*, the statutes and codes created by state and federal legislative bodies. (Again, most academic law libraries contain the statutes for all 50 states; some major law libraries have international holdings.) These are the laws passed by your own state legislature or by the U.S. Congress.

Third is *administrative law*, the rules and regulations promulgated by administrative agencies created by Congress to carry out certain regulatory functions. These agencies—the Environmental Protection Agency or the Food and Drug Administration, for example—may also be empowered by Congress to hear and settle disputes. The decisions they make are considered administrative law.

A law library also contains writings about the law: journals, law reviews, encyclopedias and dictionaries. These secondary sources are of enormous importance to the journalistic information gatherer. Encyclopedia and dictionary entries can provide quick information on terms or points of law and are particularly important aides to legal neophytes trying to make fast sense of legalese. Articles in journals and law reviews describe, interpret and comment on significant legal issues. The writers of these articles and entries often draw together, compare and make sense of laws across states and across time. This is where to start your legal research.

Major access points

Again, CD/ROM technology comes to the rescue, this time in the form of LegalTrac, a fast, easy-to-use index to pertinent journals, law reviews and assorted periodicals and newspapers. The database covers articles written about the law from 1980 to the present and operates as a simple subject index. You punch in a subject—*family violence*, for example—and LegalTrac searches its files for all relevant articles. Most libraries have a printer attached to the system, so you can print out your own bibliography.

LegalTrac has both a print version and an online equivalent, the *Legal Resource Index*, which has a more powerful, more sophisticated keyword system. Whereas a CD/ROM search is free, it costs money to go online (see Chapter 5). If you are researching a legal issue that surfaced prior to 1980, you will need to revert to the ancient technology of bound volumes. The *Index to Legal Periodicals* will be your guide.

Whichever system you use, the result will be the same: a list of secondary sources consisting of articles in journals, law reviews and an occasional newspaper. When you track down these items in the library, you will have at least three kinds of useful information:

▶ The names of legal experts who have researched and thought about the issue you are concerned with—that is, the authors of the articles. In most cases the author will be identified by the institution or firm he or she belongs to, making direct contact a simple matter.

▶ Summaries, interpretations and opinions about the issue offered by these legal experts. These will help you understand the scope of the issue, its component parts and the nature of the debate surrounding it.

▶ Citations for relevant cases and statutes (the primary sources used by the authors), which you can then look up and read yourself.

Essentially, the authors of these law review and journal articles can do much of the legwork for you. Let them.

As you read, you may need to decipher the language. *Black's Law Dictionary* is the standard reference—comprehensive, authoritative and a bit cumbersome. Consider *Oran's Dictionary of the Law*, which is not comprehensive but does cover, in highly readable thumbnail sketches, the main legal terms and issues you will encounter.

The law library staff

The more you know about what you want to know, the more the library staff can help you. Conduct background research on the legal issue, using magazines, newspapers and personal contacts, before you attempt to delve into its depths in a law library. Use the *Library of Congress Subject Headings* to compile a keyword list to use in LegalTrac. Think about what you want: Do you want to learn about individual cases or trends across time? Are you interested in decisions at the state, district or federal level?

A librarian, whether at a law school or in a state or courthouse library, can best help you if you arrive at the library with a focus, a direction and a set of questions. You might first confer with the librarian to determine if the subject headings you want to plug into LegalTrac will work. When you get your list of references, you might want to ask the librarian about the relative merits of various journals and law reviews. Which is known to be the most thoughtful? Do any have known specialties? Are there political biases you should watch out for? Finally, let the library staff (along with the maps and charts you will invariably find at the reference desk) help guide you to the material itself.

The health sciences library

Pollution in the air, pesticides in our food, radiation in our homes, cholesterol in our blood—so many of today's concerns are health-related that you are sure someday to find yourself involved in a story or information campaign with a health component. Like law, the health sciences and medical field seems daunting to the inexperienced information gatherer. Many of the basic concepts of the field are foreign to the uninitiated. Highly educated specialists who not only talk a different language (that is, jargon) but seem even to *think* differently are in charge. Information is sequestered in special libraries.

But health sciences or medical libraries are actually easy to get around in, thanks to their sensible cataloguing system and their excellent indexes to material. They are also relatively easy to find, with more than 120 academic libraries (libraries associated with medical, dental or nursing schools or health sciences universities) nationwide and some 4,000 in-hospital libraries of varying sizes. The academic libraries will generally be open to all serious researchers; access to the hospital libraries may be more problematic. Hospitals in areas with no medical school (and accompanying library) will probably be sympathetic to your request to use their facilities. Small hospitals with limited staff and resources may be resistant. But a serious journalistic researcher on the trail of important health information can usually persuade all but the most obstinate staffer. You probably won't be able to persuade a private corporation to open its in-house library to you, although pharmaceutical companies are known to have excellent holdings in the medical field.

The nation's storehouse for medical and health information is the National Library of Medicine in Bethesda, Md., part of the National Institutes of Health. With its 4.5 million volumes and 25 online databases, it is the largest health sciences library in the world. It lends material through a network of seven regional libraries, should you be unable to find something locally. How can you best prepare yourself for research in a health sciences library?

1. Understand the system.

2. Learn the access points.

3. Depend on decoders.

Understanding the system

Health sciences libraries mirror basic university or public libraries in their holdings and their system of organization. Like the familiar public library, a health sciences library contains books, periodicals (current and bound past volumes) and reference material (encyclopedias, dictionaries, etc.). Most health sciences libraries catalog their books according to the National Library of Medicine (NLM) system, a subcategory of the familiar Library of Congress (LC) system used by your public or university library. NLM uses the letter designations not already used by LC (part of Q and all of W). Books related to specific medical specialties, from obstetrics to geriatrics, carry W call letters, as do books related to body systems (cardiovascular, gastrointestinal). The NLM call number looks just like the LC number you're used to seeing. This makes locating books on the shelves quite easy.

Most health sciences libraries organize their periodicals according to an even easier system, the alphabet. If you know the name of the journal, you can find it effortlessly on the shelves. If you don't know the exact name, but only the field or specialty, the medical librarian can point the way.

Major access points

Preresearch is important to successfully using specialty libraries like law and health sciences collections. Reading secondary source material (a *Time* magazine article on diet fads, for example) will help you determine what medical and scientific questions need to be addressed and may highlight ongoing controversies. The secondary source can also pinpoint particular research you want to review or individual scientists you want to investigate. Coming to the library with a direction or with specific questions will help you expend your research time more efficiently and productively.

Because the health sciences are such a dynamic field, your research efforts will probably be directed more toward journals, which can keep abreast of new findings, than toward books, which tend to give historical overviews. An astonishing number of journals serve the health sciences. Thankfully, several excellent indexes provide easy access to this wealth of material. (Some of these indexes are available in the reference sections of larger university libraries, but you would have to go to a health sciences library to locate the journals themselves anyway.)

Index Medicus, the most comprehensive guide to journals in the medical sciences, is a straightforward research tool with good internal cross-referencing that can help point you to subject headings you might not have considered. The index, which is also available online as MEDLINE, gives you the full citation for all articles pertinent to the subject heading. In the front of each volume, you will find a complete list of journals indexed by this service. The paper version of the index is issued monthly and cumulated annually.

A number of the fields within the health sciences—biology, chemistry and psychology, for example—have separate indexes to their periodicals (some of which will also show up in *Index Medicus*). These guides are index/abstract tools that save you the trouble of hunting down citations that are not relevant, even though their titles may sound promising. You remember the procedure here. Use the index volume to locate references to articles under a particular subject or keyword. Then follow the code for that article to the abstracts volume where you will find the full citation plus a summary of the research findings. *Biological Abstracts*, *Chemical Abstracts* and *Psychological Abstracts* all work this way.

A bit more cumbersome to use, but also potentially more enlightening, is the massive *Science Citation Index* with its three interconnected parts. In part one, a subject guide, you look up the keyword related to your inquiry. What you find is a list of names of researchers who have published work in this field during the time period in question. (The index is published quarterly and cumulated annually. A five-year cumulative index is available at an astronomical price, which your local health sciences library may or may not have anteed up.) These names key you to the second part of the index, the source guide. Here, under the author's name, you find identification/affiliation information about the author (of obvious use should you want to interview the person), titles of the articles he or she produced and bibliographies from those articles. You can imagine how quickly this could add to your own bibliography on the subject. The final section is the citation index. You use this to discover the titles of other published papers whose authors cited the research you've been tracking. This particular feature may seem of limited use to journalistic researchers, but consider how it could (1) add to your bibliography on the subject, (2) help you gauge the importance of a piece of work and (3) help you locate material about a controversial finding.

Decoders

When you enter the health sciences, you enter another world. The terrain is unfamiliar; the people are strangers; the language is foreign. You need all the help you can get. Encyclopedias, dictionaries and biographical references are important "decoding" tools that can help you make sense of this specialized area. For example, before jumping into *Index Medicus* and the journal research it cites, consider referring to specialty encyclopedias like *The Encyclopedia of Biological Sciences* or *Van Nostrand's Scientific Encyclopedia*. Compilations of relatively brief articles written by experts for non-experts, specialty encyclopedias offer you authoritative summaries and overviews—just what you need before delving into the primary sources themselves.

When you do delve, you are going to need help as you go along. Frankly, the jargon is often so thick that unless you come to journalism with an extensive background in the health sciences and statistics, you are not going to understand the intricacies of what you read in specialty journals. (Neither will non-lawyers fully grasp articles in legal journals.) But it is not only possible for the journalistic researcher to bridge this gap between experts and laypersons, it is imperative. It is, in fact, one of the most important components of the media writer's job.

Specialty dictionaries can help, so keep them close at hand as you read. *Dorland's Illustrated Medical Dictionary* is a classic for good reason. The *Psychiatric Dictionary* covers not only its own field but related areas like genetics, eugenics and occupational therapy. The *Physicians' Desk Reference* (known as the *PDR*) is essentially a dictionary of prescription drugs. Its entries for more than 2,000 drugs give information on dosage, effects and precautions. These dictionaries really help the non-expert "crack the code" of the experts.

Biographical references are also important decoders. Who are these health science researchers? What else have they published (other than the one article you found)? Where did they do their advanced training? Where do they work now? *American Men and Women of Science* offers information on more than 100,000 U.S. scientists in a variety of fields. The *American Medical Directory* is a register of all physicians in the United States and U.S. protectorates.

Don't forget the most important decoder in the health sciences library: the librarian. Although people who staff small in-hospital libraries may not be specially trained, they undoubtedly know their own collections. Those who work in libraries associated with major teaching hospitals, medical schools or health sciences universities most often have undergraduate degrees in a life science and master's degrees in librarianship. Use these in-house experts wisely, remembering that focused questions bring the most useful answers.

The search

Now it's time to put some of this information to use. Let's start with diets fads and frauds and begin the search in the government documents library.

Your first stop will be the *Monthly Catalog of U.S. Government Publications*—or rather the CD/ROM version, which is so much easier to use. Here, by entering the Library of Congress subject heading *reducing diets*, you find 15 references. One entitled "How to Take Weight Off Without Getting Ripped Off" looks particularly promising (see Figure 4.2). This *FDA Consumer* article, which is simple to find in the library's stacks, turns out to be a wonderful overview of diet fads (from body wraps to appetite-suppressing eyeglasses) written authoritatively but for the layperson. A number of the other references look promising as well.

Next, you take a look at the *CIS/Index* to see whether the legislative branch has had any interest in diets fads and frauds. At first, your efforts are stymied. You use *diet, reducing diet, weight control, weight reduction* and *nutrition* as keywords, but nothing turns up the kind of listings you want. Finally, in desperation, you return to the *Library of Congress Subject Headings* to see if there is something you missed. There is: *obesity*. This one works. According to the *CIS/Index* a Senate subcommittee conducted hearings on weight reduction products. The index (see Figure 4.3) tells you where to look in the abstracts volume (see Figure 4.4). Within minutes you have the hearing itself (see Figure 4.5). Note from the table of contents what a rich source of interview subjects this document will be (see Figure 4.6).

Another likely reference guide might be the *Index to U.S. Government Periodicals*. Here, under *diet*, you find a reference to another promisingly titled *FDA Consumer* article, "Dangerous Diet Drugs From South of the Border" (see Figure 4.7). There is no abstract volume to this index, so you will have to go to the stacks to find the article and determine its relevance to your search.

Figure 4.2. *Excerpt from* CD/ROM Monthly Catalog

```
AN:  89010277
SU:  HE 20.4010/a:W 42/989
SU:  HE204010aW42989
AU:  Willis,-Judith, 1941-
CA:  United States. Food and Drug Administration. Office of
     Public Affairs.
TI:  How to take weight off (and keep it off) without
     getting ripped off.
SO:  [Rockville, Md. : Dept. of Health and Human Services,
     Public Health Service, Food and Drug Administration,
     Office of Public Affairs, 1989].
PY:  1985
PD:  [4] p. : ill. ; 28 cm
SE:  DHHS publication ; no. (FDA) 89-1116.
NT:  Caption title.
     "Updated from July-August 1985, FDA Consumer"—p. [4].
     Shipping list no.: 89-187-P.
IT:  475-H-1
DE:  Diet-United-States.
     Reducing-diets
     Weight-reducing-preparations.
     Consumer-protection-United-States.
PT:  Monograph
OC:  19476621
UD:  8903
```

After such a successful jaunt through government documents, you feel more than ready to tackle the law and health sciences libraries. At the law library your search begins at the LegalTrac computer terminal. You are pleasantly surprised to discover how easy it is to use, with its brightly colored, clearly marked keys for each major function (start a new search, enter, print, etc.) and its attached printer. But your elation soon fades when the first five keywords fail to turn up any relevant citations. Is it possible that the legal profession has had no interaction with the diet industry? No. It's got to be a keyword problem. You begin brainstorming. *Weight control* didn't work; neither did *reducing diet*. But what about *reducing* or *weight reducing*? Bingo. Under these two headings you find several interesting citations (see Figure 4.8). You now know that malpractice, products liability and false advertising suits have been mounted against diet doctors and diet products. These legal reviews should make fascinating reading.

Figure 4.3. *Excerpt from* CIS/Index

analysis and response options, S521–77.2

Terrorism trends and US countermeasures, S381–4.7

Terrorist assault and murder, Fed jurisdiction and penalties estab, S521–25.1

Oakley, Robert L.
LC program cuts to meet budget deficit reduction requirements, J891–4.2

Oakley, Willard, and Son Lumber Co.
Small business insurance programs, S721–8.2

Oaks, Robert C.
Military services recruiting and retention, S201–1.4

OAS
see Organization of American States

Oberdorfer, John L.
DC area airports transfer to and operation by independent airport authority, S261–12.4

Obergfell, Dennis A.
Student aid and higher educ programs, extension and revision, S541–44.2

Oberle, Marilyn
Income tax returns, IRS data processing problems, S521–23.4

Oberley, Terry D.
Kidney dialysis equipment reuse, clinical and regulatory issues, S141–9.2

Oberlin College
Income tax reform proposal, H781–21.9

Oberling, Pierre
Human rights violations in Cyprus, J891–6.1

Obermiller, Alan D.
Natl Guard and Reserve members employment discrimination prohibition, H761–24.1

Oberstar, James L.
Aviation programs and safety, budget deficit reduction impact, H641–16
Aviation weather hazards, detection R&D and warning systems oversight, H641–12

Budget proposal, FY87, review, H261–8.11

Canada-US Boundary Waters Intl Commission, estab, S401–22.2

Cargo preference laws, USDA and Maritime Admin programs oversight, H561–19

Commerce, Justice, and State Depts and related agencies programs, FY87 approp, H181–25.1

DOL, HHS, and Educ Dept programs, FY87 approp, H181–56.2

Energy and water resources dev programs, FY87 approp, H181–45.2

Foreign aid programs, FY87 approp, H181–92.5

HUD and independent agencies programs, FY87 approp, H181–83.1

Interior Dept programs, FY87 approp, H181–74.3

Liability insurance availability and cost, impact on transportation industries, H641–13.6

Motor carrier safety programs and regulations revision, implementation, H641–15

Trade adjustment assistance programs, review, H781–9

USDA food assistance programs, oversight and FY87 budget proposals, H161–25.5

USPS voter registration assistance programs, H621–4.1

Obert, Gerald
Medicare prospective payment system, implementation in rural areas, H781–58.1

Obesity
Children and youth health and fitness, S541–4.1
"Health Implications of Obesity", H701–8.1
Nutrition and exercise role in physical fitness and disease prevention, S541–34.3
"State of Florida School Program for Overweight Children: Program Analysis and Results", S541–4
Weight reduction products and plans, safety and efficacy, S401–3

Figure 4.4. *Excerpt from* CIS/Index *abstracts volume*

clarification of bill standard for determining liability for fraudulent claims based on knowledge or reason to know.

S401-3 WEIGHT REDUCTION PRODUCTS AND PLANS.

May 14, 15, 1985. 99-1.
v + 392 P. † CIS/MF/6
• Item 1037-B; 1037-C.
S. Hrg. 99-228.
°Y4.G74/9:S.hrg.99-228.
MC 86-7676. LC
85-603329.

Hearings before the *Permanent Subcom on Investigations* to examine the safety and efficacy of weight loss products and plans, focusing on very low calorie diet (VLCD) and dietary supplement programs marketed by Herbalife International and Cambridge Plan International.

Supplementary material (p. 271–392) includes correspondence, witness' written replies to subcom questions, and:

– "Amazing Magic of Natural Herbs" Herbalife weight control products mktg guide, with 1984 updated training booklet (p. 327–374).

S401-3.1: May 14, 1985, p. 5–14, 279–326.

Witness: **SHAPIRO. Howard L.,** Subcom Staff Counsel.

Statement and Discussion: Scope of subcom investigation into weight reduction programs, with examples of ineffective and potentially hazardous products (related advertisement, statements, p. 279, 297–317).

Insertions:

a. FTC Bureau of Consumer Protection, FTC law enforcement activities regarding advertising of weight reduction products, prepared for subcom, May 13, 1985 (p. 280–296).

b. Van Italie, Theodore B. (St. Luke's-Roosevelt Hosp Center); and Yang, Mei-Uih, "Cardiac Dysfunction in Obese Dieters: A Potentially Lethal Complication of Rapid, Massive Weight Loss" Amer J of Clinical

Nutrition, May 1984 (p. 318–326).

S401-3.2: May 14, 1985. p. 14–76.

Witnesses: **STERN, Judith S.,** prof, nutrition; dir, Food Intake Lab, Univ of Calif.

PI-SUNYER, F. Xavier (Dr.), chief, endocrinology and diabetes div; assoc dir, obesity research center, St. Luke's-Roosevelt Hosp Center.

TYLER, Varro E., prof, pharmacognosy; dean, School of Pharmacy and Pharmacal Sciences, Purdue Univ.

Statements and Discussion: Guidelines for evaluation of weight loss plans and products; possible hazards of weight loss regimens; concerns regarding weight reduction products, with detailed analysis of Herbalife herbal ingredients; contended inefficacy of and potential medical complications from Herbalife preparations; viewed deceptiveness of Herbalife advertising materials.

S401-3.3: May 14, 1985, p. 76–94.

Witness: **LOCKE, Thomas J., III (Dr.),** former member, counsellor advisory bd, Cambridge Plan Intl.

Statement and Discussion: Experiences with use of VLCDs in treatment of obese patients; assessment of medical problems associated with VLCDs; importance of medical supervision for VLCD users.

S401-3.4: May 15, 1985. p. 110–150, 379–392.

Witness: **YOUNG, Frank E. (Dr.),** Commr, FDA; accompanied by **Scarlett, Thomas,** Gen. Counsel.

Statement and Discussion: Views on weight control strategies; overview of FDA regulatory initiatives regarding weight loss products, including actions regarding advertising claims; complexities involved in FDA regulation of food and drug products, including assessment of therapeutic benefits claimed for dietary supplements.

Insertion:

– Grice, H. C. (et al., Canada Dept. of Health and Welfare), "Toxic Properties of Nordihydroguaiaretic Acid"

Figure 4.5. *Title page for Senate subcommittee hearings*

S. HRG. 99-228

WEIGHT REDUCTION PRODUCTS AND PLANS

HEARINGS

BEFORE THE

PERMANENT
SUBCOMMITTEE ON INVESTIGATIONS

OF THE

COMMITTEE ON
GOVERNMENTAL AFFAIRS
UNITED STATES SENATE

NINETY-NINTH CONGRESS

FIRST SESSION

MAY 14 AND 15, 1985

Printed for the use of the Committee on Governmental Affairs

U.S. GOVERNMENT PRINTING OFFICE

52-270 O   WASHINGTON : 1985

Figure 4.6. *Table of contents for Senate subcommittee hearings*

CONTENTS

(III)

62

Figure 4.7. *Excerpt from* Index to U.S. Government Periodicals

Figure 4.8. *Excerpt from LegalTrac database*

```
REDUCING

                    Weight loss diet malpractices, (Illinois)
          by Theodore Postel 21 col in. v136 Chicago
          Daily Law Bulletin May 17 '90 p1 col 1
                    LIBRARY SUBSCRIBES TO JOURNAL


WEIGHT REDUCING PREPARATIONS

                    Weight-loss products and Herbalife,
          (products liability) by Gail Vallot v22 Trial
          July '86 p27(3)          .
                    LIBRARY SUBSCRIBES TO JOURNAL

                    Diet pill firm agrees to pay $500,000 to
          end D.A.'s false-advertising suit,
          (Continental Health Industries) (Los Angeles)
          by Gail Diane Cox 5 col in. v99 The Los
          Angeles Daily Journal Jan 31 '86 p20 col 4


                    Reducing pills produce signs like heart
          disease, (from "Spurious Heart Disease Induced
          by Reducing Pills, Nutrition Reviews", 27,
          p.6) v31 Current Medicine for Attorneys
          Nov '84 p23


                    Agencies probe safety of cold, diet
          medicine, by Gail Appleson v68 ARA Journal
          Dec '82 p1558
                    LIBRARY SUBSCRIBES TO JOURNAL
```

At the health sciences library you go directly to *Index Medicus* to see what relevant research has been conducted on various weight-loss schemes. Under *diet, reducing* you find a number of jargon-choked entries you can't begin to understand. It's a good thing you have a copy of *Dorland's* handy. Even so, you know that as a layperson you won't be able to understand the studies. But *Index Medicus* has nonetheless performed a vital service: It has pinpointed the medical experts working in the field. Later, when you're more informed yourself, you can question these researchers directly. Two clearly stated entries in the index do catch your eye:

a study on sudden death and the Cambridge Diet and a report on gallstone formation during weight-reducing diets. These you can easily find in the alphabetically arranged journal section of the library.

Now let's consider the search for information about domestic violence. (Just for the purposes of instruction, we won't repeat government document sources used in the diet search, although all three of those sources would, in fact, net you relevant information. Instead, let's turn to three as yet untapped reference tools.) Because you are interested in any statistical data about domestic violence, you turn to the *American Statistical Index*. There, under *domestic violence*, you find a number of references to reports with potentially relevant figures, like number of arrests, number and kind of crimes and rate of victimization (see Figure 4.9). The *ASI* index volume gives you a number that you use to look up the reference in the abstracts volume (see Figure 4.10).

Using *domestic violence* again, you turn to the *GRA&I* to see if any person or agency using government funds conducted research on some aspect of this problem. As the keyword index shows, someone did (see Figure 4.11). The middle group of numbers is the code you use to find this entry in the abstracts volume. In volume 19 you find item 950,687, "Domestic Violence: Battered Women Who Kill" (see Figure 4.12). You may want to order this publication from the government (remember, the NTIS does not distribute its publications for free), or you may want to put the author's name on your growing list of potential interview subjects.

Reasoning that the regulatory arms of the federal government might well be involved in the issue of domestic violence, you try the *CIS Federal Register Index*. You're astounded at the number of separate volumes on the shelves and, once you start looking, at the poor quality of the binding, printing and paper. Remember, this publication is issued daily. Timeliness, not aesthetics, counts. Neither *domestic violence* nor any of its synonyms work here, so you move to *child abuse*, a subcategory. Unfortunately, most of the listings seem to be press releases announcing the availability of grants by the federal government to those working in the child abuse area (see Figure 4.13). But curiosity gets the better of you and, using the index code (which is nothing more complicated than the date of the report), you follow one of the listings to the *Federal Register* itself (see Figure 4.14). It is, as the index said it would be, a press release. That's no help. But you have inadvertently stumbled on some very important information: Within the cabinet-level Department of Health and Human Services, there is an agency called the Administration for Children,

Figure 4.9. *Excerpt from* American Statistical Index

Supplements 7–9   **ASI 1989**

Figure 4.10. *Excerpt from* American Statistical Index *abstracts volume*

Department of Justice

6064–27 **PROSECUTION OF FELONY ARRESTS, 1986**
Annual. June 1989.
iv + 129 p. NCJ-113248.
• Item 968-H-6. NCJRS †
ASI/MF/4 °J29.9/4:986.
LC 86-645246.

By Barbara Boland et al., Abt Associates, Inc. Annual report, issued by the Bureau of Justice Statistics, examining criminal case processing in 28 cities, 1986. Data are primarily from a nationwide computer data-base containing statistics on criminal cases.

Case dispositions are prosecutor declinations, dismissals, guilty pleas, and trial convictions and acquittals. Reasons for case declination or dismissal include insufficient evidence, due process and witness problems, interest of justice, referral, diversion, and coverage by other case.

Contents:

Introduction. (p. 1)

Chapter I-II. Overview and methodology, with 2 charts and 10 tables showing summary data for the 28 cities. (p. 2-13)

App. A. Processing statistics. Includes 14 tables showing, for 4-9 major cities, felony arrests, cases filed, and indictments, by disposition; cases declined and dismissed, by reason; and convictions resulting in incarceration by sentence length, and case processing times by selected disposition, for cases filed and indicted; all by most serious charge, and often by defendant sex, race, and age. (p. 15-94)

App. B. Jurisdictional characteristics. Narrative discussion of city judicial system characteristics. (p. 95-129)

Data are for 1986.

No separate reports were issued for 1983-85. Previous report, for 1982, is described in ASI 1988 Annual under this number.

6066
OFFICE OF JUSTICE PROGRAMS

Publications
in Series

6066–3 **NATIONAL CRIME SURVEY**
For individual bibliographic data, see below.

Continuing series of reports issued by the Bureau of Justice Statistics on the incidence of crime nationwide. Data are based on surveys of households and businesses conducted by the Census Bureau as part of the National Crime Survey, a long-range program intended to provide data on crime on a regular basis.

Surveys exclude homicide, kidnapping, commercial burglary and robbery, so-called victimless crimes, crimes against government entities, and certain types of "white-collar" crimes.

Most reports cover circumstances of criminal incidents, and victim and offender characteristics, by offense (rape, robbery, assault, larceny, burglary, and auto theft; and various degrees of each).

Reports are described below in order of receipt.

REPORTS:

6066–3.41: Criminal Victimization in the U.S., 1987
[June 1989. v+128 p. NCJ-115524. °J29.9/2:987. • Item 968-H-6. NCJRS † ASI/MF/4]

Fifteenth annual report, for 1987, presenting detailed data on criminal victimizations and victimization rates for persons and households.

Contents: introduction, summary, and guide to tables (p. 1-13); 109 tables, described below (p. 14-95); and facsimile survey questionnaires, method-

Figure 4.11. *Excerpt from GRA&I keyword index*

1989 KEYWORD INDEX

DOMESTIC ANIMALS
Virulence Mechanisms of Enteroinvasive Pathogens.
AD-A201 761/4 09-*922,685* PC **A02**/MF **AO1**

Effects of Aircraft Noise and Sonic Booms on Domestic Animals and Wildlife: A Literature Synthesis,
PB89-115026   04-*909,098* PC **A05**/MF **A01**

Effects of Aircraft Noise and Sonic Booms on Domestic Animals and Wildlife: Bibliographic Abstracts,
PB89-115034   04-*909,099* PC **A05**/MF **A01**

Animal Health, Livestock and Pets: 1984 Yearbook of Agriculture,
PB89-168611   12-*931,816* PC **A99**/MF **E04**

DOMESTIC SAFEGUARDS
UK (United Kingdom) Safeguards R and D Project Progress Report for the Period May 1987 – April 1988.
DE88706132   18-*949,919* PC **A03**/MF **A01**

Actinide Content of Spent Fuel Assemblies of WWER-1000 Type.
DE88706273   18-*949,922* PC **A05**/MF **A01**

DOMESTIC SUPPLIES
Oil Use and Oil Dependency: Long-Term Issues.
DE89014614   23-*962,413* PC **A08**/MF **A01**

DOMESTIC TERRORISM
Terrorism. January 1970 – September 1989 (Citations from the NTIS Database).
PB89-871677   22-*960,403* PC **N01**/MF **N01**

DOMESTIC VIOLENCE
Domestic Violence: Battered Women Who Kill.
AD-A208 543/9 19-*950,687* PC **A04**/MF **A01**

DOMESTIC WASTES
Glass Contaminant Removal from Refuse Derived Compost. Interim Report.
PB89-197875   20-*953,853* PC **E03**/MF **E03**

Effect of Wheeled Bins on Domestic and Civic Amenity Waste.
PB89-197891   20-*953,854* PC **E05**/MF **E05**

DOMINANT MUTATIONS
Zygote-Derived Developmental Anomalies, a New Endpoint of Mutagenesis in Mice.
DE89003929   10-*926,448* PC **A02**/MF **A01**

DOMINICA
Agricultural Sector Strategy Report (for USAID/Barbados). Volumes 1 and 2,
PB89-162622   14-*936,884* PC **A06**/MF **A01**

DOMINICAN REPUBLIC
Limited Assessment and Characterization of the Solar Radiation Energy Resources in the Caribbean Region.
DE88001133   02-*903,902* PC **A08**/MF **A01**

Establishment of a Photovoltaic Laboratory at the University of Lowell: Final Report.
DE89009040   16-*944,763* PC **A02**/MF **A01**

Dominican Republic: The Superior Institute of Agriculture-Development of a Private Institution of Higher Agricultural Education,
PB89-106405   02-*903,024* PC **A05**/MF **A01**

Fuelwood and Charcoal Research in the Dominican Republic. Results of the Wood Fuel Development Program,
PB89-160998   12-*933,328* PC **A09**/MF **A01**

Trade, Exchange Rate, and Agricultural Pricing Policies in the Dominican Republic. Volume 1. The Country Study.
PB89-162812   13-*934,563*   MF **A01**

DON SHORE BASE
Assessment of DON Shore Base Readiness Analysis.
AD-A199 868/1 04-*909,632* PC **A04**/MF **A01**

DONOR MATERIALS
Donor-Acceptor Properties of Ambient-Temperature Chloroaluminate Melts.
AD-A211 525/1 24-*964,253* PC **A02**/MF **A01**

1-Methyl-3-Ethylimidazolium Hydrogen Dichloride: Synthesis and Application to the Study of Protons in Ambient-Temperature Chloroaluminate Ionic Liquids.
AD-A211 526/9 24-*964,222* PC **A02**/MF **A01**

DONOR POLICIES
Evolution in Donor Policies for the Shelter Sector: Lessons Learned and a Case Study of Ghana.
PB89-204127   20-*953,132* PC **A03**/MF **A01**

DOOR LATCHES
Door Latch Integrity.
PB89-178347   14-*940,637* PC **A05**/MF **A01**

DOORS
Monitor for Integrity of Doors in a Shield Enclosure,
AD-A200 083/4 05-*911,058* PC **A03**/MF **A01**

WIPP (Waste Isolation Pilot Plant) Panel Entryway Seal: Numerical Simulation of Seal Composite Interaction for Preliminary Design Evaluation.
DE88008741   01-*901,960* PC **A04**/MF **A01**

Field Test Evaluation of Conservation Retrofits of Low-Income, Single-Family Buildings in Wisconsin: Blower-Door-Directed Infiltration Reduction Procedure: Field Test Implementation and Results.
DE88013344   04-*908,388* PC **A04**/MF **A01**

Usage of Radiography Techniques for Restoration of Cizre Mardin Ulucami Door.
DE88703917   07-*915,219* PC **A03**/MF **A01**

Indices Approach for Evaluating the Performance of Fenestration Systems in Nonresidential Buildings.
DE89002674   09-*921,207* PC **A03**/MF **A01**

Statement of Requirements: Hardware for Doorsets.
PB89-108161   02-*903,131* PC **E05**/MF **E05**

Analysis and Prediction of Air Leakage through Door Assemblies.
PB89-231161 22-*959,072* Not available NTIS

DOORSETS
Statement of Requirements: Hardware for Doorsets.
PB89-108161   02-*903,131* PC **E05**/MF **E05**

DOPAMINE
Studies of L-DOPA and Related Compounds Adsorbed from Aqueous Solutions at Pt(100) and Pt(111): Electron Energy-Loss Spectroscopy, Auger Spectroscopy, and Electrochemistry.
AD-A198 501/9 01-*900,489* PC **A03**/MF **A01**

Central Determinants of Age-Related Declines in Motor Function (Annals of the New York Academy of Sciences. Volume 515),
AD-A198 997/9 02-*904,550* Not available NTIS

Release of Dopamine from Striatal Synaptosomes: High Pressure Effects.
AD-A199 924/2 04-*909,597* PC **A02**/MF **A01**

Age-Related Decrements in the Muscarinic Enhancement of K(+)-Evoked Release of Endogenous Striatal Dopamine: An Indicator of Altered Cholinergic-Dopaminergic Reciprocal Inhibitory Control in Senescence.
AD-A200 642/7 06-*914,072* PC **A03**/MF **A01**

Figure 4.12. *Excerpt from GRA&I abstracts volume*

BEHAVIOR & SOCIETY

Psychology

Impact of Father Absence of Psycho-pathology of Military Dependent Children.
Doctoral thesis,
T. M. Grant. 1988, 108p Rept no. AFIT/CI/CIA-88-217

The problem of the study was to investigate the influence of father absence on the diagnosed psychopathology of military dependent children. The purpose of the study was to analyze data obtained from military medical center records for dependent children of active duty military fathers in order to answer the following questions of research: 1) Does a difference exist among GAP diagnostic groups relative to number of father absences among military dependent children under the age of 18. 2) Does a difference exist in the severity of the primary diagnoses among military dependent children under the age of 18 with regard to number of father absences. 3) Does a difference exist among GAP diagnostic groups between first-born, middle-born, and last-born children of military dependents under the age of 18 relative to father absence. Theses. (SDW)

950,684

AD-A208 771/6/GAR   PC **A03**/MF **A01**
Center for Naval Analyses, Alexandria, VA.
Maximum-Likelihood Procedure for Developing a Common Metric in Item-Response Theory.
Final rept.,
D. R. Divgi. Dec 88, 16p Rept no. CRM-88-236
Contract N00014-87-C-0001

Because the ability scale in item-response theory is arbitrary, if two item pools are calibrated in two different samples, their parameter estimates must be placed on a common metric using items administered in both calibrations. In this memorandum, a maximum likelihood procedure for doing so is derived and illustrated. Keywords: ASVAB (Armed Services Vocational Aptitude Battery), CAT (Computerized Adaptive Testing), maximum likelihood estimation, Parameters, Statistical analysis, Statistical processes, Test methods. (kr)

Social Concerns

950,685

AD-A208 444/0/GAR   PC **A04**/MF **A01**
Air Force Inst. of Tech., Wright-Patterson AFB, OH.
Parricide: Children Who Kill Their Parents.
Master's thesis,
R. A. Strong, 1988, 61p Rept no. AFIT/CI/CIA-88-206

This thesis is a scholarly investigation of adolescents who kill their parents. The research centers on who is the offender, why he or she has used parricide as a solution to an unsolvable problem, and how the criminal is treated by the justice system. Following a review of the available literature, both the issues and controversies surrounding the disposition of these juveniles are examined in detail. Based on the results of the literature review three conclusions were reached. First, adolescents who commit parricide have been victims of severely abusive home situations. The murder event is the attempt by the parricide to save himself or herself from further victimization at the hands of their abuser. Secondly, the treatment of these adolescents by the criminal justice system varies greatly depending on the willingness of the court to accept the violent family situation of the parricide as a mitigating circumstance. Thirdly, there is a visible absence of research conducted by criminal justice scholars in the area of parricide. This violent crime is a byproduct of the escalating phenomenon of family violence. Without the availability of adequate research, decision makers are unable to formulate policies which offer preventive measures which can assist juveniles at risk as well as those who have committed parricide as a solution to a life made unbearable by the subculture of violence. Theses. (sdw)

950,686

AD-A208 465/5/GAR   PC **A09**/MF **A01**
Air Force Inst. of Tech., Wright-Patterson AFB, OH.
Analysis of the Impact of Ecological Variables on Burglary Rates in Terre Haute, Indiana.
Master's thesis.
M. P. Branigan. Aug 88, 193p Rept no. AFIT/CI/CIA-88-205

An ecological analysis was conducted of residential burglaries reported to the police in Terre Haute, Indiana, during the year 1980. Research questions were developed during a review of the literature on ecological studies of crime and specifically of the crime of residential burglary. A positive relationship was hypothesized between single individual households, single parent families, density, crowding, and the distance from the center of the city and the rate of residential burglary in the study site. Multiple regression analysis, using the SPSSX Information Analysis System, was conducted. Findings indicated a negative relationship between the independent variables and the residential burglary rate, thereby failing to support the research hypotheses. Implications of the study are discussed. Keywords: Sociology, Crime, Victims, Theses. (KT)

950,687

AD-A208 543/9/GAR   PC **A04**/MF **A01**
Air Force Inst. of Tech., Wright-Patterson AFB, OH.
Domestic Violence: Battered Women Who Kill.
Master's thesis,
M. D. Cockerill. 1988, 64p Rept no. AFIT/CI/CIA-88-213

The high prevalence of domestic violence within American society indicates a problem of serious dimensions. Spouse abuse has become the norm rather than the exception due to antiquated concepts of roles in marriage and in many cases, little regard for women's rights. Despite legal precedent and protective statutes against assault, domestic abuse

Figure 4.13. *Excerpt from* CIS Federal Register Index

Child Abuse and Neglect

Child abuse and neglect
Child care (temporary) and crisis nurseries for handicapped, ill, and abused children, grants availability: OHDS *(4/7/N) 14154*
Juvenile delinquency prevention and missing children ops grants, funding priorities: Juvenile Justice and Delinquency Prevention Office *(5/9/N) 20104*
Juvenile Justice and Delinquency Prevention Coordinating Council, meeting: Juvenile Justice and Delinquency Prevention Office *(3/6/N) 9263; (3/16/N-cx) 11108*
Pornography with children, producer performer identification and recordkeeping rqmts estab: DOJ *(2/27/PR) 8217; (5/3/PR-cx) 18907*
Prevention and social svcs program re child abuse and neglect, revision: OHDS *(3/17/PR) 11246*
Prevention and treatment of child abuse and neglect, research and svcs project grants availability: OHDS *(6/1/N) 23566*
Prevention of child abuse and neglect, State challenge grants availability: OHDS *(3/30/N) 13117*

Child Abuse Prevention, Adoption, and Family Services Act
Child abuse and neglect, prevention and social svcs program revision: OHDS *(3/17/PR) 11246*
Child abuse and neglect prevention and treatment research and svcs projects, grants availability: OHDS *(6/1/N) 23566*

Child Abuse Prevention and Treatment Act
Child abuse and neglect, prevention and social svcs program revision: OHDS *(3/17/PR) 11246*
Child abuse and neglect prevention and treatment research and svcs projects, grants availability: OHDS *(6/1/N) 23566*

Child Abuse Prevention and Treatment and Adoption Reform Act
Adoption Opportunities Program minority and foster child placement and

Index by Subjects and Names

post-adoption svc projects, grants availability: OHDS *(4/25/N) 17822; (5/22/N-cx) 22021*
Coordinated Discretionary Funds Program, social svcs workshops and grants, appl deadline extension: OHDS *(4/24/N) 16407*

Child Care Food Program
Adult day care center food aid under Child Care Food Program, retroactive payment rqmts revision: FNS *(3/30/IR) 13048*
Income eligibility guidelines for school meal and special milk programs free and reduced prices, revision: FNS *(4/17/N) 15241; (4/27/N-cx) 18197*
Snack reimbursement regs, estab: FNS *(6/26/IR) 26723*
Yogurt meat alternate credit in Child Care Food Program snacks, authorization: FNS *(6/28/R) 27151*

Child day care
AFDC recipient Job Opportunities and Basic Skills Training Program, child care and supportive svcs regs revision: Family Support Admin *(4/18/PR) 15638*
Child Care Awareness Week, Natl: Pres proclamation *(4/5/PD) 13663*
DOD personnel child care programs, estab: DOD *(4/3/R) 13369*
Employee health, accident, group-term life ins, and dependent care benefits discrimination prohibition enforcement regs, estab: IRS *(3/7/PR) 9460*
Employer liability ins purchases for workplace child care svcs, restrictions review: DOL *(5/10/N) 20366*
Food program snack reimbursement regs, estab: FNS *(6/26/IR) 26723*
Handicapped children temporary care and crisis nursery grants, availability: OHDS *(4/7/N) 14154*
MiniGrant Program drug abuse educ, literacy training, family and homeless aid svcs volunteer project funds, availability: ACTION *(3/10/N) 10264*
Summer Food Svc Program and Child Care Food Program snacks, yogurt meat alternate credit authorization:

CIS Federal Register Index

54 FR 1-27853

Figure 4.14. *Excerpt from* Federal Register

Federal Register / Vol. 54, No. 51 /
Friday, March 17, 1989 / Proposed Rules

personal identifier are requested by a third party using the informant's name or personal identifier, the OIG may treat the records as not subject to the requirements of (b)(7) unless the informant's status as an informant has been officially confirmed. If it is determined that using a (b)(7) exemption would acknowledge the informant's identity, then the response to the requester will state that no records were found.

L. M. Bynum,
Alternate OSD Federal Register Liaison Officer, Department of Defense.

March 13, 1989

[FR Doc. 89-6112 Filed 3-16-89; 8:45 am]

BILLING CODE 3810-01-M

DEPARTMENT OF HEALTH AND HUMAN SERVICES

Office of Human Development Services

45 CFR Part 1340

Child Abuse and Neglect Prevention and Treatment Program

AGENCY: Administration for Children, Youth, and Families (ACYF), Office of Human Development Services, HHS.

ACTION: Notice of proposed rulemaking.

SUMMARY: The Department of Health and Human Services is proposing technical and conforming changes to its rule for the child abuse and neglect program to implement the changes made in the Child Abuse Prevention and Treatment Act (Act) by Pub L. 100–294.

DATE: Comments must be received on or before May 16, 1989.

ADDRESSES: Comments may be mailed to the Commissioner, Administration for Children, Youth, and Families, P. O. Box 1182, Washington, DC 20013, Attention: Mary McKeough.

Comments received in response to this rule may be reviewed in Room 3763 of the Donohoe Building, 400 Sixth St., SW., Washington, DC between the hours of 9:30 a.m. and 5:00 p.m., Monday through Friday except Federal holidays, beginning two weeks after the date of publication in the Federal Register.)

FOR FURTHER INFORMATION CONTACT:
Mary McKeough, (202) 245-2856

SUPPLEMENTARY INFORMATION:

I. Program Description

In 1974, the Child Abuse Prevention and Treatment Act (Pub. L. 93–247, 42 U.S.C. 5101, *et seq.*) established in the Department the National Center on Child Abuse and Neglect (NCCAN). NCCAN is located organizationally within the Children's Bureau of the Administration for Children, Youth and Families in the Office of Human Development Services.

Under the Act, the NCCAN carries out, among other activities, the following responsibilities:

• Makes grants to States that comply with Federal requirements to implement

Figure 4.15. *Excerpt from LegalTrac database*

```
FAMILY VIOLENCE
-analysis

          Protecting battered women: a proposal for
     comprehensive domestic violence legislation in
     New York, by Lisa R. Beck v15 Fordham Urban
     Law Journal Fall '87 p999-1048
          LIBRARY SUBSCRIBES TO JOURNAL


FAMILY VIOLENCE
-government policy

          Domestic violence legislation: an impact
     assessment, by Annette Jolin il. v11 Journal
     of Police Science and Administration Dec '83
     p451-456
          LIBRARY SUBSCRIBES TO JOURNAL


FAMILY VIOLENCE
-litigation

          Verdict upheld against police for failing
     to protect spouse, (New York) by Deborah
     Squiers il 13 col in. v203 New York Law
     Journal April 30 '90 p1 col 3
          LIBRARY SUBSCRIBES TO JOURNAL


FAMILY VIOLENCE
-prevention

          Helping elderly victims of family
     violence, by Janice Chapin and Eilleen Buckley
     il 37 col in. v122 New Jersey Law Journal Dec
     15 '88 p10 col 1
          LIBRARY SUBSCRIBES TO JOURNAL


FAMILY VIOLENCE
-reports

          Panel says battered women may have no
     choice but retaliation, (Committee on Domestic
     Violence and Incarcerated Women) (New York)
     v18 Criminal Justice Newsletter Aug 3 '87 p6-7
```

Figure 4.15. (*continued*)

```
FAMILY VIOLENCE
-statistics

            Guns and domestic violence, (Victoria) by
            David Neal v13 Legal Service Bulletin Dec '88
            p261


CONJUGAL VIOLENCE
-law and legislation

                Judging domestic violence, by Gail
            Goolkasian v10 Harvard Women's Law Journal Spr
            '87 p275-284
                    LIBRARY SUBSCRIBES TO JOURNAL

                Legal perspectives on family violence,
            (Seventy-Fifth Anniversary Issue) by Franklin
            F. Zimring v75 California Law Review Jan '87
            p521-539
                    LIBRARY SUBSCRIBES TO JOURNAL
```

Youth and Families—headed by Mary McKeough (address and phone number provided)—which oversees something called the Child Abuse and Neglect Prevention and Treatment Program. This agency and its director may be of great help to you.

Now, on to the law library and LegalTrac. *Domestic violence* doesn't work as a keyword here because LegalTrac uses LC subject headings. You are sent elsewhere: *family violence, abused parents, child abuse, conjugal violence* or *wife abuse.* As you might imagine, the legal system is vitally involved in this issue, and the listings are prodigious (see Figure 4.15). Note that most of the law review articles are analytical overviews—just the kind of material you need to understand overarching legal concerns. These articles will, of course, get you to specific cases if that's the direction your research is taking.

At the health sciences library you turn to *Psychological Abstracts* to see what studies have been conducted on the psychological implications of domestic violence. Under *family violence* you find more than two pages of citations, many of which look promising (see Figure 4.16). The numerical code after the entry directs you to a listing in the abstracts vol-

Figure 4.16. Excerpt from Psychological Abstracts *subject index*

Volume 76

Family Violence SUBJECT INDEX **Family Violence**

Family Violence [See Also Child Abuse]
application of U. Bronfenbrenner's social ecological hierarchy to prevention & management of physical assaultiveness, children & families, 23158
assessment & treatment issues, child witnesses of discord & violence between parents, literature review, 36745
attitudes & practices in response to wife abuse, physicians, Canada, 27468
batterer counseling, shelter outcome, battered females, 23563
causal attributions in marital violence, spouses, implications for methodological weaknesses, 1800
causation profiles, wife assaulters, literature review, 15837
characteristics consistent with personality disorder criteria, male spouse abusers, literature review, treatment implications, 12133
characteristics of domestic violence in relationships, alcoholic adults, 5437
childrearing practices & approaches to discipline & marital discord, violent conflict in homes, 13–17 yr old males, 5415
cluster analysis of abuse & antisocial behavior variables, male abusers of females, 22704
concepts of Balance Theory & General Systems Theory, understanding interactional dynamics & marital adjustment & communication patterns, father–daughter incest families, 36773
congressional reauthorization of federal family violence & child abuse prevention & treatment programs, 11640
contexts & reasons for drinking, maritally violent husbands, 15842
critique of current orientation & intervention practices of batterer programs, wife abusers, Canada, accountability implications, 27357
cultural & social stress & economics & conflict theory of family violence, 1850
definitions & development & consequences of child & spouse abuse & other violence, families, implications for legal & psychological interventions, 26231
degree of violent socialization, severity of violent behavior, male spouse batterers, 15827
demographic characteristics & MMPI profiles, males vs females convicted of murdering their domestic partners, 15857
development of family violence counseling program in rural community, battered females & their children & batterer husbands, Canada, 27133
developmental model for integrated interventions, males who batter their wives, application of L. Kohlberg's theory of moral development, 2185
domestic violence policies & increased arrests, urban police departments, 11639
dream as vehicle for retrieval of traumatic childhood memories, 49 yr old depressed female, case report, 2260
early exposure to marital violence & child abuse in families-of-origin, wife assaulters vs maritally nonviolent males, 15826
early socialization vs acute or chronic life stress, spouse abuse, married adults, 26299
ecosystematic approach to family violence, attribution implications, 36748
emotional &/or physical abuse by spouse, potential for client abuse & absenteeism & job performance, female employees of residential facility for mentally retarded, 30935
epidemiology & treatment & other issues, spouse abuse & other domestic violence, 22697
escalation & maintenance & cybernetic model of spouse abuse, 5391
establishment of batterer typologies, wife assaulters, Canada, 26221
ethics & role & utilization of nonviolent contracts, management of family violence, family therapists, 30361
evaluation of group therapy program for family violence, social functioning & cessation of violence, 23–52 yr old male abusers, 30333
evolutionary social psychology models, prediction of association of genetic relationship & migration of homicide & violence risk, families, 22695
examination of "violence breeds violence" hypothesis, abused children, literature review, 36811
extent & type of dating & parental vio-

Figure 4.17. Excerpt from Psychological Abstracts *abstracts volume*

PHYSICAL AND PSYCHOLOGICAL DISORDERS

76:    36809-36813

tishism that includes the use of abstract means to symbolically deny the female lack of a phallus. The case of a 23-yr-old male graduate student with an obscene telephone perversion is presented in which obscene words seen, heard, and spoken were used to deal with conflicts involving the dread of the sight of the "castrated" female genital. (Fench, German & Spanish abstracts)

36810. **Widom, Cathy S.** (Indiana U, Bloomington) **The cycle of violence.** *Science,* 1989(Apr), Vol 244(4901), 160–166. —Reviews the current empirical status of the hypothesis that violence begets violence, drawing on data from the fields of psychology, sociology, psychiatry, social work, and nursing. The present author suggests that methodological problems substantially restrict knowledge of the long-term consequences of childhood victimization and comments on them. Findings from a cohort study show that being abused or neglected as a child increases one's risk for delinquency, adult criminal behavior, and violent criminal behavior. However, the majority of abused and neglected children do not become delinquent, criminal, or violent. Caveats in interpreting these findings and their implications are discussed in this article.

36811. **Widom, Cathy S.** (Indiana U, Bloomington) **Does violence beget violence? A critical examination of the literature.** *Psychological Bulletin,* 1989(Jul), Vol 106(1), 3–28. —Critically examines the "violence breeds violence" hypothesis broadly defined. Organized into seven sections, the literature review includes (a) the abuse breeds abuse hypothesis; (b) reports of small numbers of violent/homicidal offenders; (c) studies examining the relationship of abuse and neglect to delinquency; (d) to violent behavior; and (e) to aggressive behavior in infants and young children; (f) abuse, withdrawal, and self-destructive behavior; and (g) studies of the impact of witnessing or observing violent behavior: A detailed discussion of methodological considerations and shortcomings precedes the re-

view. The author concludes that existing knowledge of the long-term consequences of abusive home environments is limited and suggests that conclusions about the strength of the cycle of violence be tempered by the dearth of convincing empirical evidence. Recommendations are made for further research.—*Journal abstract.*

36812. **Zagar, Robert; Arbit, Jack; Hughes, John R.; Busell, Robert E. et al.** (Circuit Court of Cook County Juvenile Div, IL) **Developmental and disruptive behavior disorders among delinquents.** *Journal of the American Academy of Child & Adolescent Psychiatry,* 1989(May), Vol 28(3), 437–440.—Medical histories, psychological tests, psychiatric examinations, and social investigations were reviewed to determine the frequency of independent diagnoses of retardation, attention deficit disorder with hyperactivity (ADD-H), and attention deficit disorder without hyperactivity (ADD). In a sample of 1,956 (384 females and 1,572 males) adjudicated delinquents (aged 6–17 yrs), 9% had ADD-H, 15% were retarded, and 46% had ADD. The   re-liabilities of the diagnoses were 0.95 for retardation, 0.91 for ADD-H, and 0.94 ADD. Retarded delinquents had the greatest scholastic delays followed by the ADD-H and ADD adolescent offenders.

36813. **Zeanah, Charles H. & Zeanah, Paula D.** (Women & Infant's Hosp, Providence, RI) **Intergenerational transmission of maltreatment: Insights from attachment theory and research.** *Psychiatry,* 1989(May), Vol 52(2), 177–196.—After reviewing evidence for intergenerational transmission (IT) of maltreatment of children as it has traditionally been viewed, the characteristics of maltreating parents that support a redefinition of IT are considered. J. Bowlby's (1969, 1973, 1980) construct of internal working models describes inferred measurement of these IT models in infants and adults. Recent findings about congruence of internal working models in parents and children and how patterns of mal-

Figure 4.18. *Excerpt from* Index Medicus

Merkel PA, et al. **N Engl J Med** 1989 Sep 21;321(12):835–6

A randomized study of maintenance therapy with ranitidine to prevent the recurrence of duodenal ulcer. Van Deventer GM, et al. **N Engl J Med** 1989 Apr 27;320(17): 1113–9

Effect of omeprazole and ranitidine on ulcer healing and relapse rates in patients with benign gastric ulcer [see comments] Walan A, et al. **N Engl J Med** 1989 Jan 12;320(2):69–75. **Comment in:** N Engl J Med 1989 Jul 20;321 (3):191–2

Ranitidine prevents postoperative transfusion-induced depression of delayed hypersensitivity. Nielsen HJ, et al. **Surgery** 1989 Jun;105(6):711–7

RANULA

ETIOLOGY

Pathogenesis and treatment of ranula: report of three cases. Galloway RH, et al. **J Oral Maxillofac Surg** 1989 Mar; 47(3):299–302

PATHOLOGY

Cervical ranulas. Batsakis JG, et al. **Ann Otol Rhinol Laryngol** 1988 Sep–Oct;97(5 Pt 1):561–2 (8 ref.)

RAPE

What causes sexual assault? [letter] Margolis LH, et al. **Am J Dis Child** 1989 Feb;143(2):137

The dark consequences of marital rape. Campbell JC, et al. **Am J Nurs** 1989 Jul;89(7):946–9

Self-cutting after rape. Greenspan GS, et al. **Am J Psychiatry** 1989 Jun;146(6): 789–90

Blitz rape and confidence rape: a typology applied to 1,000 consecutive cases. Silverman DC, et al. **Am J Psychiatry** 1988 Nov;145(11): 1438–41

Office counseling of rape victims [clinical conference] Matheny J, et al. **J Fam Pract** 1989 Jun;28(6):657–60

Anti-HIV substances for rape victims [letter] Foster IM, et al. **JAMA** 1989 Jun 16;261(23):3407

Sample sexual assault data sheet [letter] Emans SJ, et al. **Pediatrics** 1989 Jun;83(6):1073–4

Rape and AIDS [letter] Gellert GA, et al. **Pediatrics** 1989 Apr;83(4 Pt 2):644–5

The elderly victim of rape. Cartwright PS, et al. **South Med J** 1989 Aug;82(8):988–9

PREVENTION & CONTROL

Resistance to sexual assault: who resists and what happens? Siegel JM, et al. **Am J Public Health** 1989 Jan;79(1):27–31

Deadly defense? [letter] Schadler PW, et al. **Ann Emerg Med** 1988 Dec;17(12):1367

RAS GENES

Ras oncogene is expressed in adenocarcinoma of the endometrium. Long CA, et al. **Am J Obstet Gynecol** 1988 Dec; 159(6):1512–6

Expression of the ras oncogene in gynecologic tumors. O'Brien TJ, et al. **Am J Obstet Gynecol** 1989 Feb; 160(2): 344–52

Immunohistologic detection of ras oncogene products. Specific or spurious? [editorial] Wick MR. **Arch Pathol Lab Med** 1989 Jan; 113(1):13–5

Analysis of N-RAS exon-1 mutations in myelodysplastic syndromes by polymerase chain reaction and direct sequencing. Bar-Eli M, et al. **Blood** 1989 Jan;73(1):281–3

Rare occurrence of N-ras point mutations in Philadelphia chromosome positive chronic myeloid leukemia. Collins SJ, et al. **Blood** 1989 Mar;73(4):1028–32

Identification of a second transforming gene, rasn, in a human multiple myeloma line with a rearranged c-myc allele. Ernst TJ, et al. **Blood** 1988 Oct; 72(4):1163–7

Histologic typing of non-Hodgkin's lymphomas by in situ hybridization with DNA probes of oncogenes. Hamatani K, et al. **Blood** 1989 Jul;74(1):423–9

Ras oncogene mutations are rare late stage events in chronic myelogenous leuke-

ume. The *violence begets violence* idea (code 36811) looks like one you might want to pursue (see Figure 4.17). *Index Medicus*, while it has no listings under the LC headings you've been using for domestic violence, does have an interesting entry concerning marital rape under *rape* (see Figure 4.18).

Your excursion to specialty libraries has been quite productive—and much less painful than you expected! That's because you understood what these libraries had to offer and how to get it before you got there. Good work. You've found a wide range of primary and secondary material and located a number of experts you may want to interview later. But the search continues.

5

Electronic Libraries

Meet the modern media writer.

She peruses a recent Supreme Court decision, delves into the financial records of a major corporation, locates an important piece of medical research and checks on the progress of a bill in the state legislature.

He tracks a competitor's media buying patterns, studies readership response to several dozen magazines, checks last night's Nielsen ratings, refreshes his memory about a rival agency's successful ad campaign and reads a market research summary for a new product.

They do all this without running to the library, waiting for the mail, shuffling papers or rifling through reports. They never get stuck in traffic or get stranded on "hold." In fact, they never leave their offices.

Instead, they (or their media organization's resident expert) *boot up*, *log on* and tie into an electronic universe where vast stores of knowledge flash around the world at the speed of light, appearing almost instantaneously on the screen of their desktop computers. They use small, relatively inexpensive office computers to perform the most basic and important task of a mass communicator: information gathering.

Mass communication and the information revolution

Computerized newsrooms, publishing companies and ad agencies are hardly futuristic. Today virtually everyone—from back-country editors to Madison Avenue moguls—sits in front of terminals to write ad copy, edit articles and figure payroll accounts. During the past two decades computers have revolutionized how mass media workers handle information.

But the most important part of the information revolution is just now hitting the majority of newspapers, magazines, broadcast stations and ad agencies. Media writers who previously understood computers only as a way to process, store and retrieve information within the electronic boundaries of their own office systems are now learning to go beyond these old-fashioned limits. With only modest extra expense the same desktop computers on which they write their stories can be transformed into powerful information-gathering machines that tap into massive electronic storehouses of information hundreds or thousands of miles away. This sophisticated communication between an information-gathering computer and a computerized library of material (or database) is the next phase of the information revolution. Most media industries are slowly catching on as they begin to understand that electronic research has the following important benefits.

Speed

Time is the media writer's most precious commodity—and most often cited excuse for superficiality. It's deadline pressure, say all varieties of mass communicators, that keeps us from doing the complete, in-depth job we'd like to do. Enter the information-gathering computer. Assuming the writer has the option of driving to a decent library with solid reference and government documents sections—and many writers don't—a desktop computer tied into an electronic information-gathering network makes it possible to do the job both more quickly and more thoroughly. One computer expert estimates that one minute spent searching computer databases is the equivalent of one hour spent in a library. Also consider how the computer can shorten information lag time. While many computerized libraries are updated daily or weekly, the local library may receive

dors, and they offer what are known, descriptively, as *en-
database services*. DIALOG is the largest of these with more
databases containing an excess of 200 million records. The
wesome: business, agriculture, medicine, environment, science
ology, law and government. Some of the databases offer full
rs provide bibliographic references and abstracts. Other online
pecialize, like Dow Jones/News Retrieval with its impressive
of financial information and Mead Data Central with its full-
ibrary database. All vendors provide users with detailed, fre-
pdated catalogs.

cost of going online

st media writers—and more importantly, their bosses—don't
the cost of traditional information gathering. If they did, if they
the hours and the miles and the postage and phone bills, they'd
cover that a chunk of their budget goes toward gathering infor-
Online searching is not in itself cheap. But if conducted effi-
y someone who has thought through a search strategy, it is a real

cost of online searching varies widely, depending on which
es you use, how quickly you search and what you ask for. The
f *Database Searcher*, a magazine for "online professionals," re-
at she's conducted searches ranging from $1.25 (for general infor-
about a disease, easy to retrieve from an inexpensive government-
zed database) to $3,000 (for a detailed round-up of construction
s around the world, each of which had to be researched separately).
rches we reproduce later in this chapter each cost about $10.
e experienced (but harried) director of a magazine's library had
rror story to tell: He entered a database, typed in several key-
found 10 titles of articles that looked interesting and instructed
mputer to extract these articles and store them. But he forgot to
the length of the articles, several of which turned out to be more
0 pages long. The database he was using charged 5 cents per line to
ut. A minor search became a nasty $300 surprise. You can avoid
urprises by educating yourself about the databases and their costs,
ng your strategy before you go online and being vigilant about
s.

only quarterly or annual updates of certain information. Library acquisition of some government and legal documents typically runs months (or
even years) behind. These same documents may be available almost instantaneously via the computer.

Accessibility

Dedicated media writers make time to travel to the library. After an
hour of hunting, they pinpoint just the article, book or document they
need only to discover that it has been checked out, misplaced or sent to
the bindery. The same information in a computerized library is always
available. Not only can many people read the material at the same time,
but most computer libraries stay open 24 hours a day. Media writers who
don't work near well-stocked reference, law or government libraries are
not doomed to write ill-researched stories. The reporter for the *Dead
Mountain Echo* can access the same information as the journalist for the
New York *Times*. An even more compelling reason to use computer databases is that an increasing amount of information is simply not available
in any other form. You must remember, however, that computer databases generally lack historical depth. When a company goes online with
information, the most recent information is fed into the system first.
Then, slowly, the database is backdated. This means that many databases
do not have material dating back more than five or six years. In most
cases, to conduct historical research on an issue or trend, you cannot depend on online searching.

Convenience

Searching for material via computer is frequently the most convenient
information-gathering method. You stay put while the information comes
to you rather than the reverse. You draw on the computer's tireless, single-
minded energy, letting the computer dig through masses of information
that could take you hours (days, weeks) to sort through. Instead of poring
over four separate indexes, each covering only three years of material,
you use a computer service that does the combined search for you—in
minutes. Instead of looking up three related topics, cross-referencing
them and culling what you find, you instruct the computer to combine
topics and find common references. Instead of reading through entire ar-

ticles to determine their relevance, you can instruct the computer to scan for certain keywords.

Although you may not be familiar with this sophisticated "online" information gathering, you probably know its cousin: CD/ROM searching, a common technology in today's libraries. Both online and CD/ROM searching take place at computer terminals, and both involve tapping into large stores of categorized information called databases. In both searches the information gatherer types in keywords to focus and limit the search. But the CD/ROM search is self-contained. The database is on a disk stored in the computer system itself. For example, your library creates its own database of all its holdings. You come into the library, sit at a computer and, after entering a keyword that focuses your search, instruct the computer to search the database for all relevant materials. The federal government and many independent publishing companies also produce CDs (compact discs) with extensive databases you can access for free from library computers.

Online searching, on the other hand, involves communicating with distant databases. It vastly increases your access to information and allows you to conduct sophisticated searches—for a price.

Learning the lingo

Thankfully, you don't have to be a computer wizard to participate in this new phase of the information revolution. In fact, many larger media organizations are hiring computer search experts who conduct database searches for writers. *Time* magazine, for example, employs 26 computer search experts as part of its 80-person in-house library staff. University and other libraries also employ such experts who, for a fee, will make quick work of a complex search.

Free-lancers or those without access to search experts might have to do the searching themselves. Database vendors (companies that lease the rights to use databases and provide searchers with easy entry to them) offer day-long seminars in search strategies and procedures in cities throughout the country. With or without this instruction, it will help to know some basics.

Unless you are one of those who delight in talking Pascal, peripherals and parallel ports, it helps to think of the computerized information-gathering process in human rather than machine terms. Think of the

desktop computer as an extension of can make phone calls, ask questions a computer that stores masses of inform magazines, books, reference materials ink on paper but as electronic impuls your computer calls the distant librar brarian who asks what information you of light, gets it for you. Your computer, down the material.

Let's complete the picture with a mi may be a *microcomputer* (also known or, if it is connected to an office system, not describe the size of the machine but formation can it store at one time? How Can it do several tasks simultaneously? powerful type of computer, but it is still information-gathering tool.

The device that allows your computer distant computer is called a *modem*. It tra that make up your computer's vocabulary by phone lines and reverses the process for

The distant electronic storehouse of inf and it can vary in the amount of information vary in size—from a few hundred items to library that may sprawl through many large the computerized database is amazingly com size of your bathroom can store more inform versity library.

Databases most helpful to journalistic forms: *bibliographic* and *full-text*. A bibliog mous index, or set of indexes, that provides th locate the actual material. This kind of databa what article in which issue of what journal. It sentence summary of the article. But if you w yourself, you need to either locate it in the libra database. There you will find the entire conten newspapers, reports and documents.

Several companies lease the rights to a va bases, making dozens or even hundreds of them phone number and using one password. Thes

online ver
cyclopedic
than 350
scope is a
and techn
text; othe
vendors s
databases
text law
quently u

Th

M
calculate
tallied u
soon dis
mation.
ciently
bargain

Th
databas
editor
ports th
mation
subsidi
project
The se

O
this h
words
his co
check
than 3
print
such
plann
detail

Regular search costs include phone rates, vendor charges, database charges and per item fees. Phone rates can be quite low ($6 per hour, for example) if you use one of the private services instead of your regular long-distance company. In any case, the phone charge is generally a minimal part of the overall search cost because most searches are completed in 10 minutes. Vendor charges are the fees the encyclopedic database companies charge you for their services. Some cost nothing to join; others have annual subscription fees from as low as $50 to as high as several thousand dollars. You also pay a database charge (from $30 to several hundred dollars an hour) for using each information storehouse. The per item charge (from 10 cents to more than $10) is assessed for every citation, abstract or full-text document you either see on the screen or print out. Some databases, as the unhappy magazine librarian discovered, charge per line.

These costs may sound daunting but they shouldn't intimidate you. When all goes well, computer searching can be quick, making phone charges mere pocket change. Vendors frequently offer special rates, particularly if you use their services often or during off-hours. Surprisingly, old-fashioned legwork often costs more than high-tech searching.

Specialized databases

You can read the entire text of Federal Communications Commission reports, check the progress of Department of Defense programs, look up the breeding records of Kentucky Derby winners or verify Brazilian coffee prices. The online world grows more diverse every day as the information industry continues to boom. Thousands of databases are publicly available, many of which can provide journalistic researchers with the quick, up-to-date information they need to do their jobs well.

Because the online information industry is so dynamic, keeping abreast of new databases and services is sometimes difficult. Aside from the several published database directories that you can buy at your local bookstore, three magazines keep their eyes on the field: *Database*, *Online* and *Database Searcher*. The industry also has its own trade group, the Information Industry Association.

Databases of particular interest to journalistic researchers include such massive compendia of information as the following: DISCLOSURE, which provides in-depth financial information on more than 12,000 companies; ENVIROLINE, which covers environmental information from 5,000 international primary and secondary source publications; and NEWSEARCH, a daily index of more than 2,000 news stories, articles and book reviews from more than 1,700 of the most important newspapers, magazines and periodicals. These examples are offered only to whet your appetite. In this book's Glossary of Sources, beginning on page 209, you will find the names and descriptions of many more databases of special interest to media writers.

Snakes in Eden

Online information gathering does have its problems. Cost can certainly be one, particularly if the searcher is ill-trained on the system or has not thought through a search strategy. Accessibility of some databases is another. While DIALOG and a few other encyclopedic database services offer a vast array of information relevant to the journalistic researcher, some potentially important databases are available only through specialty vendors. Other databases are part of much smaller information systems or are available only through their creators. That can mean scores of different phone numbers, log-on commands, search procedures—and bills.

But these problems are mundane compared with the deeper concerns facing a society rushing headlong into an information age. Consider three of these concerns and their implications for working communicators and their audiences.

Polarization

Computerization of information, originally thought to have great potential as a democratizing force, seems to be having the opposite effect: the reinforcement and further polarization of information-rich and information-poor classes in society. More and more information is fed into databases without being published in a universally accessible form. That means that those with computers and the wherewithal to use them as information-gathering machines have access to information the rest of the public does not. Mass communicators, corporate moguls, financiers and a handful of other professionals (all of whom are members of the information-rich class already) get "richer." They may choose to share their information—or to hoard it.

Censorship

Lightning-quick, invisible censorship is possible in an age of computer-stored information. In the United States, censorship issues are generally public battles: A school district tries to purge *Huckleberry Finn* from the curriculum; Ronald Reagan muzzles the literary aspirations of FBI agents. The media report these events; the public discusses them. But in an age of digitized information, censorship can be both swift and secret. It takes only one person, a password and a few keystrokes to erase (or change) complete files. If those files exist only in computerized form, they may be lost forever.

Privacy

Computerization makes private information dangerously accessible. With patience, the right password and a bit of luck, a computer hacker can raid information from virtually any database around the world. The 12-year-olds who, for fun, penetrate sophisticated government or corporate systems have shown just how possible it is for outsiders to gain access to private information. And computers now house enormous amounts of personal information about almost all of us, from criminal records to consumer habits. This has obvious implications for all of us, as well as special legal and ethical implications for journalistic information gatherers. If it is possible—although not legal—to obtain private information about an individual, how far will the enterprising, perhaps well-meaning journalist go? Suppose quietly and unobtrusively breaking into a database means the difference between a significant investigative story and no story at all?

These are important issues to ponder, for computerization of information is more than just a new technology. The information revolution has far greater implications for our society than simply quickening the pace of communication and changing the workplace. It can change how we think, how we act and what we value.

We need to discuss and debate these thorny issues. But at the same time, we need to realize that electronic libraries are a boon to the working media writer. Their convenience and speed are unparalleled; their scope is constantly growing. They are the future. To help you see that future more clearly, let's return to our master searches.

The search

For the purposes of this search, we will log on to DIALOG, the country's largest database vendor. Before we turn on the computer (or ask an online expert to do so), we plan our strategy, focusing on answers to these vital questions:

1. What kind of material are we looking for (articles in consumer publications, primary research, government statistics, names of experts)?

2. What keywords define and limit our topic? (Remember the *Library of Congress Subject Headings*.)

3. What database or databases available from this vendor would be most likely to contain the kind of information we need? (Vendors provide detailed descriptions of all databases they offer in catalogs sent to subscribers.)

Let's begin with a search on domestic violence issues. First, we answer the three vital questions:

▶ *Kind of material.* Let's say we're looking for primary research on domestic violence, the kind found in journals that serve the fields of sociology, psychology, psychiatry, mental health, therapy and the like.

▶ *Keywords.* We know from past experience (and from looking at the *Library of Congress Subject Headings*) that a number of descriptors work with this topic: *family violence, conjugal violence, domestic violence.*

▶ *Database.* Looking through the most recent DIALOG Database Catalog, we find a number of possibilities, among them a database called "Family Resources." The description tells us that the database contains bibliographic references from more than 1,200 journals, books, newsletters and government documents on research related to the family. Dating back more than 20 years, the database covers the disciplines of medicine, psychology, sociology and education. This all sounds promising.

Follow along, referring to Figure 5.1, to see how the search progresses.

(a) We log on to the database and punch in our keywords (*conjugal* or *domestic* or *family* coupled with *violence*). Using all possible terms at once increases the efficiency of the search. After a second or two of searching, the computer responds by telling us that 1,751 items in the database contain these keywords.

(b) We ask the computer to limit these items in several ways. First, we want only journal articles (not items from newsletters or government documents). The computer finds 920 references.

(c) Now we limit the search to 1985–1990 (688 references).

(d) Now we limit ourselves to the most current material, 1988–1990 (279 references).

(e) Finally, to increase the chances of the articles being on target for our search, we ask the computer to find references that actually have the keywords in the titles (23 references).

(f) Now we ask the distant computer to send the titles of the first four of these references. (Asking for titles is free; asking for full citations costs per citation.) Looking at these titles, we find several that sound promising.

(g) We ask the distant computer to send full citations plus abstracts of those articles that sound promising.

(h) Because this database also includes "human resources" (otherwise known as "people"), we decide to use the computer to search for national experts on family violence. These people may make good interview subjects. Note that each listing gives the person's name, affiliation, phone numbers, present position and areas of expertise.

This search, from start to finish, took six minutes and cost about $10.

For the diets fads and frauds search, we will try something a little different. This is a relatively difficult topic to research via computer because so many databases may contain pertinent information. Good information may be found in medical, legal, sociological, business and news databases, for example. Which one should the searcher choose? An efficient and inexpensive way to find out is to log on to DIALINDEX, DIALOG's index of its hundreds of databases. Follow this preliminary search by referring to Figure 5.2.

Figure 5.1. *Excerpts from a DIALOG database search*

```
File 291: FAMILY RESOURCES_70-90/SEP
          (C NATL COUNCIL ON FAMILY RELATIONS 1990)

    Set   Items   Description

?ss (conjugal or domestic or family)()violence

    S1      125   CONJUGAL                          ⌉
    S2      659   DOMESTIC                          │
    S3    83829   FAMILY                            │  a
    S4     2219   VIOLENCE                          │
    S5     1751   (CONJUGAL OR DOMESTIC OR          │
                  FAMILY)()VIOLENCE                 │
?ss dt=ja and s5                                    ⌋

    S6    62835   DT=JA                             ⌉
           1751   S5                                │  b
    S7      920   DT=JA AND S5                      │
?ss py=1985:1990 and s7                             ⌋

    S8    43918   PY=1985 : PY=1990                 ⌉
            920   S7                                │  c
    S9      688   PY=1985:1990 AND S7               │
?ss s7 and py=1988:1990                             ⌋

            920   S7                                ⌉
   S10    13479   PY=1988 : PY=1990                 │  d
   S11      279   S7 AND PY=1988:1990               │
?ss s5/ti and s6 and s10                            ⌋

   S12      265   S5/TI                             ⌉
          62835   S6                                │
          13479   S10                               │  e
   S13       23   S5/TI AND S6 AND S10              │
?t 13/8/1de/                                        ⌋


 13/8/1                                             ⌉
0226043                                             │
  A FRAMEWORK FOR STUDYING FAMILY SOCIALIZATION     │
OVER THE LIFE CYCLE: THE CASE OF FAMILY VIOLENCE    │
  Section Headings: SOCIALIZATION (036); FAMILY     │
RELATIONSHIPS (022); STAGES IN FAMILY LIFE CYCLE    │
(038); FAMILY VIOLENCE (090V)                       │
  Descriptors: SOCIALIZATION FAMILY-RELATIONSHIPS   │
FAMILY- LIFE-CYCLE FAMILY-VIOLENCE                  │  f
 13/8/2                                             │
0225987                                             │
  AN ANALYSIS OF DOMESTIC VIOLENCE IN ASIAN AMERICAN│
COMMUNITIES: A MULTICULTURAL APPROACH TO COUNSELING ▼
```

Figure 5.1. *(continued)*

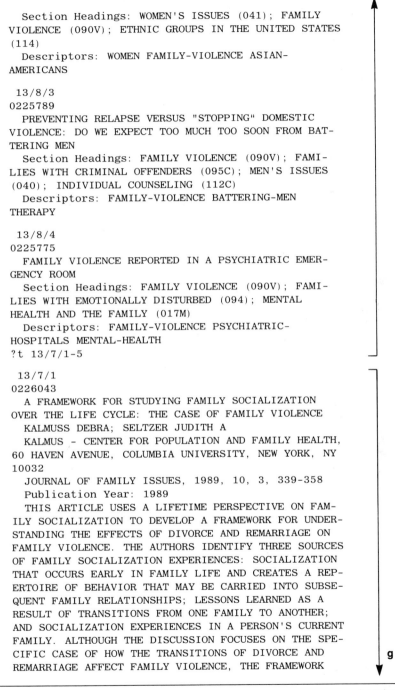

Section Headings: WOMEN'S ISSUES (041); FAMILY
VIOLENCE (090V); ETHNIC GROUPS IN THE UNITED STATES
(114)
Descriptors: WOMEN FAMILY-VIOLENCE ASIAN-
AMERICANS

13/8/3
0225789
PREVENTING RELAPSE VERSUS "STOPPING" DOMESTIC
VIOLENCE: DO WE EXPECT TOO MUCH TOO SOON FROM BAT-
TERING MEN
Section Headings: FAMILY VIOLENCE (090V); FAMI-
LIES WITH CRIMINAL OFFENDERS (095C); MEN'S ISSUES
(040); INDIVIDUAL COUNSELING (112C)
Descriptors: FAMILY-VIOLENCE BATTERING-MEN
THERAPY

13/8/4
0225775
FAMILY VIOLENCE REPORTED IN A PSYCHIATRIC EMER-
GENCY ROOM
Section Headings: FAMILY VIOLENCE (090V); FAMI-
LIES WITH EMOTIONALLY DISTURBED (094); MENTAL
HEALTH AND THE FAMILY (017M)
Descriptors: FAMILY-VIOLENCE PSYCHIATRIC-
HOSPITALS MENTAL-HEALTH
?t 13/7/1-5

13/7/1
0226043
A FRAMEWORK FOR STUDYING FAMILY SOCIALIZATION
OVER THE LIFE CYCLE: THE CASE OF FAMILY VIOLENCE
KALMUSS DEBRA; SELTZER JUDITH A
KALMUS - CENTER FOR POPULATION AND FAMILY HEALTH,
60 HAVEN AVENUE, COLUMBIA UNIVERSITY, NEW YORK, NY
10032
JOURNAL OF FAMILY ISSUES, 1989, 10, 3, 339-358
Publication Year: 1989
THIS ARTICLE USES A LIFETIME PERSPECTIVE ON FAM-
ILY SOCIALIZATION TO DEVELOP A FRAMEWORK FOR UNDER-
STANDING THE EFFECTS OF DIVORCE AND REMARRIAGE ON
FAMILY VIOLENCE. THE AUTHORS IDENTIFY THREE SOURCES
OF FAMILY SOCIALIZATION EXPERIENCES: SOCIALIZATION
THAT OCCURS EARLY IN FAMILY LIFE AND CREATES A REP-
ERTOIRE OF BEHAVIOR THAT MAY BE CARRIED INTO SUBSE-
QUENT FAMILY RELATIONSHIPS; LESSONS LEARNED AS A
RESULT OF TRANSITIONS FROM ONE FAMILY TO ANOTHER;
AND SOCIALIZATION EXPERIENCES IN A PERSON'S CURRENT
FAMILY. ALTHOUGH THE DISCUSSION FOCUSES ON THE SPE-
CIFIC CASE OF HOW THE TRANSITIONS OF DIVORCE AND
REMARRIAGE AFFECT FAMILY VIOLENCE, THE FRAMEWORK

g

(continued)

Figure 5.1. (*continued*)

CAN BE EXTENDED TO OTHER FAMILY TRANSITIONS AND BE-
HAVIORS. COPYRIGHT, NATIONAL COUNCIL ON FAMILY RE-
LATIONS (NCFR).

13/7/3
0225789
PREVENTING RELAPSE VERSUS "STOPPING" DOMESTIC
VIOLENCE: DO WE EXPECT TOO MUCH TOO SOON FROM BAT-
TERING MEN
JENNINGS JERRY L
PROVIDENCE HOUSE/WILLINGBORO SHELTER, P. O. BOX
424, BURLINGTON, NJ 08016
JOURNAL OF FAMILY VIOLENCE, 1990, 5, 1, 43-60
Publication Year: 1990
THE AUTHOR QUESTIONS THE ENORMOUS DEMANDS FOR
CHANGE THAT ARE IMMEDIATELY PLACED ON BOTH ABUSIVE
MEN AND THE CLINICIANS TREATING THEM. HE PROPOSES A
MORE REALISTIC AND HUMANITARIAN SET OF THERAPEUTIC
EXPECTATIONS FOR CHANGE, EMPHASIZING RELAPSE PRE-
VENTION AND SUPPORTIVE MAINTENANCE. COPYRIGHT, NA-
TIONAL COUNCIL ON FAMILY RELATIONS (NCFR).

13/7/5
0225217
ELDER ABUSE & CHILD ABUSE: A CONSIDERATION OF
SIMILARITIES & DIFFERENCES IN INTERGENERATIONAL
FAMILY VIOLENCE
KORBIN JILL E; ANETZBERGER GEORGIA J; ECKERT J
KEVIN
KORBIN - DEPT; OF ANTHROPOLOGY, CASE WESTERN RE-
SERVE UNIVERSITY, CLEVELAND, OH 44106; ANETZBERGER
- WESTERN RESERVE AREA
AGENCY ON AGING, 1801 ST; CLAIRE, CLEVELAND, OH
44114; ECKERT -DEPT; OF SOCIOLOGY & ANTHROPOLOGY,
UNIVERSITY OF MARYLAND, BALTIMORE, MD 21228
JOURNAL OF ELDER ABUSE & NEGLECT, 1989, 1, 4, 1-14
Publication Year: 1989
THIS PAPER SUGGESTS DIMENSIONS RELEVANT TO A COM-
PARISON OF INTERGENERATIONAL PHYSICAL ABUSE OF
ELDER PARENTS AND YOUNG CHILDREN. COPYRIGHT, NA-
TIONAL COUNCIL ON FAMILY RELATIONS (NCFR).
?ss s5 and dt=hr

```
          1751  S5
    S14    562  DT=HR
    S15     57  S5 AND DT=HR
?ss s15 and pyu1988:1990

           57  S15
    S16  13479  PY=1988 : PY=1990
    S17      2  S15 AND PY=1988:1990
?t 17/7/1-2
```

h

Figure 5.1. *(continued)*

```
17/7/1
0221743
  GOODMAN NORMAN
  DEPT. OF SOCIOLOGY, STATE UNIV. OF NEW YORK AT
STONY BROOK, STONY BROOK, NY 11794-4356; TEL: 516-
632-7750 (WORK).
  Publication Year: 1989
  TITLE OF PRESENT POSITION: DISTINGUISHED TEACHING
PROFESSOR (SOCIOLOGY). EMPLOYER: STATE UNIVERSITY
OF NEW YORK AT STONY BROOK. HIGHEST DEGREE AT-
TAINED: PH.D. YEAR: 1963. INSTITUTION FROM WHICH
DEGREE WAS RECEIVED: NEW YORK UNIVERSITY. FIELD IN
WHICH DEGREE WAS GRANTED: SOCIOLOGY. OCCUPATIONAL
SPECIALTY: SOCIOLOGICALLY- ORIENTED SOCIAL PSYCHOL-
OGIST. PRESENT PROFESSIONAL INVOLVEMENT: ANALYSIS
OF COURTSHIP, MARRIAGE, AND FAMILY PATTERNS COMMON
IN THE UNITED STATES, AND THE LIKELY FUTURE PAT-
TERNS. PROFESSIONAL ORGANIZATION MEMBERSHIP(S): NA-
TIONAL COUNCIL ON FAMILY RELATIONS (NCFR); AMERICAN
SOCIOLOGICAL SOCIETY (ASA); EASTERN SOCIOLOGICAL
SOCIETY (ESS); AND SOCIETY FOR THE STUDY OF SYM-
BOLIC INTERACTION (SSSI). COPYRIGHT, NATIONAL COUN-
CIL ON FAMILY RELATIONS (NCFR).

17/7/2
0209155
  POTHAST HENRY L
  BOX 512, HUBBARD, IA 50122. TEL. 515-864-3323
(HOME).
  Publication Year: 1988
  TITLE OF PRESENT POSITION: SCHOOL SOCIAL WORKER.
EMPLOYER: AREA EDUCATION AGENCY 6, IOWA FALLS, IA.
HIGHEST DEGREE ATTAINED: MASTER OF SOCIAL WORK
(MSW). YEAR: 1981. INSTITUTION FROM WHICH DEGREE
WAS RECEIVED: UNIVERSITY OF IOWA. FIELD IN WHICH
DEGREE WAS GRANTED: SOCIAL WORK. OCCUPATIONAL SPE-
CIALTY: SCHOOL SOCIAL WORK. PRESENT PROFESSIONAL
INVOLVEMENT: PROJECTS: HANDBOOK ON PROBLEM CONCEP-
TUALIZATION AND MEASUREMENT IN SCHOOL SOCIAL WORK;
TOOLS AND PROCEDURES FOR EVALUATION OF SCHOOL-BASED
SUBSTANCE ABUSE PROGRAMS. PUBLICATIONS INCLUDE:
SCHOOL SOCIAL WORK INVOLVEMENT IN COMBATING CHILD
SEXUAL ABUSE; INSERVICE TRAINING ON PRACTICE RE-
SEARCH; PH.D. DISSERTATION TOPIC: JUVENILE PER-
PETRATORS OF CHILD SEXUAL ABUSE. PROFESSIONAL
ORGANIZATION MEMBERSHIP(S): NATIONAL COUNCIL ON
FAMILY RELATIONS (NCFR); NATIONAL ASSN. OF SOCIAL
WORKERS (NASW); IOWA SCHOOL SOCIAL WORKERS' ASSN.
(ISSWA).
?b 411
```

Figure 5.2. *Excerpts from a DIALOG database search*

```
File 411:DIALINDEX(tm)

?sf 148,47,154,88,149,150,111,papers

?show files

FILE NAME
____  _____

148:  TRADE AND INDUSTRY INDEX_81-90/OCT
 47:  MAGAZINE INDEX_1959-MARCH 1970,1973-90/OCT
154:  MEDLINE _ 83-90/NOV (9011W5)
 88:  ACADEMIC INDEX_1976-90/OCT
149:  HEALTH PERIODICALS DATABASE_1976-90/WEEK 40
150:     *** file name banner unavailable ***
111:  NATIONAL NEWSPAPER INDEX _ 79-90/SEP
146:  WASHINGTON POST_1983 - 11 Oct 1990
492:  ARIZONA REP./PHNX GAZETTE_1988-02 Oct 1990
494:  ST. LOUIS POST DISPATCH_ 1988 - 09 Oct 1990
630:  LOS ANGELES TIMES_ 1985 - 11 Oct 1990
631:  BOSTON GLOBE_ 1980 - 11 Oct 1990
632:  CHICAGO TRIBUNE_1988 - 12 Oct 1990
633:  PHILADELPHIA INQUIRER_ 1983 - 11 Oct 1990
634:  SAN JOSE MERCURY NEWS_Jun 85-11 Oct. 90
638:  NEWSDAY_ 1988 - 10 Oct 1990
639:  HOUSTON POST_ 1988 - 10 Oct 1990
640:  SAN FRANCISCO CHRONICLE_1988 - 10 Oct 1990
641:  ROCKY MOUNTAIN NEWS_Jun 1989-10 Oct 1990
642:  CHARLOTTE OBSERVER_1988-11 Oct 1990
```

a

```
?ss diet(7n)(fad? ? or fraud?)

Your SELECT statement is:
  ss diet(7n)(fad? ? or fraud?)
     Items File
     _____  ____

       1   148:  TRADE AND INDUSTRY INDEX_81-90/
                 OCT
      18    47:  MAGAZINE INDEX_1959-MARCH
                 1970,1973-90/OCT
     147   154:  MEDLINE _ 83-90/NOV (9011W5)
       6    88:  ACADEMIC INDEX_1976-90/OCT
      57   149:  HEALTH PERIODICALS DATABASE_
                 1976-90/WEEK 40
       2   111:  NATIONAL NEWSPAPER INDEX _ 79-90/
                 SEP
      24   146:  WASHINGTON POST_1983 - 11 Oct
                 1990
      11   492:  ARIZONA REP./PHNX GAZETTE_1988-02
                 Oct 1990
```

b

94

Figure 5.2. (*continued*)

```
    15    494:   ST. LOUIS POST DISPATCH_ 1988 -
                 09 Oct 1990
    30    630:   LOS ANGELES TIMES_ 1985 - 11 Oct
                 1990
    20    631:   BOSTON GLOBE_ 1980 - 11 Oct 1990
    12    632:   CHICAGO TRIBUNE_1988 - 12 Oct
                 1990
    27    633:   PHILADELPHIA INQUIRER_ 1983 - 11
                 Oct 1990
    30    634:   SAN JOSE MERCURY NEWS_Jun 85-11
                 Oct. 90
     7    638:   NEWSDAY_ 1988 - 10 Oct 1990
     3    639:   HOUSTON POST_ 1988 - 10 Oct 1990
     9    640:   SAN FRANCISCO CHRONICLE_1988 - 10
                 Oct 1990
     8    641:   ROCKY MOUNTAIN NEWS_Jun 1989-10
                 Oct 1990
     7    642:   CHARLOTTE OBSERVER_1988-11 Oct
                 1990


File 146:WASHINGTON POST_1983 - 11 Oct 1990
         (c) 1990 Washington Post


    Set   Items   Description
    ___   _____   _____

?ss diet(7n)(fad? ?or fraud?)                          c

    S1    3877   DIET
    S2    2279   FAD? ?
    S3    7037   FRAUD?
    S4      24   DIET(7N)(FAD? ? OR FRAUD?)
?t 4/8/1-3


Diet Gimmicks.
Line Count: 27  Word Count: 304

NAMED PERSONS: WYDEN, RON
DESCRIPTORS: Diet and nutrition; Food; Food
   products industry; Advertising; Business
   regulation                                          d

FTC Charges Diet Clinics With False Claims.
Line Count: 37  Word Count: 400

ORGANIZATION NAME: federal trade commission;
   pacific medical clinics
DESCRIPTORS: Diet and nutrition; Advertising;
   Fairfax County; Fraud
```

(*continued*)

Figure 5.2. (*continued*)

```
File 149:HEALTH PERIODICALS DATABASE_1976-90/WEEK
        40 (COPR. IAC 1990)

     Set  Items  Description
     ───  ─────  ───────────

?ss diet(7n)(fad? ? or fraud?)

     S1   9613  DIET
     S2    596  FAD? ?
     S3   1135  FRAUD?
     S4     57  DIET(7N)(FAD? ? OR FRAUD?)
?t 4/8/1-5
```

    e

```
4/8/1
Automatic weight loss with Cal-Ban? Send for your
    refund now! (includes related article about
    dubious dieting aids)
COMPANY NAME(S): Anderson Pharmacals - cases
PRODUCT NAME(S): Cal-Ban 3000 (Dieting aid) -
    marketing
DESCRIPTORS: United States. Food and Drug
    Administration - management; Weight reducing
    preparations - marketing; Guar - physiological
    effect; Mail fraud - cases; Starch blockers -
    physiological effect

4/8/2
09318449 Dialog File 149: Health Periodicals
    Database
Fad diet pitfalls; a quick fix could lead to
    trouble. (Fighting Fat: The Road to a Lean
    Physique)
DESCRIPTORS: Reducing diets - physiological
    aspects; Reducing - physiological aspects;
    Bodybuilding - physiological aspects

4/8/3
09284625 Dialog File 149: Health Periodicals
    Database
The children's hour. (cooking)
DESCRIPTORS: Children as cooks - analysis; Children
    - Nutrition; Latchkey children - Life skills
    guides; Microwave ovens - safety measures

4/8/4
09230089 Dialog File 149: Health Periodicals
    Database
The syndrome syndrome: catchy names for fashionable
    diseases - but are we drowning in diagnoses?
```

    f

Figure 5.2. (*continued*)

```
DESCRIPTORS: Syndromes - names; Diseases - names;
   Nosology - analysis

4/8/5
09035761 Dialog File 149: Health Periodicals
   Database
Diets shape up: Americans are finally choosing
   facts over fads.
DESCRIPTORS: Reducing diets - social aspects;
   Somatotypes - health aspects


?logoff
```

Before we log on, we carefully scan the DIALOG catalog for potential databases. Each database has a number we type in.

(a) Note that we've found 20 databases that look like good possibilities for containing information about diet fads and frauds. Note that we've selected medical and health databases, an industry database and academic as well as consumer-oriented information collections. We type in the numbers.

(b) Now we ask the computer to scan these databases for numbers of references to *diet fads* or *diet frauds*. The numbers in the left-hand column—from 1 in the Trade and Industry Index to 147 in MEDLINE—give us an insight into how helpful each database will be. Now we can zero in on the databases that look the most promising, saving both time and money.

(c) For the purposes of illustration, let's pursue two of these databases. First, we log on to the Washington *Post* database, again using *diet fads* or *diet frauds* as keywords. The computer tells us what we already know from the DIALINDEX search: There are 24 items under these categories.

(d) We ask to see the titles of the first two. (Again, asking for titles rather than full citations is smart strategy at this point—titles are free. If one sounds promising, we can quickly get the full citation. We don't have to pay for the full citations of off-target articles.) Both "Diet Gimmicks" and "FTC Charges Diet Clinics with False Claims" sound promising. If this were a real search, we would either ask for the citations, sign off and go to the library's microform collection of the Washington *Post* or, if we had more money than time, stay online and ask the distant database to send the full text of these stories to our computer. (The description of this database in the catalog tells us that full text is available.)

(e) We also decide to look more closely at the Health Periodicals Index database. Note there are 57 references to *diet fads* or *diet frauds* in the database.

(f) We ask to see the first five—titles only. Again, for those that look promising, we can quickly call up full citations. These combined searches for diet fads and frauds research cost about $10.

Perhaps someday databases will entirely replace library collections—but that day is still in the distant future. Today's journalistic information gatherers should begin to seriously educate themselves about computerized searching while continuing to hone their traditional searching methods. Computerized and traditional methods complement each other and can lead to faster, more efficient, more productive information gathering.

6

Government: The Information Colossus

VALDEZ—On the choppy and wind-blown waters of Prince William Sound, everything had gone wrong. The oil from the tanker Exxon Valdez remained a testament to human hesitation and indecision on Day 4 of the largest oil spill in U.S. history. A battalion of state, federal and oil company officials had taken too long. The weather had taken over.

—Larry Campbell and Charles Wohlforth
  Anchorage (Alaska) *Daily News*

When 987 feet of steel ripped into Alaska's Bligh Reef in March 1989 and dumped 11 million gallons of North Slope crude oil into some of the most pristine waters in the world, the public outcry was matched only by the scrambling of government bodies into action. Consider this partial list of government involvement in this disaster by day 4 of the spill:

Federal level

U.S. Navy, U.S. Coast Guard
Environmental Protection Agency
National Oceanic and Atmospheric Administration
U.S. Fish and Wildlife Service
National Marine Fisheries Service
National Transportation Safety Board
Federal Emergency Management Administration

State level

Alaska Department of Environmental Conservation
Alaska Department of Natural Resources

Alaska governor's office

New York Department of Motor Vehicles

Local level

Homer Volunteer Fire Department

City of Valdez

Tatitlek Village Corporation

Suffolk County (N.Y.) Police Department

These government units all had a function in this disaster and were sources of varying importance in the hectic information gathering that followed the oil spill. They provided important records, documents and statements for a public eager to understand how and why this accident happened. (As you can see from the list of government bodies involved, the story stretched all the way to New York state, the home of *Valdez* skipper Joseph Hazelwood. The state's motor vehicles department and the Suffolk County Police Department confirmed Hazelwood's past arrest for driving under the influence of intoxicants.)

Understanding government organization and operations is crucial for the information gatherer, regardless of media used. Government is a pervasive servant of our society; it is a prodigious collector and consumer of information; it can also be a jungle of jargon and confusion. You must learn your way around government functions and financing in order to clearly explain the impact of government on our daily lives. Government information is not just the stuff of daily news reports, either; government actions are analyzed, supported—and castigated—in editorials, in depth pieces for magazines and in the advertising/public relations components of election campaigns. An example of the incredible range of government functions—with the obvious impact on the public—can be seen in the *National Directory of State Agencies*; here is a partial list of government activities in its index:

- ▶ Air pollution control
- ▶ Banking
- ▶ Child welfare
- ▶ Corrections
- ▶ Court administration
- ▶ Drug abuse
- ▶ Education
- ▶ Environmental affairs

- ► Food and drugs
- ► Health
- ► Labor
- ► Mental health
- ► Natural resources
- ► Police
- ► Social services
- ► Taxation and revenue
- ► Water pollution
- ► Welfare

Let's examine strategies for discovering, obtaining and evaluating government information. Because previous chapters have examined the federal government, this chapter will focus mainly on state and local governments. However, before we can begin to understand how to tap government sources, we must have a fundamental understanding of how these organizations generally operate. We'll examine the following areas: authority given to governments, their general range of activities, their financing and spending, and the records and documents they generate. We'll follow that with a brief application of this information to our two master searches. In the Glossary of Sources, beginning on page 209, you'll find a list of commonly used government sources.

To serve, protect, and . . .
The granting of official authority

Whether the government unit is a county serving 2 million people or a mosquito abatement district of 200 rural homes, its organization and functions are set forth in a constitution, charter or some form of enabling document approved by voters in a defined geographical district. To learn how a governing body is organized, your basic source is the founding document. That document may tell you, for example, that a city is governed by a council made up of elected representatives (councilors) from designated districts and a mayor elected citywide. The city council may appoint professional administrators, such as a city manager and finance director and police chief, to run day-to-day operations. Through its charter the city may also be authorized to levy taxes and enact ordinances for the benefit of its citizenry.

In addition to the constitution or charter, good sources for discovering the structure of government authority are contained in the following:

▶ **Enabling legislation.** When an elected body creates an agency or commission, its authority to act will be detailed in an act, statute, ordinance or similar piece of lawmaking. This authority is often cited in administrative and judicial decisions.

▶ **Administrative rules.** These are contained in often ponderous documents. Administrators give "life" to laws through interpretations that make such legislation operable; however, these rules can be confusing and difficult to track. It is helpful—almost essential—to develop contacts within government units to help you track this information and translate it.

▶ **Operations manuals.** Found in virtually every government agency, the manuals show lines of authority, functions and processes of the government unit. These manuals can be helpful in explaining typical "behaviors" of government. For example, how does the school district conduct its contract negotiations with its classified staff? How does the county assessor deal with an appeal of a property tax assessment?

In addition to these primary documents, the information gatherer may be assisted by these sources:

▶ **Community relations or public relations directors.** Most government units or agencies these days have some type of public relations liaison with the media and general public. These sources can help you translate the jargon of bureaucracy and find your way through the organizational maze. While you should remember that the liaison person is an official spokesperson for that unit or agency, you can mine this information treasure through persistent inquiry and the development of a good working relationship.

▶ **State "blue books."** The "blue book" is a state equivalent of the *U.S. Government Manual.* All states have them, although few of these manuals are the traditional blue color anymore. These books provide great detail on the legislative, executive and judicial functions of a state; they also list key personnel in most agencies and commissions. In addition, they provide interesting historical, geographic, economic and political information about the state. Some blue books even provide information on county, city and school governments.

▶ **State and local government directories.** Like the *Federal Staff Directory* and the *Congressional Yellow Book*, these directories (available at the government unit, the state library and many local libraries) provide detailed listings, with phone numbers, of staffers at even the lowest echelons. In addition, many of these directories contain organizational charts and listings of key contacts. Whether thick and expensively printed, as on the state level, or mimeographed and stapled, as for a local school district, these directories play an important role in tracking the source you need to have your questions answered.

Discovering government activity

Government functions are not as complex as they seem on first examination. These are the basic categories of service to the public:

▶ Public safety

▶ Public works

▶ Social services

▶ Justice and corrections

▶ Education

We authorize (and pay for) our government to protect us from crime, fire and other disasters; to build roads and maintain traffic signals; to provide a welfare system; to administer a court system and incarcerate criminals; and to offer a system of publicly financed education. In the most simple configuration we pay only for what we can afford; however, in our complex society our demand for services often outstrips our finances.

Modern government faces the unenviable task of persuading its clientele—the voters—that a needed level of service deserves to be paid for. Should the state finance more medical care for the poor? Is another fire station needed for the city? Will it really lower fire insurance rates? Will the school district's proposal to develop a multimillion-dollar computer lab improve math and reading skills of students? The information gatherer and media writer cannot explain the issues surrounding these questions without an understanding of basic government processes. Let's dissect government units to try to understand their activity. We'll examine these areas: the role of elected officials, those unsung but powerful administrators, general activities and organizational flow, relationships with workers and the electorate, and key problem areas of interest to the information gatherer.

The role of elected officials

At the head of every government unit are the *elected* representatives of the people—the governor, mayor, chair of the school board, county commissioner, state senator, prosecutor (district attorney), and in some jurisdictions, judges. These officials are responsible for setting policy through enactment of legislation or for interpreting these policies and resolving conflicts over them. Although these officials bear the ultimate responsibility for the conduct and success of their government, they are in many ways *symbols* of that government rather than its daily driving force. What really makes the traffic lights work, gets the children taught, guarantees police protection and so on are appointed, paid administrators and the legions of workers under them. This means that elected officials—or any symbolic head—may not be the best sources of information about government operations. But the information gatherer must remember the accountability of elected officials and track all activity from its source. This includes monitoring of voting records and of new policies and changes to them; it requires full understanding of legislative history and judicial interpretation of all laws. It is also important to remember that "the people" have muscles to flex, even against bureaucratic giants; the people have a notable history of rising up to remove elected officials through the recall process or to replace them in vigorous election campaigns. An important role for the information gatherer is to properly gauge the power and responsibility of elected officials and then evaluate their effectiveness.

The administrators

These are the true technocrats of modern government—the city manager, school superintendent, director of public safety, welfare manager. Government has become so technical and complicated that our bureaucrats today are highly specialized, jargon-spewing functionaries who command byzantine structures that can be difficult for even elected officials to understand. The information gatherer must discover (1) what mandates have been given to these administrators, (2) what working relationship these administrators have with elected officials, (3) what the administrators' level of expertise really is, and (4) how the administrators work with their various publics. When you consider the public's demands for government services today—ranging from mass transit to sewage treatment—you have some idea of the impact of bureaucratic administration. Administrators are masters of the paper trail; very little activity is not committed to some memorandum, record or document. The information gatherer must become familiar with this trail, as well as with the motivations of the people who create it.

The organization of government activities

Let's examine a city's organization as a method of determining areas of service and responsibility. Like most governments, a city organizes its service according to departments. This is a typical breakdown:

- ▶ **Public safety**: police and fire protection, ambulance, jail, animal control
- ▶ **Public works**: road maintenance, water and sewer, lighting, parks
- ▶ **Zoning and permits**: land-use planning, construction inspection
- ▶ **Finance**: fines, license fees, taxes
- ▶ **Other**: library, airport, civic auditorium

This is a deceptively short list. In fact, the range of activities can be staggering. However, to prevent overlap and to enjoy economies of scale, as well as to assert pre-eminence of authority, some governments control a particular activity and provide that service to a lower level of government. For example, counties—following the laws of a state—may control the assessment of property and taxation and then disburse those funds to cities, school districts, volunteer fire districts and other government units within their jurisdiction. A state may fund county prosecutors (sometimes called district attorneys or state attorneys), who conduct investigations and prosecutions of crimes committed throughout the county, including within incorporated (city) areas. By examining an organizational chart of a government unit and by familiarizing yourself with what that unit is charged by law to perform, you can avoid confusion and misdirection in what may seem an impenetrable jungle of government organization.

Relations with workers and the electorate

Government services are labor intensive; the bulk of government expenses are for salaries and benefits, with a small remainder for equipment and materials. Therefore, the relationship between labor contract negotiations and the state of government financing is an important one. As the demand for government services increases, so does the pressure on the public budget. Public employee collective bargaining, which heavily influences budgetary matters, has grown dramatically in recent years; the threat of strike by workers in essential services (police and fire) has prompted many states to choose a system of binding arbitration for wage and benefit disputes, in which an independent third party investigates and authorizes a settlement—to which both parties must agree. There is some pressure today to bring teachers and health services employees under the arbitration umbrella. In any case the political and economic power of the organized government employee deserves a careful look in any information analysis. There is little doubt that public employees today exert considerable influence on the creation and direction of government programs; they also are part of significant lobbying efforts at higher legislative levels. Not to be overlooked is the electorate, which exists in groups of varying political interest and activity. An example of these groups can be found in the crisis facing a city council when it must decide whether to annex (bring into the city) an unincorporated area that desperately needs a sewage treatment system. One group argues for relief from septic system failures; another opposes the imposition of "big government," with its larger tax appetite and its transformation of a quiet, bucolic area into an urban setting. From within the city, still another group complains that all city taxpayers will have to subsidize the sewage and water treatment needs of the annexed area, despite what this new population will contribute in taxes. Whether the information gatherer is a public information specialist for the city or a reporter for the local newspaper, he or she must be alert to the positions of these groups and to the logic of their arguments.

Problem areas

At the top of the list of problems facing the information gatherer is that of gaining access to appropriate records and documents that will reveal and explain government activity. Types of documents will be discussed later in this chapter; issues and rights of access will be discussed in the Appendix, "Access and Integrity," which begins on page 195. Another problem is that of creating an effective strategy to sort through the avalanche of government activity and its specialized language to get a clear picture of that government's actual functions. That strategy becomes more obvious as the information gatherer begins to understand government organization. However, there is little that confuses and confounds researchers and writers more than government finance—how money is obtained and how it is spent. That's a significant enough issue to examine right now.

Government financing and spending

Let's look at the revenue sources of our busy public servants. Most governments obtain their funds in these ways: taxes; fees and licenses; fines and penalties; grants from other governments; and lotteries and miscellaneous sources. These financial sources are controlled by statute, administrative regulation and the whims of the voter.

Taxes

Your tax contribution isn't confined to the money deducted from your paycheck. In addition to the income tax (which in some jurisdictions includes federal, state and city deductions), taxes also can be levied on real estate and business inventory, on retail purchases, and on alcohol, tobacco and gasoline. There is also an incredible range of special taxes on various goods and services. Some taxes are shared; for example, when a state legislature authorizes a tax on alcoholic beverages, that revenue may be distributed to counties, cities and school districts according to their relative populations. One of the most confounding and controversial of all levies is the property tax, which is based on the assessed value of homes and land. Because one's income level is not necessarily related to the rapidly inflating value of property, a growing property tax bill can cause serious financial woes—especially for people on small fixed incomes. In California, for example, a home valued in 1975 at $37,000 was worth more than $300,000 in 1990. It's not surprising, then, that California voters overwhelmingly approved a property tax limitation law in 1978 and are still amending it today.

Fees and licenses

This revenue source is part of a government's "pay as you go" program. For example, to help finance the cost of a city's inspection of a house addition, a fee is charged for a remodeling permit. Renewal of automobile licenses is tied to a payment that helps cover the administration costs of the auto registration program. Government is a prolific licenser—it controls everything, seemingly, from meat scales to elevators. You may be surprised at the large amount of revenue that fees and licenses produce for a government.

Fines and penalties

Government is a persistent regulator and disciplinarian. Whether the violation is driving five miles over the speed limit or dumping toxic waste in a river, the penalties reflect the public body's judgment of the seriousness of the infraction as well as the prevailing political and economic climate of the area. They also represent a potential treasure chest of revenue. In recent years government has been aggressive in seizing the money and property of criminal offenders; examples include the seizure of cars belonging to "johns" arrested for purchasing the services of prostitutes and of ships and planes owned by people dealing in illegal narcotics. All actions involving fines and penalties are controlled by statute and ordinance, although they often are modified by court action as well.

Government grants

Various government units are beneficiaries of a "trickle down effect" that occurs when governments disburse their general funds for use by other governments. One of the best examples of this is the public works grants given to states, counties and cities for projects such as road and sewer construction and for development of low-income housing. States also get in the philanthropy act, sharing part of their revenues for local education and police support. Local governments often refer to this as "soft money" because its continued provision is not assured.

The lottery and other monies

A recent entrant in the government revenue scramble is the state lottery, an institutionalized form of the urban numbers-running game. Revenues that come from state-sanctioned gambling generally go toward education and economic development programs. Although several states have generated a great deal of money with lotteries, the method is often criticized because of contentions that people who are least able to afford it are putting their money into government coffers, hoping to strike it rich on that $10 million jackpot. In addition to the lottery, there is a host of miscellaneous revenue sources. One of the most typical is a payment in lieu of taxes to counties and school districts from revenue generated by the federal government on its lands within those local government areas. An example in Oregon is the 50 percent share of revenue that the federal Bureau of Land Management gives to local governments from sales of timber in their jurisdictions.

The preceding section has outlined basic government activity. As you will soon discover, this activity generates mountains of paperwork that may or may not be within easy reach. The next section will examine the records and documents that you may need in your search.

Government's long and winding paper trail

Searchers learn their true mettle when they face the government paperwork colossus. The federal paper machine was discussed in Chapter 4; the discussion here will be limited to state and local records. All governments keep records on their transactions, inspections, investigations and findings. In most cases these records are open to public scrutiny—not just to the review of the media. Here's a listing of just some of the records and documents that government bodies produce:

- ▶ Minutes of all official meetings
- ▶ Statutes, codes, bills, ordinances and resolutions
- ▶ Budgets and expenditure reports
- ▶ Arrest reports and criminal court records
- ▶ Reports of agency investigations
- ▶ Records of tax assessments, tax payments and sales of real and business property
- ▶ License and permit applications
- ▶ Inspection reports (for example, nursing homes, restaurants, plant safety, etc.)
- ▶ Bid reports and awarded contracts

All of these records have a natural storage place and an obvious care-taker. Using a variant of "every topic has a home," ask yourself the following questions: (1) What kind of records does this government unit produce? (2) Who has the most ready access to this information? and (3) What is the natural storage place for these records? First, statutes and enabling legislation often prescribe what records must be kept and how they must be published and stored. On the state level many of these records and reports are filed with the state library or archives. On a local level city and school clerks maintain a fairly complete filing system on major records as well as minor memoranda.

The information gatherer must follow the trail between what a government unit is authorized to do and what it actually does. Reports on and records of government activities are helpful guides along this trail. For example, the natural home for information on local crimes is the police department or sheriff's office. Most of these records are public, of course; exceptions could include information dealing with juveniles and incidents that are the subject of a current criminal investigation. However, the criminal court system would deal with that information as well. Higher-level authorities may also be interested in this information; the state police and federal government may want statistical information on local crimes to help compile a broader picture of current trends in crime.

Check your state's public records law to get a good overview of which records are available and which are exempted from public view. In addition to schooling yourself on an important law, you will have given yourself a solid orientation on the types of records produced in your area. Also, read an analysis by the state attorney general of your area's law.

Most high-level administrators will have copies of this analysis; so will law schools and various media. It will give you a sense of government's attitude toward its records and documents.

The search

Now you're ready to apply this knowledge of government systems to the master searches. To see how various government organizations are connected to the topics of domestic violence and weight-loss fads and frauds, the information gatherer should follow several steps to identify the government unit, activity and records related to the search.

Step 1: Learning the organization

Your state blue book tells you that a Department of Human Services provides casework and shelter assistance in cases of domestic violence; its Department of Public Health controls the licensing and regulation of weight-loss clinics. A county organization manual shows a local variant of state services: Children and Family Services and the Department of Health Services. Consulting both state and local government directories provides the names of officials who can further explain their departments' responsibilities and services. Connected to both of these topics is the possibility of criminal prosecution and civil litigation; state and local police and county courts will be heavy contributors of statistics and records. *Note*: While much background research on various topics can be done in the reference rooms of libraries, a great deal of organizational, statutory and administrative information may only be found at the governments themselves or through their officials. Make it a point to develop good working relationships with key sources in the government units you are researching.

Step 2: Determining regular and special activity

For both of these topics, the central government activity is *protection* and *regulation*. You must track all work—and reports—that involve investigations, licensing, controls and prosecutions. For example, on the state level the Department of Public Health may investigate complaints about a lack of medical supervision for certain liquid-diet programs; the department may then move to suspend or revoke the licenses of the companies providing these services. In addition, local courts may be the first place that consumer complaints surface (as lawsuits)—dealing, for example, with serious damage to health, such as the loss of gall bladder function from use of these liquid diets. In the family violence search the information gatherer may discover from police reports that very few domestic disturbance reports result in immediate arrests; from a county family services division that shelter housing for battered spouses and children is woefully inadequate; and from a state department of human services that abused children are too frequently removed from foster care (which the state finances) and returned to the care of abusive parents, who apparently have promised to seek counseling.

Step 3: Extracting needed information

A basic assumption in gathering government information is that public disclosure is presumed. Information that is withheld or exempted from disclosure needs to be carefully listed and explained by a government unit. You must stay in regular contact with appropriate government agencies to determine what records and documents are available and/or forthcoming. You also need to contact sources who can place these records in context. It's not enough to wait for the issuance or publication of a record. For example, regular contact with the casework coordinator of the child abuse program in your county might alert you to a soon-to-be-issued report on a dramatic increase in child abuse reports and on new strategies for combating this epidemic of violence. Remember also that government units whose programs are funded by higher-level governments (for example, a federal grant to create temporary shelters for battered spouses) are required to issue progress reports and audits to those governments. They can be very revealing.

Step 4: Evaluating that information

You must carefully examine all government information to assess its sources and political agenda. What motivates the writer of this information? What appears to be missing from this assessment? Exactly what do these statistics mean? Consider a set of statistics compiled by your county: that the circuit court has issued 420 restraining orders against husbands, to prevent them from seeing their estranged spouses, as compared with 180 orders issued for the same period one year ago. Ostensibly, this legal order is intended to prevent further cases of violence. But does it really work? Has the number of assault cases still risen? Does the county sheriff admit that a court's order is not the same as a bodyguard service? Do records show that 30 percent of the spouses who sought the order petitioned within two weeks to have it dropped? The point is that official information should not be accepted at face value. Information needs to be poked and probed; it must be examined from top to bottom.

Developing a mastery of government organization and information is a long-term project. Remember that the use of these institutions is just part of your search strategy—but the technique and philosophy are the same, regardless of who or what is providing the information: (1) Have I targeted what I need to know? (2) Have I identified who or what can provide it? (3) Do I know where and how to get this information? and (4) Do I understand what this information really means?

7

The Culture of Commerce

Capital. Investment. Production. Sales. Profit. Dividend. The cycle of business is predictable and unrelenting. Money is constantly sought to develop organizations that produce goods and services. If these products and services are successful in the marketplace, they should yield a profit, which will encourage further investment.

Incorporation. Directors. Proxy. Governance. Our commercial institutions follow a pattern of organization and activity not unlike that of government bodies. They create policy, form budgets and engage in conduct that has a significant impact on economics, politics and family.

Like those of government, the activities of business profoundly affect both society and public policy. Consider these issues: increasing labor costs and declining worker productivity; a dramatic shift from a manufacturing economy to a service one; mortgage interest and property inflation rates that threaten home ownership; the care and rehabilitation of displaced and injured workers. Like that of government, the world of business is complicated, and it can be secretive—despite a host of public disclosure requirements.

Understanding our commercial culture requires a mastery of the processes that fuel an economic machine of gargantuan proportions. Fortunately, the business world is not a totally closed society. The days of tight-lipped robber barons and their Machiavellian lieutenants are over, for the most part. More than 50 million Americans own stock in corporations; many business activities are subject to government scrutiny and regulation; and the trade press constantly reports on our commercial culture.

This chapter will examine the organization of business, its most significant issues, common documents and records, and the advertising and public relations function. It will end with a sample search on one of our master topics.

The organization of business

Many of our commercial institutions bear a striking resemblance to government units. Their similarities include the following:

▶ **Organization and functions outlined by a charter.** When a business incorporates (in the state of its choice), it reveals its intended functions, its capitalization and its directors. This is similar to the incorporation of a government entity—for example, a city, which lists its geographical boundaries, its functions and its method of governance (by councilors, commissioners or perhaps even directors). Like a government's constitution, a corporation charter is the founding document.

▶ **Governance through an elected body, with major issues controlled by a special electorate.** All publicly held corporations are managed by a stockholder-elected board of directors, which, like government, will appoint its administrators (executives). This configuration is guaranteed when a business offers its stock for public sale. When enough stockholders (who control enough voting stock) object to the activities of their corporation and directors, they may be able to vote in a new slate—in effect, creating a successful recall movement.

Private vs. publicly held businesses

A private, for-profit corporation is a business that does not issue stock to the public. Such firms are generally owned by family members or a limited circle of investors. As a result, the public reporting required of these firms is quite limited when compared with the almost 20,000 publicly held companies required to make regular public disclosures to the federal Securities and Exchange Commission (SEC). When a corporation "goes public," it asks for public investment so that it can expand and better capitalize its operations. In exchange, the "publicly held" firm is under legal obligations to make regular reports of its operations to the public. (More on this on page 121.) For example, while Exxon is a publicly held business that sells its stock through the New York Stock Exchange, Advance Publications is not. The latter firm is closely held by several members of the Newhouse family, which owns, among other things in its $10 billion media conglomerate, 26 newspapers, 40 magazines (including *The New Yorker*) and four book publishing firms (including Random House). Very little information on the Newhouse operations would have been available had it not been for a dispute in U.S. Tax Court in 1989 involving several billion dollars. In arguing against the court's financial assessment of their father's vast estate, the Newhouse brothers were forced to disclose earnings, actual operations and projections of their many media businesses. In the end the court found for the Newhouses. However, much proprietary information was disclosed in the process.

The not-for-profit corporation or foundation

A non-profit organization is created to provide an important public service. Examples include a Rape Crisis Center and a Famine Relief Network. The non-profit organization may also be a philanthropic group, such as the Gannett Foundation, which funds various community groups from its non-taxable holdings in the Gannett Corporation. These organizations pay no federal or state taxes on their revenues, which may come from contributions, fees and grants. (However, the salaries of people working for these tax-exempt groups are taxable.) Such organizations are under great public scrutiny. The most important public document related to their operations is the Internal Revenue Service's Form 990, which is a public record listing all annual revenues and expenditures. (More on this on page 125.)

Discovering corporate organization

The information gatherer has a wide range of sources available for learning how businesses are organized and who runs them. These sources can be found at three levels: (1) published directories, (2) state documents and (3) the corporations themselves. (A number of corporate sources are listed in the Glossary of Sources, beginning on page 209.)

Directories

Examples are *Standard & Poor's Register of Corporations, Directors and Executives* and *Ward's Business Directory of U.S. Private and Public Companies.* Such directories list major directors, officers and executives; the corporation's basic operations and sales; and its affiliates, divisions and subsidiaries. Updated at least annually (some computer database forms of these directories are even updated quarterly), these sources provide an excellent overview of who owns and runs these corporations and what businesses these corporations conduct.

State documents

In every state of the union, the office of the corporation commissioner or the corporation division of the secretary of state's office can provide substantial information about the organization of corporations doing business in the state. Much of the information in basic directories is available at the state level; a copy of the corporation charter, with other filing information, should also yield important information on the organization. Articles of incorporation, for example, could reveal the true ownership and financing of privately held firms, which have no reporting requirements to the SEC.

Corporations

Public relations officers of corporations often are effective conduits of information about the firms they represent. They can provide copies of charters, SEC registration statements, annual reports and organizational charts, among other things. Although the PR function obviously reflects the vested interests of a corporation, a firm is unlikely to decline to reveal information that could be discovered, for example, in the office of the state corporation commissioner. Finding PR directors of businesses is not difficult; many are listed in directories as vice presidents for public affairs. One phone call can do wonders.

Common issues and themes in business

The activities of business inevitably fall into one of three categories: (1) performance, (2) competition, and (3) impact. Let's examine the issues and themes in these categories.

Performance

The final judgment of a company's success or failure is based on the anxiety-producing "bottom line." Have strong markets been developed for a firm's products and services? What is the state of profitability and productivity? Has the company actually lost money or just suffered a drop in earnings? If the company has losses, what is its explanation? Is the company operating with little or no labor problems? Have certain company activities come under government scrutiny? Are stockholders pleased with the company's performance?

Competition

In an ideal arrangement of a free-market economy, vigorous competition should ensure quality products at attractive prices. The competitive behavior of industries and individual firms reveals much about the business environment—its pressures as well as its regulation. The information gatherer must be alert to these behaviors, which speak of innovation and industry, as well as ruthlessness, price discrimination and restraint of trade.

Impact

As this nation learned in its Industrial Revolution, great social and economic costs were associated with a move from an agricultural to a manufacturing economy. Issues such as worker and product safety, environmental concerns, employment practices, advertising claims and stockholder security should be part of any evaluation of corporate activity. Serious social, political and economic consequences occur when business behavior drifts into zones of harm, fraud and greed. Conversely, exemplary corporate behavior results in positive public attitudes and a move away from government regulation. As the shift from a manufacturing economy to a service-based, "information age" economy picks up momentum, the information gatherer must be alert to both the positive and negative effects of our new business "revolution."

These themes and issues are regularly covered in the trade press and in the general media as well. Using common keyword strategies, the information gatherer can easily track the work of trade and institutional journals through common indexes like *Predicasts F&S Index*, *The Business Index*, *Business Periodicals Index* and the ABI-Inform database.

Business records and documents

Many printed and electronic sources are available to the information gatherer. In this section we'll examine government sources, corporate-offered information, and the work of the media, specifically the "trade" press. (More on these sources on page 127.)

Government sources

As Chapters 4 and 6 showed, government is a tireless player in the country's political, social and economic activities. In the business arena a number of government agencies regulate and otherwise influence corporate activities. These include, on the federal level, the following:

- ▶ Securities and Exchange Commission (SEC)
- ▶ Federal Trade Commission (FTC)
- ▶ Internal Revenue Service (IRS)
- ▶ Antitrust Division of the Department of Justice
- ▶ Department of Labor
- ▶ Food and Drug Administration (FDA)
- ▶ Federal Communications Commission (FCC)

- ▶ Occupational Safety and Health Administration (OSHA)
- ▶ Interstate Commerce Commission
- ▶ Environmental Protection Agency (EPA)
- ▶ Equal Employment Opportunity Commission (EEOC)
- ▶ Consumer Product Safety Commission

On the state level a number of agencies and departments can provide helpful information on corporate activity, including the following:

- ▶ Secretary of state
- ▶ Corporation Commission
- ▶ State Department of Revenue
- ▶ State Department of Labor (Wage and Hours)
- ▶ State insurance commissioner (Workers' Compensation)

Check your blue book or state directory to determine which agencies are most active in business regulation.

Let's examine the most important federal sources here—the SEC, FTC and IRS. The other federal sources listed also will be briefly discussed.

The Securities and Exchange Commission (SEC)

The largest information source about publicly held corporations comes from the SEC, which was created in 1934 to provide, according to the *U.S. Government Manual*, "the fullest possible disclosure to the investing public." Located in Washington, D.C., with a helpful public reference room, it also has nine regional locations with some library service. Many SEC documents also are available at government depository libraries and at other libraries that subscribe to the Q-Data or Disclosure services, which reproduce corporate reports in microfiche and electronic database forms. To discover which corporations are required to file SEC reports, consult an annual publication, the *Directory of Companies Required to File Annual Reports with the Securities and Exchange Commission*. This publication is available at many library reference rooms and at all government document depositories. You may find it at large brokerage firms in your city as well.

The "founding document," as far as the SEC is concerned, is the Registration Application or Statement, which must be completed by all corporations that want to have their securities (stock) registered and listed for public trading on a stock exchange. This basic record often contains more financial and director information than the corporation registration filed with a state. After completing the SEC statement, the publicly held firm is required to file at least four reports on its performance every year. In practice, however, many more reports may be filed—most of which will be bonanzas for the information gatherer. Let's examine the following SEC reports: the 10K, 10Q, 8K, 14D1, 13D and 6K, as well as the prospectus and proxy. Don't be put off by all these numbers and letters—just consider them a convenient filing system for busy bureaucrats!

10K, the annual report.   This is a lengthy, detailed report of a corporation's activities during its entire fiscal year. (Many firms do not follow a typical calendar year in their accounting, but may begin their year on July 1.) The 10K is far more comprehensive than the often glossy annual report sent to all stockholders—the SEC wants facts, not the gilding of any lilies. Among other items, the 10K will inform the information gatherer about the following:

- ▶ The company's complete financial statement, including profit, loss, cash flow, working capital, shareholder dividends, debts and any "extraordinary" items contributing to profits or losses
- ▶ A summary of all operations during the fiscal year, including all foreign operations
- ▶ Principal stockholders and shares owned
- ▶ Salaries and benefits received by all directors and major officers of the corporation
- ▶ The results of any legal proceedings or hearings resulting in damages, fines or penalties as well as a summary of any pending legal proceedings
- ▶ Forecasts about future operations and any information about issues that may affect these operations

10Q, the quarterly report.   Although this information is less formal than that contained in the annual report, it does provide updated financial data for each of the three business quarters after the filing of the 10K. This form can signal pending problems (such as lawsuits or product recall) or improving prospects for a company. In the first-quarter report after the company's annual meeting, the results of issues voted on by stockholders are reported in the 10Q.

8K, a warning flag. This filing is an important signal that significant changes are taking place in the firm. Changes in ownership, assets, or debts, pending bankruptcy, and lawsuits must be reported to the SEC within 15 days of the event. Obviously, such information alerts investors, who can then make their best financial choices. The *Valdez* oil spill, discussed in the previous chapter, was prime 8K material because of the dramatic increase in cost and legal liabilities for Exxon.

14D1 and 13D, the takeover alert. An offer to purchase a publicly held firm must be reported on the 14D1. This reveals interesting information on the potential purchasers, their form of financing and the proposed purchase price. Another signal of a takeover attempt could be found in the 13D, the filing of which is required of an individual or firm attempting to buy more than 5 percent of the stock of a publicly held company. Both these notices are important because investors can benefit from the increased value of stock that often occurs in a takeover try.

6K, the foreign connection. Foreign firms that sell their stock in the United States are required to file this form annually.

The prospectus and proxy. When a private company goes public, or when a publicly traded firm wants to issue new securities to raise capital, the company must file the S-1 form, the *prospectus*. This form is helpful because the company must reveal how it intends to use the capital it raises and what its future operations will look like. It must provide enough financial information for investors (and their brokers) to determine the worth of this investment. Although the prospectus is available through the SEC and the corporation, it also can be found at various brokerages. The *proxy* is a request to permit directors in a firm to vote their preferences on behalf of the stockholders at the annual meeting. Obviously, most stockholders don't attend annual meetings, and many never even vote their shares. However, when a company is beset by troubles and stockholders are upset, it is not unusual for a group of those stockholders to propose a new slate of directors. In these situations a "proxy battle" is underway.

Other services of the SEC. In addition to its excellent public reference room, the SEC provides valuable information on investigations and prosecutions through its Division of Enforcement. It also provides special publications and analysis; for example, when the stock market suffered a serious drop in prices in 1987, the SEC prepared a mammoth document called "The October 1987 Market Break," which analyzed the factors that led to the crash. The most useful regular publication of the SEC is *The Daily News Digest*, available at government document depositories.

The Federal Trade Commission (FTC)

The FTC was created in 1914 to be a tenacious business watchdog. History has proved that the FTC's tenaciousness has varied according to the current political administration, but the commission still has these tasks:

▶ Promoting fair competition

▶ Preventing dissemination of false advertising

▶ Preventing price discrimination and other deceptive business practices

▶ Regulating certain aspects of packaging and labeling

▶ Protecting consumers against circulation of obsolete or inaccurate credit reports

Unfortunately, not all business information held by the FTC is open to public inspection because the Freedom of Information Act exempts the release of certain financial information and confidential trade secrets. Still, much of the FTC's investigations and prosecutions, in addition to the agreements it negotiates with businesses, are available to the public. Many of the FTC's decisions and regulations, such as those involved with advertising claims, can be tracked through the *Federal Register Index*. Some cases make their way through the court system, as when a federal judge in 1989 ordered the Ralston Purina Company to pay $10 million in damages for false health claims for its Alpo pet food.

In addition to the *Federal Register Index*, FTC actions can be tracked through the public reference service of the commission, through the federal *Monthly Catalog*, through databases like ABI-Inform and LegalTrac, and through various business periodicals indexes, including the *Wall Street Journal Index*.

The Internal Revenue Service (IRS)

You won't learn much about corporate life from the IRS—unless a tax dispute forces parties into U.S. Tax Court, as it did in the Newhouse case mentioned previously. Both the claims and contested records will be in plain view. If a company has allegedly defaulted on payment of personal, corporate or employee withholding taxes, that also will be a matter of public record because the IRS will go to court to seek a lien against assets and property in order to recover its money.

Most public IRS information comes from the annual 990 form required of all not-for-profit groups (990PF if the group is a private foundation). These forms are filed at the IRS regional office nearest the group's headquarters. Not-so-recent filings are stored at federal regional record centers.

These documents reveal several things:

▶ All revenue sources

▶ Employee wages and benefits

▶ Total expenditures and overheads

The information gatherer can learn, for example, which African famine relief organization has the lowest administrative overhead, which foundation provides the most money for literacy training and which trade association has the highest political lobbying fees.

In many cases the not-for-profit organization will make its 990 form available for inspection on request. It should also provide its Application for Recognition of Exemption, an IRS form in which the group makes its case for non-profit status, which permits contributions to the group to be tax-deductible. The IRS routinely reviews all 990s to see whether the spirit of the group's application is being maintained.

The IRS has a large Criminal Investigation Division (CID). The CID offers workshops in financial investigative techniques for law enforcement agencies and financial institutions. These workshops are especially important in these days of the cash-based drug economy and the extensive money "laundering" that takes place at banks. Information gatherers interested in the investigative techniques of these workshops should contact the public affairs officer at the nearest regional office of the IRS for further information.

Other federal sources

Antitrust Division of the Department of Justice. As the enforcer of the nation's antitrust laws, this agency monitors and prosecutes monopolistic practices and other activities in restraint of fair trade. It pays careful attention to corporate mergers and suspicious patterns of industry pricing. The closest regional office of the U.S. attorney is a good source of information on this divisions's activities.

Department of Labor.   Unions, management, collective bargaining, mediation and pension plans are closely monitored and recorded by this far-flung department. Its Bureau of Labor Statistics is an exhaustive fount of data on employment, prices, productivity, family expenditures and other economic issues.

Food and Drug Administration (FDA).   Because its activities affect the health of its citizenry, the FDA often finds itself in storms of controversy. One of its main functions is to certify prescription drugs for use; in recent years, criticism of delays in certifying drugs for the treatment of Acquired Immune Deficiency Syndrome (AIDS) has been rampant. Other controversies have included non-release of medication for sufferers from Alzheimer's disease and an abortion-inducing pill from France. The FDA also is involved with lesser questions, such as how much sugar should be contained in breakfast cereal. An important information source is the FDA's Center for Food Safety and Applied Nutrition. Many trade journals track the activity of the FDA, but the *Federal Register Index* and the *Monthly Catalog* are again excellent sources for commission activity.

Occupational Safety and Health Administration (OSHA).   Worker health and safety, plus workplace conditions, are the focus of this agency, which also has a state counterpart. Records and investigations of occupationally related accidents and illnesses are available at both the state and federal levels. For example, the growing incidence of "repetitive motion syndrome" related to day-long keyboarding at a computer terminal is under investigation by OSHA; changes in furniture design and keyboard adjustment and adjusted break periods have been some of the changes mandated by OSHA.

Interstate Commerce Commission.   This agency regulates rates and routes of trucking companies, railroads and bus lines. The commission collects quarterly and annual reports from these public carriers, which reveal much about a firm's operating and financial history. It also publishes helpful public advisory bulletins about current transportation problems. On the state level a public utility commission may oversee rates and routes of public carriers.

Environmental Protection Agency (EPA). Now enjoying full cabinet status, the EPA is busier than ever attempting to maintain acceptable air and water quality levels and to investigate and prosecute illegal discharges of wastes and toxic material. The use of millions of dollars in EPA "superfund" monies to help clean up housing complexes built over toxic waste dumps is now an all-too-familiar story. The EPA has four main departments: Air and Radiation, Water, Solid Waste, and Pesticides and Toxic Substances. As an example of its record keeping, the EPA maintains a "Toxic Chemical Release Inventory" from all firms that have released any chemicals into the environment, whether as part of regular plant operations or by accident. Environmental quality and natural resource departments exist on state and county levels as well.

Equal Employment Opportunity Commission (EEOC). The EEOC investigates discrimination in hiring, promotion and pay. It focuses on sex-based pay differences and on discrimination against the handicapped. The commission regularly publishes data on the employment status of women and minorities.

Consumer Products Safety Commission. Although it may seem that people only hear from this commission around Christmas, when it announces its list of unsafe toys, it is busy setting product safety standards and conducting investigations on hazardous products all year.

The trade press, trade associations and industry analysts

When you consider that the *Wall Street Journal* is the largest-circulating daily newspaper in the United States—selling 800,000 more copies than the nationally circulated New York *Times* and 500,000 more than *USA Today*—and when you consider that more than 1,000 business and specialized periodicals report and analyze corporate activity, you realize that information gatherers have a legion of informed researchers at their disposal. In addition, many daily newspapers and general circulation magazines are increasing their coverage of business and economic issues.

The best starting point for tracking the work of the trade press is the appropriate index. These are listed on page 120 in this chapter and on page 214 of the glossary. All of the periodical indexes work on the key-word system and provide only title and subject information. However, a database like ABI-Inform also provides a useful abstract for the 800 periodicals it cites, which is essentially the same number as the microform *Business Index* and the printed *Predicasts F&S Index*. Read the introductory information in all of these indexes to help you determine whether the periodical coverage and historical depth are what you are looking for.

Two other reference works are helpful in tracing trade sources:

▶ *Business Information Sources* (2nd ed.), by Lorna Daniells. This is a voluminous compendium of reference works, directories and associations by the business bibliographer of the Harvard Business School. It is well worth reading to get an information overview of the business or industry being examined. The informal narrative helps you make comfortable, informed choices about sources in a wide variety of business and industrial categories.

▶ *Encyclopedia of Business Information Sources*, by Gale Research Co. Issued every two years, this volume provides brief but nonetheless helpful listings of more than 1,000 information sources in business and economics.

Using the trade press can be full of pitfalls. First, some trade journals are uncomfortably close to the industries they cover, which makes their objectivity suspect. Second, the writing can be riddled with jargon and technical terms that may not be fully explained. Third, some publications may unabashedly copy information unearthed and produced by others. It is important for the information gatherer to learn the publication's track record for serious research, objectivity, clarity and originality. Much of this information about performance is anecdotal, but there may be some formal, published criticism and review of a publication's work as well. A natural pecking order generally emerges quickly.

Industry and trade groups

These groups produce great quantities of information about products and services and about industry trends. Many associations advertise their information services in such publications as *Advertising Age*, *Quill*, *Columbia Journalism Review* and *Washington Journalism Review*. (*WJR*, in fact, publishes an annual listing of business information sources.) Here, for example, is a pitch from the McKesson Corporation:

Writing a wrap-up? . . . A trend story? . . . Need a quote? . . . An industry expert? . . . A photo? . . . On deadline? We can help. We can provide information and experts on the drug and health care industry . . . the beverage business . . . the chemical industry.

Many industries and associations produce source books as well. Two of the most prominent come from the insurance and chemical industries. Not all source books and information services come from for-profit corporations, however. Many services are offered by non-profit associations, such as the Consumer Federation of America, the Center for Science in the Public Interest and the Environmental Health Center.

Industry and trade groups can be found through two sources:

▶ *The Encyclopedia of Associations,* by Gale Research Co. This volume lists more than 20,000 association sources. Their regular publications also are listed.

▶ *The National Trade and Professional Associations of the United States,* by Columbia Books. An annual publication, it is similar to the Gale book, but it adds an extensive listing of union and labor sources.

Industry analysts

Industry experts make their living by accurately evaluating and forecasting business performance and trends. In general, these experts are not industry apologists; they are voracious researchers and analysts who value their reputation for giving sound investment advice. Several types of experts are available:

▶ **Financial analysts.** Many brokerage houses and large investment firms employ these analysts, who prepare reports and forecasts on specific businesses for clients. A brokerage firm like Salomon Brothers, for example, may prepare an analysis of the market for the artificial sweetener NutraSweet and assess its impact on the U.S. sugar beet market. The business media routinely call on these analysts for commentary; however, much of their detailed work is proprietary and seen only by clients. A good listing of these analysts can be found in the *Financial Analysts Federation Membership Directory.*

- ► **Trade and industry economists.** Many large banks and investment houses have staff economists who analyze industry conditions and trends. Like psychiatrists arguing over the sanity of a criminal defendant, these economists may not always agree. However, their observations and opinions will be based on solid research, which may provide new directions for the information gatherer.

- ► **Local stockbrokers.** You might be surprised at the information and expertise some of these brokers possess. Many do their own research in order to make a favorable impression on their clients—and to gain commissioned sales. They also subscribe to expensive reports from Dun and Bradstreet and Moody's and may also obtain SEC filings on the firms they are monitoring. They can be an excellent local source and should be able to direct you to other sources.

One area of industry research made available to libraries on microfiche is *Corporate and Industry Research Reports,* which contains thousands of analyses of business activity by more than 60 investment firms nationwide. *CIRR* is indexed annually by J. A. Micropublishing. This is where the information gatherer might find projections on the $30 billion nutrition and weight-loss markets in the 1990s as well as projections for specific firms.

The advertising and public relations functions

In our commercial culture, successful marketing, high profitability and attitude change are closely tied to success in advertising and public relations. At the heart of the advertising and PR functions are information and promotion; without a solid base of information, a campaign of influence and promotion simply cannot succeed. In this section let's examine the roles of advertising and public relations and the methods their practitioners employ to obtain and use information. In the Glossary of Sources on page 214, key advertising, public relations and media sources are listed.

Whether their goal is to affect a consumer decision or to change an attitude, advertising and public relations have an underlying sales function. Public relations pioneer Edward Bernays called his work "the engineering of consent." The chief difference between advertising and public relations is, of course, how these persuasive messages are used and what control the "author" of the message has. Advertising pays for the space and time it uses. A staggering bill of $300,000 for 30 seconds of television prime time is not unusual. Public relations, on the other hand, offers both information services and access to media and other groups by "releasing" news to media outlets and responding to crisis situations (such as the *Valdez* oil spill) when the media are urgently pressing for information and comment. However, because the PR function does not involve a payment to media for space and time, publication editors consider PR material fair game for change and even non-use. A leading electronic PR service, PR Newswire, compares itself to a news service by using satellite communications to reach more than 1,500 U.S. newsrooms. This is part of PR Newswire's pitch to customers:

> Whether you are seeking to reach a broad audience or a narrowly defined one, whether your release is business or financial, a press advisory or a news story, for immediate release or a seasonal feature, you'll find the precise service for your needs at PRN.
>
> More than 15,000 news sources rely on PRN each year. They range from local elected officials to presidential election committees; from labor unions to employers' associations; from large universities and teaching hospitals to local philanthropic organizations; from the one-person PR shop to the world's largest public relations agencies.

Because of the greater financial investment behind the advertising message, much care is taken to ensure that the message will reach the right audience through the appropriate media, be properly comprehended and easily recalled, cause the hoped-for response and improve the economic or political status of the client. For this reason the advertising industry is highly dependent on the following:

- ▶ Pretesting and post-testing of messages for recall and attitude measurement
- ▶ Assessment of demographic and psychographic profiles of people for classification as potential buyers and voters
- ▶ Evaluation of the effectiveness and "reach" of different media in delivering advertising messages to various publics

In many ways the need for information is as important in public relations. The PR practitioner must identify the proper audience and media outlets for the client's message or campaign. The practitioner must do a creditable job of information research in order to be both logical and persuasive. And the persuasion doesn't always take place in the media. Consider this excerpt of a report to Exxon stockholders several weeks after the disastrous Alaskan oil spill in March 1989:

> . . . Exxon attempted to promptly mitigate the spill's effects by burning or dispersing the floating oil with chemicals. This effort was frustrated by delays in securing the necessary permissions and, later, by the development of adverse weather conditions.
>   . . . What exactly caused or contributed to the accident is the subject of ongoing investigations by Exxon and various government authorities. But, so far, it appears that the tragedy resulted from human error. . . .

Resolving conflicting information is not necessarily the role of the PR client; it is the function of the information gatherer and media writer. For example, the media professional had quite a task resolving statistical discrepancies between Exxon and Center for Marine Conservation (CMC) figures after the oil spill; almost two months after the spill, Exxon contended that only 37 percent of the oil slick remained, while CMC estimated that 72 percent remained.

Media professionals—and media consumers—must remember that advertising and public relations can be helpful sources of information. But what is not being revealed is often more important than what is being "released." Release implies control. The flow of information from corporation to media outlet can be carefully orchestrated. The information gatherer must work hard to gather a wide range of evidence in order to put together a cohesive, logical and truthful picture.

The search

Now let's turn to our master search on weight-loss fads and frauds. The family violence issue is more suited to public policy searches than to commercial applications; however, it is worth noting that even a brief review of the trade press reveals that progressive corporations are beginning to provide assistance to workers who are the victims of family violence or who may be committing that violence. By offering counseling and other support, trade journals say, these corporations may help reduce absenteeism, decrease medical insurance claims and increase productivity.

To begin the weight-loss search, we educate ourselves first on corporate organization. We'll use two of the largest weight-loss companies as a continuing example—Nutri/Systems and Sandoz Nutrition. Checking the *Directory of Companies Required to File Annual Reports with the SEC*, we find that Nutri/Systems is required to file but Sandoz is not. That could mean three things about Sandoz: (1) Its valuation and number of stockholders are below SEC minimums; (2) it is not a publicly traded corporation; or (3) it is a foreign corporation that does not trade its stock in the United States. We'll now turn to some directories to fill in the blanks on Sandoz and to learn more about Nutri/Systems.

Standard & Poor's Register of Corporations reveals that Sandoz Nutrition is part of a foreign conglomerate—Sandoz, Ltd. of Switzerland. The parent firm does not trade its stock in the United States and is therefore not subject to major SEC reporting requirements. However, the S&P source tells us that Sandoz Nutrition is headquartered in Minnesota; we make a note to check with the state's corporation commission. S&P also tells us that while the nutrition firm did only $120 million in business in fiscal 1988 (mostly for its Optifast program), the parent firm had a total of almost $7 billion in sales for a wide variety of chemical and agricultural products in the same period. *Ward's Business Directory* tells us that Nutri/Systems is headquartered in Pennsylvania and that it was founded in 1976. (We make a note to start tracking SEC filings on Nutri/Systems; we'll use Q-Data as our source.) Finally, because we are curious about a large number of references to Weight Watchers International (WWI) in the trade press, we check the *Directory of Corporate Affiliations* and learn that WWI is a subsidiary of the ketchup and processed food giant H. J. Heinz, whose stock is publicly traded.

So far we have used some basic directories to help get a sense of business organization. Along the way we have obtained names, addresses and phone numbers of key sources as well as some basic operating data (annual sales, number of employees) on the subjects of our search. Now we'll review the trade press and other media to get a current overview of themes and operations within these firms and the industry.

A search through the ABI-Inform database (which covers only the last five years in the CD/ROM form), the microform *Business Index*, the CD/ROM form of LegalTrac (see page 51) and the printed *Predicasts F&S Index* is revealing. It tells us, among many other things, the following:

▶ Competition is heating up in the liquid diet business; more than 2,600 hospitals have entered the weight-loss-center business, which in 1989 reported $5.4 billion in gross revenues.

▶ Nutri/Systems has come under fire as a result of lawsuits filed by several Florida women who allege that the liquid diet program has damaged their gallbladders.

▶ Sandoz Nutrition has no reported diet-related litigation yet, but its international image is taking a beating over a toxic spill of 30 tons of pesticides from its Swiss plant into the Rhine River—killing a half million fish in four countries. The *Wall Street Journal*, among other publications, discusses Sandoz's much-heralded drug Clozaril for treatment of schizophrenia but reveals lethal side effects and a much higher price tag for the medication in the United States than in Europe.

▶ Hospitals are reported to be charging as much as $3,000 for Sandoz's Optifast program, although less than $500 is for the powder, which provides only 80 calories per serving.

▶ Nutri/Systems has filed suit against WWI for allegedly appropriating trade secrets.

▶ In order to maintain its market share, the Sandoz Optifast program is now trying to target consumers who need to lose only 25 pounds or less.

This material gives an interesting overview of the competition and litigation in this business. To further sample some sources, we now turn to government and the SEC.

We'll try to find filings from Nutri/Systems. Using the Q-Data microfiche system, we look up the firm's 1989 10K filing. That complete annual report reveals some interesting data:

▶ The firm had more than 1,300 weight-loss centers.

▶ Gross revenues exceeded $200 million.

▶ Net profit was $11.6 million.

▶ The chief executive officer earned a salary of $1.7 million.

To check on other possible sources in government, we quickly scan the *Monthly Catalog* and the *Federal Register Index*. The *Monthly Catalog* tells us of a congressional hearing that began in March 1990 on weight-loss programs. It also cites a periodical from the Food and Drug Administration, *The FDA Consumer*. The title of the cited article is "How to Take Weight Off Without Getting Ripped Off." Reminding readers of a number of deaths as early as 1978 from liquid protein diets, it alerts them to an FDA regulation that requires warnings on labels when a diet product's calories come from protein. The *Federal Register Index* cites a proposed consent decree between the Federal Trade Commission and an Arizona company over allegedly fraudulent advertising involving a Band-Aid-like patch to be worn on the skin—a patch "guaranteed" to help one lose weight.

To get an overview of the positions and research of several trade and professional associations, we check the *Encyclopedia of Associations* and the *National Trade and Professional Associations of the United States*. Here we find names, addresses, phone numbers and lists of meetings and publications of these groups:

▶ The American Dietetic Association

▶ The American Society of Bariatric Physicians (specialists in the treatment of obesity)

▶ The National Nutritional Foods Association

Finally, to get a view of one firm's marketing plans, we turn to the *Standard Directory of Advertisers*. We find Nutri/Systems and discover that its 1990 ad revenues are projected to be $80 million—with half of those expenditures in newspaper space. We also learn who the firm's communications vice president is and which advertising agency represents it.

Of course, this is not an exhaustive search, but it does reveal that a methodical use of such diverse sources can yield a range and depth of information that news releases and the trade press alone can't provide. Whether your information output is an in-depth story or an advertising campaign, you must be thorough and exploit the information capabilities of all possible sources.

8

Experts and Where to Find Them

When three Portland *Oregonian* reporters started researching a series on the Hanford Nuclear Reservation across the Columbia River in Washington state, they didn't know the difference between radiation and radioactivity. Like most people in the Pacific Northwest, they had no idea what went on at the $975-million-a-year facility. "I didn't really understand whether Hanford was a place or a building or quite what it was," confessed one of the reporters.

A few months later, they produced a 15-part series that coherently examined the massive nuclear power institution from environmental, technological, political and economic perspectives. How did they do it?

They relied on experts. During the course of their research, the reporters compiled a source list of nearly 400 names, conducted hundreds of hours of interviews, attended special briefings and waded through a 20-foot-high stack of reports. They became students in the best tradition: curious, inquisitive, skeptical. Many of their expert sources acted as teachers.

The *Oregonian* reporters may have had more time and a more complex assignment than most journalists, but the challenge they faced is basic to all those who create media messages: tackling an unfamiliar subject and understanding it well enough to write about it accurately and coherently.

This is the same process Los Angeles advertising copywriter Ann Keding went through when she was hired to create a campaign for a battered women's hot line. Keding depended on the experts—from hot line personnel to local and state crime fighters to the women themselves—to gain an understanding of the problem. Only after extensive research was she ready to create the campaign that eventually earned her two awards and a special citation.

Every day, media writers are put in the difficult but exciting position of trying to make sense of an increasingly complicated and specialized world they themselves don't understand. True, some writers are experts—economists hired to write about economic issues, health care professionals selected to create information campaigns about health issues—but most are not. Most are as unfamiliar initially with the subjects they cover as are their audiences. It is the ability of media writers to identify, locate and question experts that allows them to do their job with a degree of confidence. It is their healthy skepticism that allows them to use—and not be used by—the experts they consult. Experienced media writers know that experts can range from knowledgeable, helpful guides to self-serving and manipulative sources. That's why no serious media writer depends on a single source of information, and why no writer goes into an interview unprepared.

This chapter will detail how to find experts and use them in your work. The following chapter will discuss the logistics of actually interviewing these experts.

Finding experts

The first and most important step in using experts in finding them. A media writer who can combine curiosity, resourcefulness, perseverance and common sense with solid researching skills will discover rich sources of information for every imaginable assignment.

Defining experts

With our penchant for inflated job titles and our abiding faith in formal education, it's no wonder we tend to define experts by the words and initials surrounding their names rather than by their actual knowledge.

But experts may or may not have elaborate titles and advanced degrees. It's possible that the executive director of the state Department of Fish and Wildlife—an impressively titled, multidegreed official—doesn't know as much about the effects of industrial pollution on fish as some untitled, lesser-degreed field researcher. The local Vietnam vets counselor may be able to answer questions about delayed stress with more clarity and depth than a top executive in the Veterans Administration.

It's possible, even likely, that the top person in an organization knows less about any specific area relating to the organization's activities than does an underling. That's because chief administrators, if they are effective, delegate authority. Their assistants and subordinates grapple daily with specifics. They know the ins and outs of the issues and problems in their domain. Perhaps once a week, they brief the boss. Some bosses have a good general feel for the organization's activities; others, isolated by their very power, may have a distorted perspective. Whatever the case, the person at the top of the hierarchy is often not the expert you're looking for.

Who are the experts? They are the people who have information on and experience with the issue you are researching. They exist in government and the private sector at all rungs on the bureaucratic ladder. They may be associated with well-known organizations, little-known groups or neither. They may be designated official spokespersons or people hidden deep within some corporate labyrinth. It is their knowledge that makes them useful to you, not their titles, affiliations or degrees.

Digging for experts

Good journalistic researchers are rarely content to skim the top layer of officialdom for expert sources. They look elsewhere for people who can help them understand and report on complex issues. And they use all their research abilities to meet the challenge. Digging for experts means using the information-gathering skills and tools you have learned in previous chapters.

The federal government is one place media writers repeatedly turn to in their quest for specialized information, expert testimony and knowledgeable commentary. Within the bowels of the bureaucracy, you can find experts on subjects from organized crime to organic fertilizers, from franchise practices to foreign travel. In addition to gathering information that is national and international in scope, the federal government serves as a key source of detailed local, state and regional data, through either main agency offices in the Washington, D.C., area or regional offices scattered throughout the country.

Chapter 4 helped guide you through the paperwork labyrinth of the federal government, using reference tools commonly found in depository, university or public libraries. But the federal government can also be successfully plumbed for people, as you will soon discover.

City, county and state governments are good hunting grounds as well. As discussed in Chapter 6, these entities are concerned with a variety of vital issues including public safety, education, social services, public works and the environment. Most governments publish directories of their services with the names and phone numbers of personnel. Many department numbers are published under city, county and state headings in local telephone directories. In addition, a growing number of government units employ public information officers who can be helpful in directing the journalistic researcher to experts and specialists.

Keep in mind that the government is only one of several major institutions that can be mined for expert sources. As Chapter 4 detailed, medicine and law have their own experts who can easily be identified as the authors or cited sources in articles indexed by basic research guides like *Index Medicus* and LegalTrac.

As Chapter 7 showed, private industry can also be a gold mine of experts, particularly if the media writer is savvy enough to use these sources in a way that avoids puffery. Calling a business executive at a book publishing company and asking for information on the future of that company invites meaningless self-promotion. Calling the same person and asking questions about the impact of computers on the publishing industry may get you detailed information from an expert.

To find the experts you're looking for, use your researching skills and remember these guides:

- ▶ *Directories in Print*
- ▶ *Encyclopedia of Associations*
- ▶ *National Trade and Professional Associations of the United States*
- ▶ *Moody's Manual of Investments, American and Foreign*
- ▶ *Poor's Register of Corporations, Directors and Executives*
- ▶ *Thomas' Register of American Manufacturers*

Perusing trade magazines (see Chapter 7) is another method of locating industry experts. Numbering in the tens of thousands, each devoted to the special interests of a particular trade or profession, these magazines regularly profile, quote and refer to industry experts. Trade magazines and professional journals are also good places to find the names of experts on particular issues or problems.

Institutional and "outsider" experts

Although conceivably you can find an expert just about anywhere, let's concentrate on three particularly important sources of experts not yet explored in detail in previous chapters.

Experts within the federal government

With its 62 independent agencies, boards, commissions, and corporations and its 51 congressional committees, 13 departments and three branches, the federal government employs almost 3 million civilian workers. According to Washington, D.C., research expert Matthew Lesko, some 710,000 of them are information specialists. Imagine every man, woman and child in San Francisco working five days a week to collect, analyze and evaluate information, and you begin to get an idea of how vast a resource the federal government is. As a taxpayer you may shudder. But as an information gatherer, you have to cheer.

Skilled journalistic researchers appreciate the resources of the federal government. Always skeptical, always alert to hidden agendas, conflicts of interest and other problems that might interfere with honest responses and accurate information, they use government sources wisely. They have learned that the agencies of the federal government collect information about regional, state and even local concerns. They know that regional offices of federal agencies are prime information centers. Unlike lazy or ill-prepared media writers who settle for a call to an "authorized" government spokesperson, these researchers know how to dig for information below the top layer of officialdom.

Although the federal government is an unparalleled source of information, it can also be an unparalleled source of frustration to the journalistic researcher looking for fast answers. It's easy to see why. The bureaucracy is so vast and so tangled that few understand it. Cabinet-level departments are composed of divisions, which themselves contain offices that include agencies made up of bureaus that contain departments. Information offices and information experts exist at all levels. In so complex a system, workers may not know of the existence of other specialists working in their field but not physically in their office. Agencies with overlapping expertise and information may be found in several different departments.

It is difficult for people—including most novice journalistic researchers—to know where to begin looking for experts to talk to. Mercifully, the government understands the problem and publishes guides to its own organization and workings, from general directories to agency-by-agency phone books. A handful of independent publishers are also in the business of deciphering the bureaucratic maze. Some of these federal guidebooks can be found in the reference collections of newspapers, magazines and broadcast stations. Most or all, depending on the size of the library, can be found in the government documents section of public or university libraries.

By consulting these books, a researcher can start with little understanding of the federal government and end with an impressive list of experts' and specialists' phone numbers.

The basic source is *The United States Government Manual,* the official handbook of the federal government. It offers descriptive information on the agencies of the three branches of government, as well as independent and quasi-official agencies, boards, committees and commissions. Each listing includes a description of the agency's purpose, programs and history as well as a roster of the agency's top officials. The information here is broad but shallow. It's best to use the *Manual* for basic education about government structure, the kind of information you will need to effectively tap other directories.

With fundamental knowledge of the bureaucracy, you are ready to delve into more detailed guides like *Congressional Quarterly's Washington Information Directory,* a guide to 5,000 information sources in the legislative and executive branches. Conveniently divided into major subject areas (science, defense, housing), the book lists key agencies and committees, and names and numbers of people working in each area. To locate sources working for the federal government's vast regulatory apparatus, the book to use is *Congressional Quarterly's Federal Regulatory Directory.* Here you will find extensive profiles of the 13 largest, most important regulatory agencies and abbreviated entries for 93 others. If you know which agency deals with the issue you are researching, this book can point you to an array of experts.

Other references, organized like phone books, are extremely valuable—but only to those who already know what they're looking for. Because they contain more information and are more likely to be in a nearby library, these directories are superior to individual agency or Washington, D.C., phone books. For example, *The Congressional Staff Directory* is a comprehensive guide to the thousands of people who work in the House and Senate. Senators, representatives and their staffs—including such excellent, overlooked sources of information as research and legislative assistants—are listed with addresses and phone numbers. *The Washington Monitor's Congressional Yellow Book* covers the same turf in loose-leaf form, which makes constant updating possible. *The Federal Staff Directory* lists 27,000 decision-makers in the executive branch, including key administrators and their staff assistants. Another entree into the executive branch is *Washington Monitor's Federal Yellow Book*.

Experts at the university

Like most things right under our noses, university experts are often overlooked. These men and women have invested years becoming knowledgeable in their fields and spend their days reading, researching, writing and talking about their subjects. They are accustomed to explaining complex subjects to novices and, compared with some government or industry experts, are far more likely to be impartial. All these characteristics make academic experts attractive sources for a wide variety of information quests, from background on a statewide economic concern to the latest research on an herbicide being used within the city limits.

How do you locate academic experts? Annually published university catalogs will tell you the names, academic backgrounds and teaching/research specialties of faculty members. University phone directories often publish both work and home numbers for all staff. These important research tools should be a part of your reference library. But sometimes the descriptions of specialties are too vague or the university too immense to make reading the catalog an efficient way of locating sources.

You might want to contact the dean, director or chairperson of the relevant department or school. That person is generally quite familiar with the specialties, interests and current projects of faculty members and can offer referrals. If the university has a public information department or news bureau designed to handle such requests efficiently, use it. The department may maintain an updated list of all faculty members qualified to answer questions on certain subjects. Sometimes one phone call will get you a complete list of academic experts on the desired topic.

"Outsider" experts

"Outsiders" exist apart from established institutions like government, education, law or medicine. They may be members of non-profit organizations, special interest and consumer groups, or a wide spectrum of community and activist groups. Such groups have a particular, visible focus (for example, the environment) and sometimes an expressed advocacy position (for example, the promotion of solar energy). Whether acting as advocates, central clearinghouses or research agencies, these groups have devoted much time and many resources to gathering a wealth of information on the issues that concern them. Their members may be particularly well-informed, articulate and candid. Because their biases are generally known, they can be used wisely and cautiously as sources.

Where do you find such people? There are many places to look, but you must expect to spend some time digging. Outsiders, by definition, often do not have high visibility and cannot be found by going through the regular channels we've already described in this chapter. But there are a few standard library tools that can help. Both the *Encyclopedia of Associations* and the *National Trade and Professional Associations of the United States* may pinpoint likely organizations. *Directories in Print*, which lists many of the thousands of directories published in the United States, may point you to a specialty directory that could open up a whole world of new sources. Computer database searching may prove productive as well. Some databases (like ENERGNET) are set up specifically to identify experts in a given field; others have "human resources" components (like the Family Relations database we searched in Chapter 5).

Special interest magazines and newsletters may also help you identify outsider experts. Writers and editors at these publications may themselves be experts. Certainly, in the course of their work, they would be in contact with experts. Consider asking for referrals from more well-known "outsider groups" like the Sierra Club, Common Cause or Planned Parenthood. Also remember that the assistants and researchers who work for legislators at both the state and national level are often in a position to know about all the players—insiders and outsiders—involved in a particular issue.

Most states have PIRGs (Public Interest Research Groups) that gather and disseminate information about vital consumer issues. Tap these groups for their own internal experts or ask them for names of people they contact when they want quality information. Pay attention to the calendar listings section of your local newspaper. Many groups you've never heard of (and that have never been reported on or plumbed for sources) will show up there. Keep your eyes open when you pass public bulletin boards. Special interest groups, especially those with little funding or those in the midst of a controversy, often post announcements and leaflets. Finding outsiders may take a bit more time than rounding up experts within accepted and visible institutions, but the benefits—freshness of vision, candor—may be considerable.

Other strategies for finding and using experts

When digging for knowledgeable experts below the top layer of officialdom, journalistic researchers need to employ many different strategies. Learning to use PR departments to get at sources (rather than using a PR person *as* a source) is an important tactic. Other strategies include asking for referrals, using hot lines and choosing sources that more accurately reflect our diverse society.

Using public information and public relations departments

PR departments are a fact of modern life. Most government units have them. So do virtually all corporations, foundations, universities, agencies, associations and major non-profit organizations. PR people have a well-defined mission: to tell the story of and promote the organizations that employ them. This mission may or may not conflict with the media writer's quest for information. PR departments can act as either facilitators or obstacles in the research process; the choice often depends on the kind of information you're after.

Their helpfulness in locating experts is often tied to the information the journalistic researcher is pursuing. Two recent dealings with a hospital PR department illustrate the point. In the first case the writer was looking for a medical expert on athletic injuries for background on a story about the risks of overexercising. The PR staff found the expert and returned the journalist's call within the hour. The second story involved the hospital's battle against the opening of an independent medical clinic.

The writer wanted to talk with hospital business personnel about the potential economic effect of the clinic on the hospital. After five days and numerous phone calls, a PR staffer called to say that the business experts were unavailable and the hospital would have no comment on the matter.

At their best, PR departments can be vital links between complex bureaucracies and information-hunting writers. They can quickly locate experts, help set up interviews and even provide background reports, usable photos and other important material. At their worst, they can stonewall requests and construct a difficult-to-penetrate barrier between the organization and the media.

Getting referrals

An efficient, common-sense way of locating experts is to ask for referrals from any number of different people and organizations. When you are wracking your brain for names of specialists, ask yourself these questions:

1. Would any of my colleagues, because of past assignments or personal interest, know of experts in this field?
2. Could specialty reporters for the local media offer referrals?
3. Is the subject I'm interested in covered by a trade publication or research journal? If so, would an editor be able to direct me to the specialist I need?
4. Is there a relevant association or society that can put me in contact with experts?
5. Have I remembered to ask every expert I talk with for the names of others in the field?

Following up on any or all of these questions may net you just the expert you're after.

Calling hot lines

Usually set up as adjuncts to public affairs departments, industry hot lines are designed to answer specific questions quickly. They can also be important sources of experts. A recent issue of the *Columbia Journalism Review*—an excellent place to find out about industry hot lines—contains hot line ads for a drug company, a health care corporation, a chemical company, an insurance company and the Tobacco Institute. Obviously, some hot lines are more self-serving than others, but that doesn't necessarily diminish their usefulness as locators of experts.

The federal government also operates a number of hot lines with free "800" numbers. Among the potentially useful ones for journalistic information gatherers are numbers to call for information on dangerous chemicals, runaway children, cancer, political fund-raising laws and energy conservation. These and other hot line numbers are listed in Matthew Lesko's *Information U.S.A.* The directory assistance operator for 800 numbers (call 1-800-555-1212) or the published directory of 800 numbers will also be helpful.

One of the most important hot lines operating today, in terms of both its scope and credibility, is the Media Resource Service (MRS). Established by the Scientists' Institute for Public Information and funded primarily by foundations, MRS (1-800-223-1730) is a free referral service for all members of the media seeking reliable sources with scientific and technical expertise. Acting on your request, the MRS staff searches a computerized list of nearly 15,000 scientists and engineers who have agreed to participate in the program. Often within an hour, MRS returns your call with a list of experts. In the case of controversial issues, the names of representatives from all sides are provided along with a summary of each person's position on the issue. Because of its large database, policy of providing experts with conflicting views and lack of ties to industry, MRS is a highly trustworthy guide to sources.

Avoiding sexism

Many writers are conscious of—and assiduously avoid—sexist language in their writing. But few are conscious of inadvertent sexism in their choice of experts. When media writers consistently quote male experts with regard to politics, business and science and confine female experts to commenting on nutrition, child rearing and domestic affairs, they help perpetuate oppressive, restrictive, out-of-date stereotypes.

If the mass media are a mirror of our society, then the reflection should show female scientists, lawyers, business executives, doctors and athletes. It should show men competent and interested in child rearing, family affairs and household management. That doesn't mean story after story about "the first woman/man who . . ." It means integration of the sexes into all relevant media messages. The balance of experts is one simple way media writers can help make the media a truer reflection of reality.

This certainly does not mean choosing a less qualified source in the quest for male-female balance in the message. It does mean being conscious of societal realities, being wary of stereotypes and making an effort to show in your choice of experts that both men and women are competent in a wide range of human affairs.

Using experts in your work

What place do experts have in your message? How can you help your audience understand what experts are saying? Using experts in your work is a more complex process than you might imagine.

Attribution

Good media writers also attribute a comment, opinion, inference or judgment to its source. But there is more to attribution than merely identifying a source as Senator So-and-So. Media writers have an obligation to give their audience identifying information that will help readers or viewers evaluate the source's remarks and think independently about them.

Consider the difference the additional information (highlighted in italics) makes in the following attributions:

> "This is the safest, most effective weight-loss formula ever invented," says Patrick Donnell, *president of the pharmaceutical company that will begin marketing the formula next month.*

> "This is the safest, most effective weight-loss formula ever invented," says Patrick Donnell, *a National Institutes of Health scientist involved in obesity research for more than three decades.*

Full attribution can help put an expert's remarks in context, clarify an expert's position and identify the motivation for the comment. Identification is particularly useful to the public when experts disagree. Suppose you wrote the following:

> "The president's plan to do away with the federal tax deduction
> for state income tax is an abomination," says Sen. Tom Thompson,
> D-N.Y. But Sen. Roberta Roberts, R-Alaska, disagrees. "This plan
> will be a great boon to the hard-hit taxpayer," she says.

Considering these two statements, readers or viewers might dismiss the conflicting remarks as typical party squabbling. Generally, this pairing of "yes it is/no it isn't" is of little real help to those who want to understand and form their own opinions about issues. Suppose, instead, you added this additional information (again, in italics) about the senators:

> "The president's plan to do away with the federal tax deduction
> for state income tax is an abomination," says Sen. Tom Thompson,
> *whose New York constituents pay the highest state income tax in the
> country.* But Sen. Roberta Roberts, *whose Alaska constituents pay the
> nation's lowest state income tax,* disagrees. "This plan will be a great
> boon to the hard-hit taxpayer," she says.

Help your audience make informed decisions about the comments of experts. Include all pertinent identification as part of the attribution. Also, when relevant, include information explaining the conditions under which the information was obtained. If you've spoken directly to a source, make that clear in your story. If you've culled a statement from a memo, press release, wire service story or other source, mention that too.

Jargon slaying

Experts often talk their own language. It's both a shorthand by which they communicate with one another and a barrier to their communication with those outside the field. Be it the secret tongue of butchers or bureaucrats, jargon has little place in mainstream media writing. On the contrary, the writer's job is to cut through jargon to communicate clearly and effectively with the audience.

The writer who interviews a banker and then writes about "downturns in commercial lending package applications" (jargon) instead of "fewer businesses applying for loans" (translation) is doing no one a service. Jargon is not impressive; lucid explanations are.

There may be times when knowing a bit of jargon can help you establish rapport with a source or communicate more quickly. Specialty encyclopedias and dictionaries are particularly helpful tools (see Chapters 3 and 4). But regardless of your own mastery of the special language, you owe your audience a jargon-free message.

Problem experts

In the best of all possible journalistic worlds, expert sources are co-operative, articulate, honest and accessible. They are interested in communicating complete, accurate, timely information that helps others understand and function in society.

But it doesn't always work out that way. Let's consider some sources who present problems.

The rehearsed spokesperson

These sources are generally closed to two-way communication. They have a message to relate, most often dictated to them by a higher-up, and their job is to relate it. Their major concern is media coverage for that message. Presidential press secretaries and corporate media liaisons—especially during times of trouble and tension—are often good examples of this type. Although rehearsed spokespersons frequently must be contacted for "official comment," they are generally not good sources for anything other than their rehearsed message.

The well-used expert

Information gatherers can be lazy. Instead of digging for information, they wait for it to be handed to them. Instead of cultivating new sources, they return repeatedly to the same ones. A trusted expert is a person to hold on to, but the search for new sources of information should never stop. The well-used expert can quickly become the overused expert, thus unintentionally narrowing the scope of the information the writer gathers and the audience learns. Is Ralph Nader the only consumer advocate in the nation? Is Sam Donaldson the only in-house network news critic? Sometimes it seems so. Journalistic researchers who talk exclusively to the mayor about city affairs or to the police chief about crime are doing their audiences a similar disservice. The promise of American journalism is that it can be a forum for a wide range of voices. It can't fulfill that promise if researchers consistently rely on well-used experts.

The self-interested expert

The self-interested expert operates from a personal agenda that may get in the way of complete, accurate, honest communication. Media writers can protect themselves and their audience against potentially manipulative or deceptive information by recognizing self-interest (in themselves as well as others), backgrounding themselves thoroughly before questioning sources and using the "bull's-eye strategy" described on page 153.

Battling experts

It's both exciting and frustrating to encounter experts who categorically disagree. Spirited debate can help crystallize the issues, and controversy certainly can create exciting copy. But conflict does not necessarily promote understanding, and media writers have a responsibility to do more than let experts battle it out within a story. Not all experts are equally knowledgeable or trustworthy. It is the media writer's job to confirm information and give the audience concrete ways to judge the value of various experts.

Equivocating experts

Even more frustrating than experts who disagree are experts who do not offer straightforward responses. Some who respond to questions with ambiguous answers or seeming double talk may be acting out of self-interest. These people are truly problem experts and should be approached as such. But others may be responding honestly with no hidden agenda. Media writers often crave black-and-white answers to complex problems, and the mass media are in the habit of trumpeting simple, definitive statements (*the* cure for the common cold, *the* cause of teenage suicide). The truth is, few questions have simple answers, and the more expert an expert source really is, the less likely he or she is to offer an emphatic, unequivocal statement. Media writers should think of using experts to explore questions as well as answer them, to report uncertainty as well as fact.

The search

Let's look at the function of three different kinds of experts in the information-gathering process while referring to our master searches.

The background expert

Background experts are behind-the-scenes sources you use early in the information-gathering process, not to amass quotes or settle controversies but to educate yourself and begin formulating intelligent questions. They are people you can trust to give you initial guidance, offer a crash course on a subject and point you to helpful references and sources. They are people in front of whom you can shamelessly parade your lack of knowledge. Often, they are people with whom you have already established a rapport.

One of the best places to look for background experts is the university. Professors, as we've mentioned before, are generally good at explaining the basics, accustomed to talking to people who know little about their field and often less self-interested than those directly involved. Another obvious place to look is within your own professional and social circles. Wherever you find them, background experts can be exceptional front-line sources.

Who might serve as background experts for our continuing exploration of diet fads and frauds? The media writer's own physician might be a likely candidate. Nutritional science professors at the local college or university could be important sources. For the domestic violence issue, professors from sociology, counseling or law might be a good place to start.

"Expert" experts

After the writer is thoroughly backgrounded and understands the outlines of the issue, the time has come to consult with those who have particular expertise. These are people with credible credentials, although they may not carry the most impressive titles. These are people with proven expertise and/or experience who have been involved in or have been studying the issue for some time.

Where are the "expert" experts on diet fads and frauds? Think back to the information-gathering techniques discussed in previous chapters and you will see that you can readily answer this question. Consider, for example, what Chapter 4 taught you about specialty sources. The scientists and researchers who have published studies on weight-loss schemes and their consequences would make highly credible sources. So would those who have appeared as witnesses in congressional hearings. Remember that the federal government's regulatory agencies are involved in monitoring both weight-loss drugs and publicly held companies that operate weight-loss clinics and programs (see Chapter 7). The MRS hot line (see page 147) might also be an excellent referral service for this issue.

You already have a head start on the family violence search as well. Again, your specialty library research (see Chapter 4) has already identified an impressive list of physicians, psychologists, legal scholars and others with expertise you will want to tap into. Don't forget the experts at all government levels (see Chapters 4 and 6) as well as those involved in non-profit and special interest associations.

Experts at the bull's-eye

All of us, from time to time, are guided by self-interest. Your sources may have their own agendas, regardless of the information you're pursuing: politicians who seek positive media coverage to boost their campaigns, business executives who believe good stories can lead to promotions, scientific researchers looking for publicity to help them secure grants. Others may be impelled by institutional loyalty: the college president who glosses over the resignation of an important faculty member or the hospital administrator who releases only those statistics that show cost containment. Media writers need not be suspicious or distrustful of the motives of all sources. But they must realize that the information flow can be affected by forces unrelated to the information quest.

Knowing this, careful, sensibly skeptical media writers will devise an information-gathering strategy that helps prevent them from being manipulated by the self-interest of others. This plan, which we'll call the "bull's-eye strategy," is simple: Contact sources beginning with those least personally and professionally involved in the story (those with the least to gain or lose by it). The background expert is the natural first stop. Then, after establishing the outlines of the story, begin contacting people with increasing involvement (and potential self-interest). You will be better able to question the self-interested sources and evaluate their responses if you speak to them last. Thus, the information search follows the perimeter of the target, spiraling in to the bull's-eye (those at the center of the controversy or most likely to be professionally or personally affected by what you write).

Consider the diet fads/frauds search and the domestic violence issue. For both, the information quest begins on the perimeter with background sources and moves to "expert" experts with increasing involvement. At the center of the bull's-eye sit those with the most to gain or lose. For the diet fads search, this might be the manufacturer of a weight-loss pill or the executive of a corporation that runs weight-loss programs—both of whom have considerable financial interest in making sure information about their products and services is positive. For the domestic violence search, one bull's-eye source might be a person on trial for committing domestic violence (and his or her attorney), who would have an obvious stake in presenting the case in a certain light. Other potentially self-interested sources might include those who operate domestic violence programs and shelters (and who are fighting for scarce funding dollars).

A word about "the involved" vs. "the dispassionate"

"The dispassionate" are sources knowledgeable about but not directly involved in the issue you are researching. "The involved" are in the thick of it. Both have their place in the information-gathering scheme, providing information and insights germane to their different positions. In general, those directly involved provide the intimate details only they can know, as well as the fiery quotations their involvement may fuel. Those not directly involved provide background, perspective and context, helping both you and your audience better understand an issue. Sometimes, but not always, those not directly involved will be less self-interested "perimeter" sources while those involved will be more self-interested, "bull's-eye" sources. This seems to be the case with our two master searches, as we've just described.

The important thing to remember is that experts need to be chosen well and cautiously, with an eye to what they know, not just who they are, and an understanding of where their self-interest might lie. How do you deal with them once you've identified them? Read on.

9

Interviewing

This is a true story.

An author, on a promotion tour for her latest book, arrived at a newspaper office in time for a scheduled interview. The reporter, a 25-year veteran at this metropolitan daily, kept her standing by his desk while he finished what was clearly a personal phone call. Finally, hanging up the phone and turning from his cluttered desk, he motioned her to sit. He rolled an ancient typewriter table over to his desk, placed it between himself and the author, inserted a sheet of paper into a vintage Smith-Corona and typed for a minute or two. Then he looked up, training his eyes about three inches above the author's head, and said: "I haven't gotten through much of your book. I get almost a hundred books a week in the mail. You know, it's an interesting job but . . ." And he proceeded to discuss the details of his job, what he liked and disliked about it, how he got it, how he wished he had time to write himself—while the author sat there wondering whether *she* should be the one taking notes.

This terrible tale proves that interviewing does not come naturally to all who attempt it (including those who have been attempting it for decades!). Interviewing is *not* a natural act. It is a learned skill. When done well, it may look effortless—like a spirited conversation between two informed and enthusiastic people. But it's hard work, demanding not just preparation but also restrained intelligence, not just practice but also sensitivity. The information in this chapter should give you a running start at learning vital interviewing skills. But first, let's put interviewing in the larger context of information gathering.

The perils of people as sources

Whether it's a journalist interviewing a source or an advertising copywriter quizzing a client, media writers often converse with and question those who have specialized information. Interviewing may be a common way to get information, but never forget that it is only one way among many. More important, always be mindful of its basic limitation: People are generally *not* good sources of factual information. They *are* good sources for opinions, comments, rebuttals, denials, analysis and, of course, personal experience. They can help explain complexities. They can point you to other sources of information. But when you need facts, when it's "hard data" you're after, go to documents. When deciding whether a person would be the best source for a particular kind of information, keep in mind the following:

▶ **People may not know.** Most facts and figures are not likely to be carried in the head of any particular person.

▶ **People may think they know but don't.** A confident but ignorant, misinformed or forgetful source is worse than no source at all. People remember selectively and often inaccurately.

▶ **People may know but not want to tell.** Remember that self-interest—from basic corporate survival to dreams of glory—can be a powerful motivating force.

▶ **People may inform you selectively.** Everyone has his or her own agenda working at certain times.

▶ **People may lie or misrepresent the facts.** To project a certain image, to protect themselves, their reputations or their careers, some people may deliberately give you erroneous information.

Let these caveats guide you as you decide the best way to use people as sources. Remember that locating the right expert (see Chapter 8) is half the battle.

Types of interviews

Interview is a generic term for everything from a five-minute phone conversation to a five-day follow-'em-everywhere marathon. Interviews differ from one another in at least two important ways that have implications for how you prepare for the session and how you conduct the conversation: purpose and form.

Purpose

What is the purpose of the interview—a quick comment, some background, answers to some controversial issue or in-depth material? Your answer will help determine how you proceed.

Quick-comment interviews

In the course of your work, whether it's putting together a story or preparing an information campaign, you may find it necessary to consult briefly with various sources. You may be checking a simple fact, asking for a quick reaction, touching base with trusted sources or making that obligatory call for an "official comment." Whatever the case, the conversation is brief and to the point and is generally conducted by telephone.

Backgrounders

These are the interviews, sometimes quick, sometimes lengthy, conducted relatively early in the information-gathering process. They are designed to educate the writer by delving into context, explanation and analysis.

Combat practice

Controversy, drama and tension are at the heart of many media messages. After thorough backgrounding, and mindful of the "bull's-eye strategy" (see page 153), information gatherers may find themselves interviewing those at the core of a controversy. These interviews often involve asking tough, challenging questions that sources may perceive as combative or hostile.

In-depth interviews

These are more leisurely—but still tightly orchestrated—sessions with sources you are striving to understand in some way. You have many questions to ask and much ground to cover. You want not only to hear responses to these questions but also to see reactions. For this reason it is preferable for in-depth interviews to be conducted face-to-face.

Form

What form will the interview take—through the mail, by phone, face-to-face or in the field? Often deadline pressure or geography determines this. But frequently you (or your subject) control the choice.

Mail interviews

This may sound absurdly dated in an age of satellite communication and fax transmission, but there are several reasonable applications for this "old technology." Suppose, for example, you want responses to 10 brief questions from 100 people? A mailed questionnaire is definitely the way to go. Suppose you are dealing with a reclusive subject? (The author Vladimir Nabokov demanded that all interviewers submit questions in writing and wait for his considered responses by mail.)

Phone interviews

Some people hate the phone and feel no real rapport can develop when interviewer and subject are physically apart. Others say that "phone friendships" (long-term relationships with people you speak to but have never met) are so common in today's world that phone interviews can be as satisfying as face-to-face encounters. Regardless of your view, "phoners" are a fact of life. In fact, a recent survey of reporters at four major metropolitan newspapers found that these journalists used the telephone for a full two-thirds of all their interviews. Phone interviews often fit into busy people's schedules better than do face-to-face meetings. They can be real time- and money-savers too.

Face-to-face interviews

This is what most people think of as an interview: an information gatherer, nodding and scribbling notes, seated across from an animated source. Because face-to-face encounters have great potential for gathering rich data about a person, from physical appearance to mannerisms to environment, they are the preferred form for depth interviews.

Field interviews

A variation of the face-to-face encounter, the field interview takes place outside the office, restaurant or hotel lobby and on the home turf of the interview subject. That sometimes means interviewing a cattle rancher while on horseback or conversing with an artist in the midst of a deafening gallery opening. Field interviews sorely test the interviewer's skills but are often an incomparable way of gaining insight into a subject.

Preparing for the interview

Thorough backgrounding, intelligent formulation of questions and mastery of information collection techniques will prepare you for your interview.

Backgrounding

He was a well-published science writer with two advanced degrees—an expert compared with his general assignment colleagues—but when he readied himself to interview Nobel laureate scientist Linus Pauling, he prepared as if cramming for a final exam.

"I read everything I could get my hands on," says Tom Hager, author and magazine journalist whose focus on medical issues brings him into contact with a wide range of experts. "You don't want to be caught short talking to a man of his reputation. You want to be able to ask good questions. At the very least, you don't want to embarrass yourself."

Not every writer interviews big-name experts, but all deal regularly with people who know more about their own field than does the writer. That's the nature of working for the mass media. What allows the writer to deal with these sources professionally and obtain quality information is solid backgrounding. At its most fundamental this means several things:

▶ A reasonable understanding of the basics of the field

▶ Sufficient depth of knowledge specific to the issue you are researching so that you know what questions to ask

▶ A working vocabulary of the jargon related to the field

Without this background, communication is difficult and information gathering is, at best, inefficient. This doesn't mean you have to be a trained criminologist to talk intelligently with the local police chief. But it does mean you have to know enough that your eyes won't glaze over when the chief begins talking about "class A misdemeanors" and "DWI citations."

How can you prepare yourself to get the most out of your interviews with experts?

1. For basic background, skim general and specialty encyclopedias, almanacs and other reference tools (see Chapters 3 and 4).

2. Read newspaper and magazine articles on the subject (see Chapters 3 and 5 for how to locate them).

3. Read trade magazine and journal articles on the subject (see Chapters 4 and 7).

4. Check government documents for helpful material (see Chapter 4).

5. Ask sources, including the person you intend to interview, for suggestions of relevant special reports and publications you should read before the interview.

6. Contact knowledgeable colleagues or dependable "background experts" for information (see Chapter 8).

You cannot become an instant expert by doing background research for a few hours or a few days, but you can create a solid basis for questioning experts. You can improve communication and increase the chances of conducting an intelligent interview.

Formulating questions

As you read and talk informally to others about the issue you are researching, you will naturally begin to formulate questions. Some of these questions will be easily answered as you continue your background work. Others will be best answered by delving deeper into written sources. But some questions—particularly those involving opinion, commentary and analysis—will be suitable to ask during an interview.

What makes a good interview question? A good question is straightforward. It is not vague, equivocal or wordy. A good question asks for a specific response and is phrased so that the respondent is neither boxed in nor asked to make meaningless, sweeping statements. A good question never seeks information that basic background sources can readily provide. (This only shows your own lack of preparation.) Instead, it strives to explore new terrain, to elicit fresh responses. Compare the following examples:

VAGUE: **What do you think about family violence?**
(May elicit a general, sweeping statement that lacks focus.)

MORE FOCUSED: **In your therapy practice you've worked with brothers and sisters who are violent and abusive toward one another. Why does this happen? What are some of the common patterns that emerge?**
(Asks specific question targeted to the expertise of the source.)

One way of identifying what makes a good question is considering what makes a bad question. Here are four all-too-common varieties of bad questions:

▶ **The pointless platitude.** This is the banal question that invariably elicits the banal, clichéd response. It asks the obvious—and that's what it gets, as in "How did you feel when you reached the summit of the mountain?" ("Tired but happy.")

▶ **The preachy preamble.** Here the interviewer delivers a little lecture before getting down to the actual question. Of course, you may feel passionate about the issue you're researching; that's only human. But prefacing your question with a sermon is a sure way to horrify the interviewee while severely tempering his or her response.

► **The triple-decker memory strainer.** You've all heard these seemingly interminable multipart questions. They're common at presidential press conferences: "Tell me, Mr. President, how would the United States respond if . . . , and if the response was diplomatic would that mean . . . , and should the response be military, could you elaborate on . . . ?" The interviewee cannot possibly keep track of all these questions.

► **The whining apologia.** Here the interviewer profusely apologizes for the question he or she is about to ask. ("I know this is a dumb question. I really should have done my research better, and I'm sorry to take up your time with such trivial matters, but . . .") After such a setup, what kind of response might the interviewer expect? And what impression would the respondent be left with?

Bad questions invariably elicit poor responses. If you pose a vague, hazy question, you will generally find yourself listening to a vague, hazy answer. If you pose a close-ended question ("Tell me, do you believe A or do you believe B?"), you will generally get nothing more than is already inherent in the question. If you pose a yes/no question, you give the interviewee the opportunity to respond monosyllabically.

Good interview questions do not exist in a vacuum. They are part of the whole interviewing dynamic, which means a good question might be

"Really?" or
"Could you elaborate on that?"

because a question often picks up on a previous comment, asking for details or making an explicit transition between two ideas. In this way, an interview is like a conversation: It flows from idea to idea. It is not a series of completely preformulated questions fired at an individual in a preformulated order. There is give-and-take; there is flexibility.

This brings us to the two major problems novices experience when formulating interview questions: *over*preparation and *under*preparation. If you overprepare, you write out all questions, word for word, and create an immutable order for them. Having done this, you preclude the possibility of real communication taking place during the interview. On the other hand, if you underprepare (also known as "winging it"), you risk asking ill-informed questions, creating uncomfortable silences—and making a fool of yourself. There is a happy medium. Solid background research and practice in the field will help you reach it.

Mastering information collection techniques

How will you record what your interviewee is saying? You have several options: pen and pad, computer or tape recorder.

Pen and pad

Some writers swear by pen and pad. There are no batteries to wear out, no tape to break, no static to interrupt. You can take a pen and pad anywhere, they argue. And people who shy away from being electronically recorded don't seem to be intimidated by a writer holding a pen. These are all good reasons to master the art—and it *is* an art—of note taking, even though easier technologies exist. Most experienced writers take notes even if they are simultaneously recording a conversation on tape.

Writers like to use stenographer's notebooks both because the small size is convenient and because the pages are designed to be turned easily. Over the years they learn to develop listening skills that allow them to hone in on "good quotes" as they occur in the conversation and paraphrase all else. Most writers also develop some sort of shorthand or system of abbreviation that allows them to write far more quickly than the average person. You are undoubtedly familiar with this practice, as students often develop swift note-taking skills to follow fast-talking lecturers.

Computers

Some writers replace pen and pad with computer, typing in notes as the interviewee speaks. This is very efficient but oftentimes not very pleasant. If the interview is by phone, if the phone is equipped with a receiver shoulder rest (so both hands are free) and if the computer keyboard is relatively silent, this is not a bad method. But for face-to-face interviews, the interjection of a major piece of machinery and the sound of the keyboard (however quiet) can be a real obstacle to decent communication.

Tape recorders

Many writers use tape recorders during interviews. Although they also take notes, taping relieves the pressure of having to catch every word and allows the interviewer to make more eye contact with the subject.

Assuming that the tape recorder is relatively small, is placed inconspicuously and is used with the full agreement of the interviewee, the atmosphere can be quite relaxed. On the other hand, taping doubles (or sometimes triples) the time needed to collect information, for the interviewer must listen to the entire tape again and take notes from it. Also, as any veteran of this technology will tell you, strange and awful things can happen to tape recorders, tapes and battery recharge units. Always double-check equipment, always operate with fully charged batteries (even if you expect to plug in), always buy decent-quality recording tape (no longer than 45 minutes a side)—and always be prepared to rely on pen and pad.

Whether you're interviewing in person or by phone, you will need to secure permission from the interviewee to record the conversation on tape. In a face-to-face interview you want to place the recorder between the two of you and resist the temptation to stare at it during the interview. If you're familiar with the machine (you know how far away someone can be from the microphone and still be heard), if you've checked your equipment and if you use audio sensor tapes (they beep just before the tape runs out), this will help.

If you want to record a telephone interview, you have two choices: the cheap and the good. The cheap choice is a small cord with a jack on one end that plugs into the recorder and a suction cup on the other that attaches to the telephone receiver. Sound quality is mediocre to awful, depending on the quality of your telephone equipment. The suction cup has a terrible habit of falling off during the earth-shaking part of the interview. Much better but a bit more expensive is a telephone recording accessory you can buy at your local electronics store. It plugs into the phone line like a telephone answering machine and delivers good-quality sound.

Whatever "technology" you choose, from pen to pocket Sony, learn how to use it *before* you go out for the interview. Don't let the process of collecting the information interfere with the dynamics of the interview. It's hard enough asking penetrating questions of a total stranger without adding complications.

The interview

You've done your homework: You've located a worthy expert, backgrounded yourself on the subject, formulated intelligent questions and mastered (or at least practiced) information collection. Now it's time to conduct the interview. How is it done?

Making contact

First, of course, you have to arrange the interview. This is almost always done by phone, even if the interview is to take place face-to-face. What your parents told you about phone etiquette goes double here: Speak up; never mumble. When calling for an interview, be sure you do the following:

1. Introduce yourself and state the organization you work for and the project you're involved in.
2. Explain the purpose of the interview.
3. Be specific about the amount of time you're requesting.
4. Give the person your telephone number(s) in case plans change unexpectedly.

It's often a good idea to pose a sample question or two, or at least to go over the terrain of the interview, as in, "What I'd like to concentrate on in the interview is . . ." If you will be talking to several experts in the field, mention that fact to your potential interviewee. Knowing that he or she won't be the sole representative in a field often eases some anxiety.

Unless time pressure, scheduling difficulties or geography dictates a phone interview, be sure to discuss and decide on an appropriate place to meet. The interviewee's office is most convenient for the subject (and much can be learned from observing a person's work environment), but it is also full of distractions. It is the rare person who won't answer the phone or a knock on the door during an interview. Your office, if you have one, might be a good choice if it's convenient for the interviewee and has a relatively quiet corner. Restaurants are generally a bad choice. Clanking silverware and other people's conversations muddy the recording; all those dishes on the table make note taking awkward. It's also difficult to eat and talk simultaneously. If the purpose of the interview is to gain insight into the individual, then conducting the session at the interviewee's home or, if relevant, "in the field" may be a good choice.

Setting the ground rules

Sometimes before and often during the interview, you and the interviewee must agree on the ground rules. For example, during the initial conversation to arrange the interview, your subject says, "I'll agree to this, but only on deep background." Or, you arrive at the session and are quickly informed by the interviewee that the conversation will be "off the record." What do these statements mean?

Writers frequently face situations like this, and reaching agreement on the ground rules governing the conversation is vital. Unless you and the interviewee understand each other perfectly from past experience, do not take anything for granted. Your definition of terms may differ from those of your source. Here are some common ones:

▶ **Deep background.** When an interviewee agrees to give you information for "deep background," it generally means the information is to be used only to help you understand an issue. The source does not want the information published or broadcast in any form. Sometimes the source doesn't even want you to use the information in conducting interviews with other sources. Make sure you know the conditions.

▶ **Background.** By "background" your interview subject probably means the information is not to be used for publication in any form. However, the source may not object to your using the information to question others.

▶ **Off the record.** This confusing phrase can mean at least three things: (1) You can't publish or broadcast the information in any form; (2) you can weave the information into your message if you make no mention whatsoever of where you got it; or (3) you can use the information if you do not explicitly mention the source. Because "off the record" is both vague and commonplace, you need to discuss its meaning with the source.

▶ **Not for attribution.** In this case, generally, the interviewee will allow you to use the material if you don't attribute it directly. How vague does the attribution have to be to satisfy the source?

▶ **Don't quote me.** Another hazy phrase, this can mean you can't use the quotation at all or you can use it but can't attribute it directly. Make sure you know what interpretation you're consenting to.

Agreeing to one of these "deals" can help you get information that would otherwise be unavailable. Such agreements may encourage interviewees to talk more freely and candidly. They can lead to tips, leaks and sensitive information while protecting sources from retribution. On the other hand, unattributed information often lacks credibility (see Chapter 10). Fabricated, distorted or self-serving information can be transmitted more easily when the source is not made publicly accountable for the remarks. It is *always* preferable to attribute.

When you are faced with a demand from a source, first make sure you know what the source is asking for. Next, use every argument you can muster to get the material on the record and for attribution.

Managing the dynamics

Although, in a sense, every interview is unique, all interviews also have some basic similarities. The interviewee will change, the relationship between the questioner and respondent will differ and, of course, the subject matter will vary—but let's concentrate on the commonalities.

Anatomy of an interview

Except for those two-minute phone conversations when all you want or need is a quick comment, most interviews, whether phone or face-to-face, seem to go through these stages:

▶ **Phase 1:** Meeting the subject and engaging in conversational ice-breakers ("small talk")

▶ **Phase 2:** Settling in, including establishing rules ("Do you mind if I use a tape recorder?" "My understanding is that this conversation is on the record."), arranging the means of information collection and reviewing the purpose of the interview

▶ **Phase 3:** Asking relatively easy or unchallenging questions while attempting to establish a rapport

▶ **Phase 4:** Asking increasingly more challenging or provocative questions

▶ **Phase 5:** Backtracking to make sure all bases have been covered, all follow-up questions asked

▶ **Phase 6:** Concluding the interview

Let's consider the stages one by one. When meeting a person, remember that first impressions (in person or via the telephone) are lasting impressions. Arrive (or call) on time; dress appropriately; conduct yourself professionally. You will want to ease into conversation as you walk in the door (or first get the person on the line). This is the purpose of small talk, that short burst of idle chatter about the traffic, the weather or mutual acquaintances that allows two strangers to begin talking while they size each other up and get comfortable. Small talk should never go on for more than a minute or two, but should simply bridge the gap between your arrival and the beginning of the interview.

Next, you settle in, open your pad, plug in your tape recorder and make sure you and the interviewee are operating under the same assumptions about the interview. Remember to summarize why you're conducting the interview, what ground you hope to cover and how it fits into the larger project you're doing.

Then, the questioning begins. Remember, the key is to maintain a balance between control and flexibility. You have certain areas you want to cover and a direction you would like the interview to take. But you also must realize that an interview can take on a life of its own. Allow yourself to be surprised. Make sure you *listen*. Your questions should reflect not only the direction you've planned for the conversation but also the evolving conversation itself.

The notion of asking less challenging questions first is just common sense. For one thing, a person is far more likely to answer a sensitive question *after* rapport has been established by talking about less sensitive issues. For another, if an interviewee is going to react with hostility to a certain question, it's best that the hostility surface late in the interview after you have been able to extract some information. Beginning with a tough question (unless that's the only question you have to ask or you know the source well) can create an insurmountable obstacle to communication.

Before you conclude the interview, take a moment to review your original list of questions and whatever you've jotted down under the "be sure to ask" category during the conversation. Your source won't mind a minute of silence as you look over your notes. When you do conclude, make sure you leave the door open for a follow-up phone call, should you need to check a fact or clarify a response.

Body language

Up to 90 percent of what is communicated during a given conversation has nothing to do with words, say interpersonal communication experts. It's arched eyebrows, crossed forearms, drumming fingers, tone of voice, pace of speaking—any one of hundreds of attitude cues we (usually unconsciously) send to others. Those who specialize in interviewing have a healthy respect for the power of body language. They understand, for example, that *eye contact* is probably the single most important component to a successful face-to-face conversation. Establishing eye contact is the first step to establishing rapport. It communicates to the interviewee that you are interested in what he or she is saying, that you're paying attention, that this conversation is important to you. Looking someone squarely in the eyes also communicates forthrightness and honesty.

Common nonverbal cues like *nodding* and *smiling* are also important conversational tools. When you briefly nod as someone is talking, you show, once again, that you're paying attention. You give the person the message that you understand what he or she is saying. Both nods and smiles encourage the person to keep talking.

The position of your body also communicates. If you lean forward, you show interest, eagerness and sometimes (whether you want to or not) impatience. If you lean back, you create a more relaxed atmosphere that may allow your respondent to be more expansive. Some communication specialists suggest attempting to mimic the body language of the person you're interviewing. The theory is that people feel most comfortable talking to people just like themselves. So, if your respondent is a fast-talking, forward-leaning hand-wringer, you should be too.

This is probably not bad advice—within reason. For example, each person has a "comfort zone" for face-to-face communication, an optimum distance that must be maintained between him- or herself and others. If your respondent needs only a relatively narrow space to feel comfortable and you draw away (because you need a wider space), this can send an inadvertently unfriendly message. If, on the other hand, your respondent needs a relatively wide space and you impinge on it (because your space needs are more modest), you send a message of aggression. You certainly would not want to overdo the mimicking idea, for it can quickly turn into parody.

Silence

Probably the most important non-verbal tool to keep in mind is *silence*. The general rule is that most people will fill a silence when it stretches beyond what seems comfortable. You can use this to your advantage in an interview by remaining silent (and perhaps leaning forward in expectation) after your respondent has stopped talking. This is often one of the most effective ways of encouraging people to expand on their answers.

Obviously, body language cannot be "spoken" over the phone, but silence, tone of voice and pace of speaking can all be used to enhance communication.

Learning to listen

Many people's stereotype of a good journalistic interviewer is a hard-nosed interrogator who fires volleys of tough questions (Mike Wallace on CBS's "60 Minutes," for example). But the truth is, learning to listen is just as important as, if not more important than, learning to ask questions. Good interviewers are active, engaged listeners who don't just nod along distractedly but who truly hone in on the conversation. Because they are attentive, they pick up conversational clues others miss. They can structure follow-up questions and forge links between ideas. And, because they are perceived by their respondents to be interested and concerned, they are able to establish an easier rapport and get a better interview.

Special problems

If you've selected your person well, backgrounded yourself thoroughly and practiced the skills of interviewing, you can reasonably expect to have a good experience. But sometimes, even when you've done everything right, something still goes wrong. Consider these five troublesome interviewees and some suggestions for how to get the interview back on the right track.

The silent interviewee

You ask what you think are wonderful questions and get monosyllabic answers. You ask a question you thought would trigger a lengthy response and get a one-liner. What do you do? First, don't lose patience. Some people take a long time to warm up to a conversation. Second, make sure you ask open-ended questions that cannot be answered by a yes or no. Third, follow up each too-brief response with another inquiry. This may be as simple as saying "and then?" or "uh huh," nodding encouragement and waiting. If all else fails, you might try to beat the person at his or her own game by using silence. Don't jump in to ask another question; rather, let the silence expand and see what happens.

The wandering interviewee

Every interviewer has had this experience: You ask a question and the respondent takes off on an interminable, unrelated tangent. You are simultaneously aware of the need to keep the conversation focused and the desire to be polite. You don't want to interrupt, clear your throat or drum your fingers on the desk, but you do want to bring the respondent back to earth. What do you do? Try giving this nonverbal cue: Stop taking notes. This is a dramatic (but somewhat subtle) hint that the person has ceased to be interesting. It works.

The evasive interviewee

The key to dealing with the evasive interviewee is thorough backgrounding. If the interviewee responds, "I really don't know much about that," you can come back with, "But your three-year involvement with the Committee on X must have given you some insights." It's a common strategy to bring along memos, published stories, manuscripts of speeches—anything that documents the thoughts, opinions and ideas of the interviewee. To jog the memory of an evasive interviewee, you might want to read from one of these documents. It is also important to understand from the outset why an interviewee might be evasive. Does this person have something to lose by responding to a certain line of questioning? Get a fix on motivation. It will help you structure questions.

The hostile interviewee

Generally, interviewees will be hostile if they are under fire for being part of some current controversy or if they have been (or perceive themselves as having been) mistreated by the media in the past. Clearly stating the purpose of the interview at the outset may help alleviate hostility related to the first circumstance. Your own credentials as a respected professional may help the second. But sometimes nothing helps. Remember to come prepared, remain unflappable and save your toughest questions until last.

The well-rehearsed interviewee

We've already discussed the phenomenon of the media-savvy spokesperson who is not open to two-way communication (see page 150). Some well-rehearsed interviewees calculate every word and gesture to achieve just the effect they desire. A good interviewer stays away from these master manipulators, using them only when "official comments" are absolutely necessary.

The search

Let's consider how to prepare to interview a key subject in the diet fads and frauds search: the manufacturer of a weight-loss product, an over-the-counter pill that promises to dramatically curb dieters' appetites. You can locate this person by any number of means previously mentioned. For example, this person may have been mentioned in a magazine or newspaper article (see Chapter 3) or in a legal case (see Chapter 4). He or she may have been a witness at a congressional hearing (see Chapter 4). In the absence of any reported mentions, you can identify this person by consulting various business directories (see Chapter 7).

The first step is thorough backgrounding. Find out as much as possible about the company, its products and profits, and its method of operation in the marketplace (see Chapter 7). You will need to refer to government documents and conduct legal research (see Chapter 4) to investigate whether the company has been involved in lawsuits or other actions. You will also want to background yourself on the biochemistry of the product. The packaging label will tell you what it contains; a background source (see Chapter 8) will explain what all those unpronounceable words mean. As you are preparing, keep in mind that this person is probably a "bull's-eye" source (see Chapter 8). That means you want to interview perimeter sources first to maximize knowledge and minimize the possibility of being manipulated.

It's time to call for an interview. You introduce yourself and your organization and summarize your project. Next, you detail the purpose of the interview; for example: "As you know, there's been quite a bit of controversy over your product. The published medical studies I've seen question its effectiveness. Your own literature cites other studies and claims great effectiveness. I'd like to talk about those other studies and any other data you have on the product. I'm interested in getting to the bottom of the question, 'Does it work?'" Because the company is located in a distant city and because the company source is a busy person, let's assume you arrange a phone interview.

You spend considerable time going over your background material and constructing questions. Some may be in the form of questions: "Do you have your own in-house chemists who develop and test products?" "Tell me about the studies you cite in your promotional brochure. Who conducted them? How many people participated?" Others may address general topics you want to cover: competition from other pill manufacturers, threat of FDA regulations. With your questions and topics before you, your telephone recording device plugged in and your tape recorder checked, you are ready to make contact at the decided-upon hour.

YOU: Hello, Mr./Ms. Smith, this is _____ from the _____ (*introduction*). You remember we set up a time to talk this morning about the effectiveness of Lard-B-Gone (*purposes of the interview*)?

SMITH: Yes.

YOU: Good. I'm glad we were able to set this up before you take off for Europe next week (*small talk*).

SMITH: Yes, it is a busy time for me.

YOU: Well, let's get right to it, then. I was talking with Jones at Weight-Off, Inc. and s/he mentioned two new weight-loss pills that are about to come on the market. I'd like to talk about competition in the industry as well as your product in particular (*what terrain will be covered*). I'd like to tape-record this conversation if that's alright with you, Mr./Ms. Smith (*setting the rules*).

SMITH: Yes, fine. I'll be recording it, too, from my end.

YOU: Let's start first with the competitive nature of the industry, okay? Ten years ago, yours was the only nationally advertised over-the-counter diet pill. Today there are more than a dozen such products. What's happening to the industry (*unthreatening question that gets the interviewee talking*)?

The interview continues as you ask about the studies cited to prove the effectiveness of the pill. You save the toughest questions—the lawsuit, the accusations by doctors that the pill is unsafe, and so on—until the end. Although the telephone prevents you from using the full range of non-verbal tools, remember that tone of voice and silence are powerful communicators. Also keep in mind that an interviewee can only be as evasive as you allow him or her to be. If you go into the interview prepared, you can ask (and re-ask) pointed questions that make it difficult for an interviewee to bob and weave around the subject.

> YOU: Mr./Ms. Smith, how do you explain the tremendous difference in results between the tests your own chemists ran on the pill and those conducted by scientists at the National Institute for Obesity Research?
>
> SMITH: I'm not familiar with that study.
>
> YOU: Let me refresh your memory. It was big news when it was published last year in the *American Journal of Weight Research*. *Time* and a few of the women's magazines picked up on it. Anyway, the study concluded that your pill had no greater effect on suppressing appetite than a sugar pill placebo.
>
> SMITH: Well, that study was not really comparable at all with the studies we did. It's an apples and oranges thing.
>
> YOU: I don't think so, Mr./Ms. Smith. In the published study, doctors gave 100 obese women your pill and 100 obese women a sugar pill. Your own study looked at a group of obese women too, about the same age range and just about as overweight as the group the scientists studied. Both groups didn't go on a special diet or do any exercise they weren't already doing. The studies were about as similar as they could be. So how do you account for the major discrepancies in findings (*now you've got him*)?

An interview can be nerve-wracking or relaxed, hostile or amiable, emotional or sedate. But it is always challenging—and often fun. Choosing the right person, backgrounding thoroughly and listening intently are the keys.

10

Trust, Truth and Thoughtful Assumptions

nformation gatherers are not robots. They are not objective, disinterested transcribers of whatever is delivered to them. They are not infallible humans who never get confused, bored, anxious—and hoodwinked.

However, information gatherers can rise above some of these mortal failings. They can be discerning, skeptical and cautious. They can be hounds for detail.

Being such an information gatherer is not simply a matter of talent and experience; it also is an attitude. Learning about credibility and reliability as well as bias and conflict will help you develop such an attitude. This chapter will set an agenda for what should be expected from a thorough and ethical information gatherer.

Let's begin with the collection and evaluation of evidence. We'll follow that with these topics:

- ▶ Searching for detail and context
- ▶ Dealing with conflict, bias and deception
- ▶ Reacting when information gathering falls short

Collecting and evaluating evidence

Consider all information as evidence: It can solve a puzzle, prove a point, refute an argument or answer a hurried question. So far, this book has stressed strategies for collecting as much relevant information as possible. Now it's time to discuss evaluating the worth of various pieces of this evidence and to examine what might be described as "getting a fix on the truth."

A nautical analogy may be helpful here. When sailors near land, they face new dangers as threatening as gale-force winds on open seas. Shallow water, reefs, riptides and poorly marked channels can spell a tragic end, even this close to port, to a difficult voyage. To avoid such a disaster, sailors need to establish exactly where they are. To do this, they take a navigational fix to determine their location. The most accurate fix is obtained by taking several lines of position, using reliable navigational aids as reference points. Establishing these points against, for example, a lighthouse, buoy and breakwater marker will give a reliable fix of position—if the sailors are precise. When that fix is plotted on a navigational chart, these three lines of position should intersect at the same point. That is where the sailors are—and away from danger, they hope.

Establishing validity for collected information is much like taking the correct navigational fix. If a sailor's technique is poor and the charts are flawed, the lines of position won't properly intersect—forcing the crew to make a dangerous guess. The information gatherer must work precisely and check the validity of information in order to trust that material. An obvious lesson is not to depend on just one source; a more hidden one is the need to rigorously evaluate one's information—how it was obtained, how complete it is and what it means.

Smoking and mortality

Here's an example to illustrate the breathless pursuit of truth. For many years the Tobacco Institute, a lobbying group for tobacco growers and manufacturers, has argued that no proven link exists between the use of tobacco and premature death. The entire scientific and medical community has disputed this, and now it points to a recent report from the federal Centers for Disease Control: CDC's computer analysis of death records from all states shows that in 1985 more than 300,000 Americans

died from smoking. So—is this statistic the link that will refute the Tobacco Institute's position?

To answer this question, the information gatherer must understand
two critical points about the evaluation of evidence:

- ▶ There are precious few simple truths or obvious facts.
- ▶ One should never underestimate the influence of language and
  source on perceived levels of truth of a statement.

No matter what perception the information gatherer may have about
the self-interest of a tobacco-lobbying organization and about the presumed higher goals of the medical community, he or she must be tenacious in pursuing further information and context. For example:

1. Was smoking actually listed as a cause of death on all the death
   certificates analyzed by the CDC?

2. If not, *how* did CDC determine that a death was related to
   smoking?

3. What was the average age on the death certificates?

4. Did all states follow similar reporting practices so the CDC did
   not have to make unnecessary assumptions?

When these questions cannot be properly answered, the information
becomes suspect. Obviously, the information gatherer must get more
background on what the method of investigation was and how it was determined that smoking was directly related to these deaths.

Language and source also are important issues. For example, in an
earlier paragraph, the authors said the CDC's computer analysis shows
that in 1985 more than 300,000 Americans died from smoking. "Shows"
is a pretty powerful word here. It suggests that the authors believe the
truth of the statement; however, until the information gatherer can get
closer to the facts, "purports to show" or "contends" is more accurate
language. Writers must be very careful about the signals they send because, although their confidence in the truth of their statements is high,
their "evidence" may be too easily attacked—thereby crumbling the credibility of their presentation. Often the problem is a lack of follow-up; ac-
cepting information at face value and without tough questioning is a dangerous practice indeed.

The media professional also understands that certain sources carry
a higher "natural credibility" than others. In extremes, that certainly is
true: Nobel Prize-winner Mother Teresa naturally would be more trusted

on a variety of topics than would mass murderer Charles Manson. But most credibility calls are much closer than that; for example, while some people would argue vehemently that the Tobacco Institute is going to say anything to stave off diminished tobacco advertising and use, others would say that a government agency like the CDC is a self-serving bureaucracy that just wants to perpetuate itself and force government's will on the people. And some people do not assume that a government entity is naturally more credible than a commercial one. What really makes the government's study more reliable, they ask. So, more information about sources and their agendas must be made available to the public. That is also part of the information package.

The Rashomon dilemma

In 1951 the Japanese director Akira Kurasawa created a classic inquiry into truth with his film "Rashomon," in which four people give four different versions of a murder and a rape that have occurred in their presence. Kurasawa's intent was to let the audience decide the truth of what really happened. There was more to his story than the fact of a murder and a rape; context, cause and blame became elusive factors. So it can be with the information chase. Our audiences may agree, for example, that an oil spill has happened in Alaska, that the United States is spending money way beyond its means, that family violence must be eliminated. But they will not all agree on the causes of or cures for any of these problems. They need more information, more context in order to make these decisions and to develop a meaningful consensus.

Information can be a powerful persuader in the search for even a portion of "the truth."

Searching for detail and context

Here's the quintessential human interest story—sad to some, funny to others:

> LOS ANGELES—Actress Barbara Bain's dog was killed when a delivery person heaved a copy of the Los Angeles Times toward her front lawn and it landed on her animal, her agent said yesterday.
> Agent Marty Blumenthal said the accident happened last week.

"They offered to make restitution, but how do you put a price on a pet you've had for 14 years?"

The Times' circulation department declined to comment on the incident.

This is, obviously, an unusual death. However, the story is incredibly sketchy; you don't have to be an information hound to pursue the following questions:

1. How big was this unfortunate dog?
    ► Consider the implications if it was a Great Dane. If it was a Toy Poodle, then the story's impact (!) is lessened.

2. How big was the newspaper?
    ► Perhaps it was a 7-pound Sunday edition, with 346 advertising inserts. If it was a light edition, then more questions arise.

3. Was the newspaper purposely thrown at the dog? From what distance? With what force?
    ► These facts may be harder to ascertain, but they are natural questions.

Pursuing detail on such a story may seem far-fetched, but it illustrates the trouble a body of information causes when it creates more questions than it answers. Detail and context are the keys to information that the media audience can use—without having to say, "Huh? What does this mean? I'm not sure I understand this."

Let's examine two pieces of information to show the need for greater investigation.

The case of the "neglected" aircraft

Imagine the panic and anxiety at ABC Airlines when this broadcast information hits corporate headquarters:

> The Air Transport Association today reported that ABC Airlines has the worst record of aircraft maintenance in the domestic airline industry today. Its study contends that ABC spends the fewest number of hours on jet aircraft maintenance of all 15 major U.S. carriers. . . .

If the basis for a judgment of the "worst record" is hours of maintenance alone, this information could be in jeopardy. Surely these questions would have to be answered, in order to provide more detail and context:

1. **What is the age of ABC's aircraft?**
   ▶ If these aircraft are relatively new, perhaps less maintenance is required.

2. **How much maintenance and analysis is controlled by computer?**
   ▶ Newer aircraft may have more computer-assisted maintenance, which may not be reflected in a company's quarterly reports to the U.S. Department of Transportation.

3. **What is the experience level of ABC mechanics?**
   ▶ If ABC has mostly highly experienced mechanics (more than all its competitors), these people may work more efficiently and expertly, resulting in fewer needed hours of maintenance.

4. **How many planes are still under factory warranty?**
   ▶ Maintenance of these aircraft might be separately reported.

If this information is available but simply not reported, false and harmful impressions may result. The information gatherer, in analyzing this report from the ATA, must be careful to understand the report and not create erroneous linkages. The information gatherer must pursue detail and context by asking sources these questions:

1. How did you obtain this information?
2. What does it mean?
3. What might be wrong with your analysis?
4. What could be missing here?

This is more than an issue of fairness. It is one of completeness and professionalism.

More special deliveries?

What should the average citizen make of the statistic contained in the following statement?

> In the last 20 years, the percentage of Caesarian-section births has more than quadrupled; today almost 1 in 4 women have this surgical procedure to deliver their children.*

---

* National Center for Health Statistics.

Several possible conclusions can be drawn: (1) that physicians are performing more C-sections because the procedure provides more revenue than does a normal birth; (2) that mothers are becoming less healthy; (3) that babies are becoming larger; or (4) that with the alarming increase in both malpractice suits and malpractice insurance premiums, the C-section delivery lessens the chance for a malpractice action against a physician.

Remembering the first maxim about evaluation of evidence—that there are precious few simple truths or obvious facts—the information gatherer realizes that one cannot draw a conclusion from a single piece of even the most startling data. The experienced media professional knows that portions of several possible conclusions often combine to form the closest approximation of the truth of an issue. For example, consider the following data also from the National Center for Health Statistics:

▶ In the last 20 years, deaths of infants at birth have been cut in half.

▶ The maternal death rate today is only 30 percent of what it was 20 years ago.

The combination of all these statistics offers context for the C-section statistic. Obstetricians today will argue that medical technology is at such a level that fetal monitoring—including the measurement of oxygen in fetal blood—provides more information about possible distress of a fetus, which may prompt a decision to perform the C-section.

These physicians probably will agree that the soaring increase in malpractice claims and premiums has led to more "defensive medicine," which might lead to the decision to perform a C-section in situations where a team of physicians might not all agree. To give more substance to this issue, the information gatherer should obtain data on the number and rate of malpractice lawsuits relating to all births.

Lastly, a conclusion—or allegation—that physicians perform these procedures mainly for economic gain treads on dangerous legal and ethical grounds. The proof of such a charge may be difficult to obtain, which could have the information gatherer looking down the barrel of an expensive defamation lawsuit. This proof requires demonstration of a lack of medical need to perform these procedures. Also, it is reasonable to assume that professional associations and regulatory agencies would monitor unethical or unprofessional behavior and discipline offenders— records that are supposed to be public. So, if the information gatherer wants to pursue the economic gain conclusion, some hard facts about medically unnecessary procedures must be found.

The pursuit of detail and context may be time-consuming and run counter to the needs and interests of those media pressured by relentless deadlines. However, fragments of information often lead to only slivers of the truth. That simply won't do. We must always ask, "Now exactly what does this mean?"

Conflict, bias and deception

For some, determining the validity of information is a matter of instinct. Pulitzer Prize-winning reporter Joel Brinkley uses a finely meshed filter to detect bias and deceit. In an interview situation, he says,

> the first and most important thing is to figure out what motivates the person, what he hopes to gain or fears he might lose as the result of the piece I am writing. For most people, everything they say to a reporter is run through that filter.
> As to when I trust a source, if it's a one-time interview with someone I don't know well, it is when I have been able to confirm with other sources large elements of what he said. If it is someone I use all the time, I begin trusting him and may not feel as compelled to confirm every little element, after we have worked on a few stories together and he has established a clean record of reliability.

Some factors that aid the filtering process include an assessment of what the source might gain or lose with the release of information and how that information is attributed. But a tenacious pursuit of facts often will speak for itself. When the United States invaded the Caribbean island of Grenada, the media were denied access until the military action was completed. However, the U.S. government did "release" these "facts": Three thousand troops landed to protect the lives of 1,000 citizens. Their lives were in danger from a Cuban occupation of more than 1,000 troops who were setting up a terrorist center. Calling its Grenada operation a success, the U.S. government contended that only eight American service personnel had been killed and that damage had been kept to a minimum.

What more could be said after this official version? Plenty, say communications scholars Everette Dennis and Melvin DeFleur:

There was a lot more. Reporters went to Grenada after the ban on their travel was lifted and unearthed a number of discrepancies between what they saw and the government's reports. For instance, 6,000 American servicemen were on the island on October 25, not 3,000. On October 30, the State Department admitted there had been only 700 Cubans there, all but 100 of whom were in fact construction workers. Similarly, the alleged cache of weapons was found to be much smaller than the president had indicated, and there was no evidence of a terrorist training base on the island. Papers released by the government did not show that any Cuban takeover had been planned or that the Soviets had been involved in any way with the prime minister's [Maurice Bishop's] murder. Some of the returning American citizens, while grateful to be safely at home, admitted that they had never been aware of any danger, and journalists found that the Cuban government had given assurances several times that they would not be harmed. American casualties were eventually listed at 18 dead and 89 wounded; most of these had been sustained on the first day of the invasion. And a Canadian reporter discovered that a mental hospital had mistakenly been bombed, resulting in the deaths of 17 civilians, which the government never reported. . . . In the confusion over the facts, one point about press censorship became clear: Americans learned only what the government told them.*

The lessons here, some of which were reinforced in 1985 with the government's reluctance to release information on the explosion of the space shuttle Challenger and in 1989 with the Panama invasion, include the following:

▶ Sources will seldom reveal all they know.

▶ Sources generally will release information according to their own needs and agendas.

▶ In the face of conflicting information and outright deception, the information gatherer must chip away with pieces of detail that will undermine the misinformation that is being generated.

A key element in resolving conflicting and slanted information is attribution—giving authorship or sponsorship to statements or to a body of information. When a source will speak for attribution, he or she in

* Melvin DeFleur and Everette Dennis, *Understanding Mass Communications*, 3rd ed. (Boston: Houghton Mifflin, 1988), 122.

effect stands behind that information. Obtaining attribution for information helps the information gatherer and the audience; among other
things, it does the following:

- ► Provides the audience with another source to evaluate
- ► Shows the audience that the information gatherer has been
  working to show authorship of information
- ► Adds to message credibility and fairness
- ► Shores up media credibility

The information gatherer must be alert to reasons for incomplete,
slanted, deceptive and unattributed information. Learning motivations
can be helpful in setting a level of validity and credibility for that information. For example, reticence or deception on the part of a source could
be linked to (1) protection of a special interest, (2) a need to delay action,
(3) the floating of a "trial balloon" to determine how the public will react
to that information, or (4) embarrassment with or fear of the source, who
may not have confidence in this information or who may fear retribution.
Asking a source, "Will you stand behind this information?" and "What
attributed facts can you provide to back up your information?" is a direct challenge to the source to be a visible, responsible author of that
information.

When information gathering falls short

Overstatement, generalization and incompleteness can plague the
information gatherer; these problems become especially evident as the
writing process begins. Look at these examples and try to imagine what
brought writers to these points:

> **Like many who teach at the university, Sara Thomas espouses radical
> politics in the classroom.**
>
> (So—exactly how many is "many"? How did the writer confirm these
> numbers? This surely seems a gross overstatement, with other proof to
> the contrary. Further, exactly what is "radical politics"?)
>
> **The majority of pit bull dogs are dangerous, which is the fault of
> their owners, many of whom are into drugs.**
>
> ("Majority" would be at least 50.1 percent of the field—is that really true
> about these dogs? What authoritative source said so? And how is it pos-
> sible to track down information of drug use of a dog owner?)

Jurors, while assuming the defendant is innocent until proved guilty, often assume the rape victim is lying about the crime.

(This is a gross generalization. How is it possible to know what anyone, let alone jurors, is assuming?)

A recent study at a major university reveals that American voters support an increase in the use of nuclear power for energy transmission.

(This is deception by vagueness. What study, exactly? What university? Exactly what did the study find? How did the study define "support"? Who was surveyed?)

The search

An audience wants to know that information is complete and that sources are identified; it doesn't want to be assaulted (and insulted) by sweeping, fantastic statements that can't be corroborated. Solid information gathering is the key—when a message contains too many "holes," more information and context are needed.

An example from one of our master searches may be instructive. Consider this advertising claim by XYZ Weight Reducers Inc.: "We can report a success rate of 80 percent with our clients in keeping their excess pounds off." Data that our master search has uncovered so far runs counter to such a claim—that medical studies show as high as a 95 percent "recidivism" rate (a return to previous weight levels) after one year. In the face of this information, what conclusions can we draw about that advertising claim? Here are several possibilities:

▶ The advertised success rate was for a period shorter than one year.

▶ The data was based on clients' self-reporting, with little or no substantiation by the company.

▶ The success claim is pure puffery.

▶ Something truly amazing is happening with XYZ Weight Reducers!

In any event, more information is needed to substantiate such an amazing claim. In the advertising world, regulatory agencies like the Federal Trade Commission and the Federal Communications Commission monitor such claims and punish false ones; in these and other media arenas, the public and other institutions can also be stern judges of the quality of the information offered and the premises based on them.

Credible information carries great power. It serves a public hungry for context and detail, a public that can use help in its decision making. Shallow information undermines public confidence in our media institutions; the use of unattributed sources and sketchy detail can be a form of demagoguery. Although the information gatherer is often rushed, and time pressures may not always permit the ideal presentation, an attitude that fosters thoroughness and fairness will lead to quality results—information that the public can use.

Writing:
Visions and Revisions

The information search is over. You've finished asking questions of others. Now, before you transform that information into a well-crafted message, it's time to ask questions of yourself:

1. What am I trying to say?
2. How do I begin?
3. What should I emphasize?
4. What can I leave out?
5. What's missing here?

Welcome to a world of anxiety, frustration and great rewards: the challenge of putting order and logic into your information collection, of touching the minds and hearts of an audience with what you know and believe.

The writing task is more than a mechanical assembly of data and words. It is (or should be) a rather complex piece of architecture that, to be successful, requires a firm foundation, strong structural support, clean lines and, never to be overlooked, a distinctive style. The writing process cannot be separated from information gathering and synthesis; without a well-organized body of information that provides detail and context, the mass communicator writes around a subject, not about it.

Thus far in *The Search*, you have learned techniques for information identification, collection and evaluation. This chapter focuses on the organization and presentation of your information. It will examine these topics:

▶ Selecting your focus

▶ Developing a thesis

▶ Outlining priorities in presentation

▶ Stressing detail and context

▶ Looking for "holes"

The search for a focus

Anyone who has embarked on an information search of even moderate length realizes that the writing process develops in tandem with that search. The searcher—the writer—is guided by a central issue that will be the focus of the writing. For example, in the weight-loss master search, a focus begins to emerge after you evaluate the material you've gathered on several key questions:

1. How many weight-loss programs are there in the United States today?

   ▶ This is a direct, factual question. Obviously, it is an important issue, as it provides both background and context. But it is also a relatively easy question to answer; therefore, it really doesn't qualify as a central point of inquiry and writing focus.

2. Are these programs harmful?

   ▶ This may be too simple a yes/no question. Once it is answered, other more important questions emerge. You are left with too narrow a focus. Still, this can be a helpful point for part of your writing, as you must establish the fact of any harm in order to demonstrate a problem.

3. How effective are these weight-loss programs?

   ▶ With a more expanded question than the previous one, you enter an area of conflict, of opinion, perhaps of advocacy. Although the answer to this question requires a lot of detail and analysis, it may not be a wise choice for focus because it may ignore a deeper inquiry into what to do if these programs are judged to be ineffective *and* harmful.

4. How have research and public policy protected society from harmful weight-loss programs?

  ▶ Now you have a focus that will permit you to answer all of the previous questions and to provide an analysis that will be of service to your audience. Indeed, the previous questions should have guided your information gathering as well; certainly they will contribute to your writing.

In selecting a focus, you aim at a compelling issue, but you hope to be as comprehensive as possible. In that sense your focus is a big umbrella—it covers you wherever you go.

The thesis

Having chosen your focus from the material you have gathered, you next begin to develop a thesis. It becomes the answer to your main question. In the weight-loss search that thesis—or position statement—might look like this:

> Weight-loss programs are generally expensive and ineffective. Agencies at various government levels have not protected society from the physical and financial harm caused by these programs.

This raises several questions about thesis statements:

1. Can a thesis be subjective and opinionated?
2. Must the writer substantiate every part of his or her thesis?
3. Should a thesis provide for discussion or exposure of divergent views?

In every case the answer is yes. Very few pieces of writing are totally objective; after all, people also write to persuade, not just inform. The selection of sources, the emphasis of the material, the decision of what to underplay or omit and even the choice of verbs and adjectives contribute to the writer's position on issues. This does not mean, however, that the message is unfair; balance is not the same as focus. Advertising copywriting may be an exception to the issue of balance; not many consumers expect an advertisement to expose all the "warts" of an advertised product.

Still, the careful and responsible writer will address all major parts of an issue. The effective professional writer deals with all aspects of a thesis—leaving nothing to an unintended interpretation or inference. Failure to do so creates a suspicion about unfairness and about incomplete information gathering.

If your information is complete, if you have found appropriate detail and context, the development of a thesis is a natural and almost obvious step. Amazingly, you can see your position developing before you complete your information search.

The outline

In its most traditional and direct form, the information outline looks like this:

INTRODUCTION

THESIS STATEMENT

BACKGROUND/HISTORY

BODY #1: PRIMARY PROOF OF/SUPPORT FOR THESIS

BODY #2: DISCUSSION OF CONFLICTS/OTHER VIEWPOINTS

RESTATEMENT OF MAIN POINTS

CONCLUSION/CALL FOR ACTION

This outline reflects a gradual development of a position and a release of information in stages. However, it shouldn't be confused with the exact outline of a writing plan. As a method of information organization, this outline is in marked contrast to the so-called news-burst organization, where the presentation begins with a truncated summary of the most important information ("three people dead in arson-caused fire that destroyed two buildings"), followed by a statement of related facts in descending order of importance. No conclusion is stated—the information merely runs out of steam and importance.

The persuasive nature of the advertisement, coupled with the audience's limited attention span for such messages, calls for information that quickly attracts attention, makes a key point and then exits in hope that the audience will remember the focus of the message.

Media form dictates the information search as well as the outline. The most helpful example here is an outline that expands the traditional form, to provide greater analysis. Let's look at a possible information organization for our weight-loss search:

INTRODUCTION

▶ Growth of the weight-loss industry

▶ Highlights of concerns about its programs

THESIS STATEMENT

▶ Government has not properly protected society from the physical and financial harm caused by some weight-loss programs

▶ Other key points that the writer will introduce and later discuss

BACKGROUND/HISTORY

▶ History of the development and of successes/failures of these programs

▶ How society has embraced the concept of fitness and of the need for an "ideal" body weight

ANALYSIS OF PROBLEM

▶ Media projections of the ideal body and of quick-fix approaches to weight loss ignore genetics and psychological issues that affect how and what we eat

▶ Statistics

▶ Statements from authorities

▶ Rebuttal from selected weight-loss firms

▶ Discussion of the role of government regulatory agencies

▶ Restatement of the problem

BODY #1: case studies of problems associated with these programs

▶ Inability to keep weight off after initial loss

▶ Associated health problems and deaths

BODY #2: role of government agencies in the regulation of these programs

▶ Description of government agencies charged with regulation

▶ Evaluation of agencies' work: successes and failures

▶ Opinion from a variety of sources on what needs to be done

RESTATEMENT OF MAIN POINTS

▶ Substantiating thesis with summary of points that reinforce it

CONCLUSION/CALL FOR ACTION

▶ More oversight on dietary supplements is needed from the Food and Drug Administration

▶ Federal Trade Commission and Federal Communications Commission must more carefully monitor advertising claims and demand greater substantiation of those claims

▶ Educational institutions must work harder to discuss health issues and self-image

This outline shows how extended an analysis can be and how information sources can be used. It certainly illustrates how a written presentation must have logic and order. Now let's turn to another use of your message organization—to show how detail makes your information more persuasive.

Detail and context

Authoritative writers don't explain issues with generalities. They don't withhold the identities of sources from their audiences. Instead, they present information with a precision and a context that give the audience confidence in it. Here are some examples:

▶ Instead of stating that there are a growing number of lawsuits against manufacturers of certain dietary supplements and against weight-loss companies, the effective writer discusses a selection of relevant cases and the reasons these cases are having such an impact. In addition, he or she provides comparative statistics on the number of complaints and claims filed in recent years.

▶ Instead of generalizing that weight-loss programs don't work over a long period, the effective writer cites studies—mentioning also the credentials of the researchers and the way these studies were funded and conducted—showing that more than 80 percent of clients return to their previous weight, especially those on liquid-only diet programs.

▶ The effective writer brings in credible, authoritative sources to give examples and to explain why government regulation in this area is failing.

Appropriate detail helps answer questions before they are asked. It can be an effective persuader. The key is that the writer's audience shouldn't have to ask for more examples, more sources, more facts. An experienced writer has an intuition about when the story is complete.

Context helps clarify meaning so a writer's intentions aren't mistaken. For example, writers discussing the effectiveness of weight-loss programs must first establish the actual claims of these programs and then measure the programs' successes, failures and complaints within the framework of what these programs say they will do. Proper context also involves an evaluation of sources. Do some sources appear to be biased? Do they have hidden agendas? Make sure your audience is clear about their meaning—and yours.

Discovering what's missing

A valuable benefit of organizing your writing—a process some call prewriting—is recognition of holes in your story or message. When you have trouble bringing a sense of order to your outline, it may be a sign that your information gathering is incomplete. You may find, for example, that you do not have enough data about health problems associated with special diets; you may be depending on too narrow a range of sources; or you may have overlooked the nutrition counseling benefits of certain programs.

Often you aren't aware of the deficiencies in your search until you begin the writing process. As you gain experience, you will recognize what's missing in your search long before that search is over. That's because you will be thinking about writing even while you are gathering information. This is the ideal; your information directs your writing, and your writing reflects the accuracy and strength of that information. When that information is published, a final judgment is made: If your audience understands, if it agrees, if it is moved to action, you're on the road to success.

A note on clarity and style

Good writers don't let form interfere with the function of their information. They realize that clear, concise expression serves that information—and the audience—best. When the information is complete, the writer's next obligation is to ensure that it is presented in a direct, orderly fashion. However, this doesn't mean the writing must be bland.

Effective writers choose words carefully. These words should represent exactly what writers mean. Strong writers use lively words and vary sentence length to create an easy, inviting rhythm. Innovative writers develop a style that is fresh, original and playful. It should not be forced.

Does all this sound impossible? It shouldn't—because it isn't.

Good writing follows a precise blueprint. It depends on reliable information to lay a firm foundation. It uses information to create an orderly inquiry that can be forceful and persuasive.

The reward of well-presented information is power. An audience is empowered by what it reads and hears; the writer gains confidence and builds his or her reputation. A society is dependent on clear, detailed information that provides context. Providing less than that creates the opportunity for misinformation, deceit and demagoguery.

The media writer has a vital, important calling. This is not high-blown rhetoric but a simple truth in a society so dependent on information in its daily functioning.

Information—accurate, complete and contextual—is the key. Please don't settle for less.

Access and Integrity

Free expression. Open government. Information gathering without fear of harassment or prosecution. In a free society these principles and standards are supported by constitutions, charters, statutes, judicial decisions and administrative interpretations. These principles are sustained and fought for because they are an integral part of the human spirit.

One may be tempted to argue that such principles are a matter of common sense; after all, the public is entitled to know the public's business, right? People should be able to speak their piece, right?

Yes—most of the time.

No right is completely unfettered. Any society of laws must balance the public welfare, individual rights and its own security. And with most of those rights come corresponding responsibilities. In such a complex society we also balance our laws and our ethical principles; it is in this environment that we must view our rights and responsibilities as information gatherers.

This appendix will outline and briefly discuss issues of access and integrity in information gathering. Specifically, we will examine the following:

▶ Public records and freedom of information
▶ Open meetings legislation

- ▶ Federal standards of access
- ▶ The harm that can occur in the information-gathering process
- ▶ The various protections afforded the media professional
- ▶ Important ethical concerns for the information gatherer

Letting the sun shine in

It is curious that many states had public records and open meetings laws in place long before any equivalent federal rules were passed. It took the federal government almost 200 years to put into operation a broad-scale Freedom of Information Act, whereas Florida enacted such legislation at the turn of this century. With this in mind, let's examine how states' public records and open meetings laws operate and then turn to several federal acts relating to access.

State public records laws

A "public body, public funding" test is applied to state and local government records, whether that information is a typewritten report, chart, photo, map, magnetic tape or computer database. All states and the District of Columbia have public records laws; these *presume* open access to all citizens, with certain exemptions specified by statute. (Idaho, for example, has passed more than 70 exemptions to its open records law.) Such exemptions typically include the following:

- ▶ Ongoing criminal investigations
- ▶ Personnel matters, including hiring, discipline and firing
- ▶ Real estate and appraisal matters involving government property
- ▶ Juvenile criminal records
- ▶ Adoption and welfare records

This means, then, that the citizen—as well as the media professional—should have generally unrestricted access to such information as minutes of government committees, commissions, districts and councils;

government budgets and expenditures; police and court activity, including indictments and affidavits for search warrants; motor vehicle registrations and driving records; and property assessment records.

All this may seem to present a rosy picture to the information gatherer. However, in reality the process is studded with obstacles, as some government officials look for new ways to restrict the use of open records laws. For example, it took a dogged fight by reporters for the Charlotte (N.C.) *Observer* to get the University of South Carolina to reveal the lavish spending practices of its president. The Lakeland (Fla.) *Ledger* had to sue to get a sheriff to provide records on his office's activities. And in an example related to one of our master searches, researchers and reporters in Georgia, Florida and New York have encountered stiff resistance in getting information on child abuse deaths, whereas Colorado has been much more open. The lesson here is that for open records laws to work, both citizens and the media must press for their rights—to "remind" public officials of their obligations under the law and to take the conflict to court if necessary.

Media professionals should be thoroughly conversant with their states' open records laws and with the judicial and administrative interpretations of them. These laws are part of states' statutes, codes or consolidated laws. State newspaper publishers associations, law schools and the offices of state attorneys general are excellent sources for this information. Wisconsin media have set an excellent example with their creation of a Freedom of Information Council, which coordinates research and response to violations of records and meetings laws. In addition, there are at least 20 state freedom of information (FoI) telephone hot lines.

This may come as a surprise to the information gatherer, but government officials and employees often need to be educated or at least "reminded" about the provisions of a state's open records law. With this in mind, the media professional should always do the following:

1. Ascertain a government's understanding of and response to the law.

2. Press for a proper and reasonable opportunity to inspect records that should be open under the law.

3. Seek a reasonable and speedy appeals procedure in case of a denial of access.

4. Where applicable, ask for the imposition of reasonable fees for searching and copying.

State open meetings laws

Although all states have statutes mandating public access to most government meetings, the range of coverage and the amount of exemptions vary widely. In addition, the use of the so-called executive or closed session appears to give the media information-gathering rights not available to the average citizen and provides an opportunity for government abuse. Let's examine the general nature of these laws first.

The assumption underlying most of these laws is that a public body must discuss its business in public, with certain statutory exemptions. Bodies that create laws and policy, whose actions have a fiscal impact on the public, normally are covered by these laws. This coverage obviously includes state legislatures (but not necessarily their committee meetings), city councils, school boards, county commissions—even the local mosquito abatement district! On the other hand, most of these laws do not apply to appointed advisory bodies, to government groups and to private groups to whom a state or local agency may have contracted services.

These laws specify certain exemptions from a public meeting, with the stipulation that although *discussion* on exempted matters can be held in private, any *decision* on those matters must be made in a public meeting. These exemptions include the following:

- ▶ The hiring, disciplining or firing of a public employee
- ▶ Labor negotiations
- ▶ Real estate appraisals and pending transactions involving a government body
- ▶ Discussion with the public body's legal counsel on legal strategy or pending litigation
- ▶ In certain jurisdictions, deliberations of parole and workers' compensation boards

Examine your state laws carefully to discover which groups and proceedings are exempt from the statute, and which items can be discussed in the executive or closed session. Again, the office of state attorney general (state's attorney in some jurisdictions) will be helpful in providing guidance as well as published opinions about such closures of meetings.

The executive session is a curious compromise. In some states the media are permitted to attend a closed meeting with the understanding that they will not reveal the content or the nature of the discussions. The general public, however, is excluded from these sessions, which sometimes may be as little as a five-minute "recess" in a four-hour open meeting.

The benefit is that the media can serve as a watchdog and alert the public to any improperly called executive sessions. As in the case of open records disputes, some arguments over the executive session make their way into the courtroom. Consider this scenario that illustrates a problem with the closed session:

A reporter attends a regular meeting of a county commission. She remains while the commission excludes the general public from a 15-minute closed portion to discuss assessment problems with a large body of real estate that provides property tax revenues. The reporter properly sees this as an area that should be *publicly* discussed—it doesn't really relate to property acquisition—so she objects to the proceedings, and with the support of her editor, she reports on these proceedings. In retaliation the commission bans her from the next closed session; when she won't leave that session, the commissioners have her arrested for trespassing and disturbing the peace. Her publisher, furious, sues the commission and asks for a court order to restore closed session access. To consider its new legal problem, the commission—you guessed it—holds a closed session, to which the reporter obviously is not "invited."

The media must monitor meetings that are improperly called—those held privately, those called without proper public notice (as specified in the statutes), and those that skirt the law with such creative contact as a telephone conference call connecting elected officials. Not surprisingly, several states now have legislation prohibiting such surreptitious electronic contact. As a general strategy the information gatherer should question every attempt to close any portion of a meeting and be alert to any meeting called without the notice required by statute.

Federal laws of access

Although our Constitution clearly provides for a large measure of free expression, it does not specify any guaranteed right of access to federal government information. Earlier statutes relating to specific agencies and presidential executive orders may have provided some small measure of access, but it took the 1966 passage of the Freedom of Information Act (FoIA) to provide a direct path for citizens to obtain information not specifically exempted by this legislation. One example: The FoIA made possible the release of a 541-page FBI file on former U.S. Supreme Court Justice Potter Stewart; the material revealed, among other things, that Stewart was rejected for a job with the FBI after law school because his mother had been a member of the League of Women Voters. It's noteworthy that users of the FoIA are not always media professionals; state and local governments have used it to discover needed information, as in 1990 when Washington state's Ecology Department pressed the U.S. Energy Department for documents about a 1-million-gallon wastewater spill at the Hanford nuclear facility.

This act, amended in 1974, 1976 and again in 1986, mandates the federal government to make available to anyone records, documents and proceedings in any form (including computer tapes) that are in the public interest. As with similar state laws, this act provides for exemptions; the federal legislation has nine:

► **Information classified or kept secret to protect national security.** Much of this exemption is based on the president's ability, through executive order, to have information classified. This has always been a highly restrictive exemption, but actions taken during the Reagan administration created even more difficulties, as presidential directives ordered previously unclassified or declassified material to be reclassified and therefore out of the reach of the public and the media. However, thanks to a 1974 amendment, courts may inspect classified documents in order to rule on whether those records have been properly classified or whether they should be open to public scrutiny. As it stands today, however, it wouldn't be unusual to obtain a document released by the CIA with these authorized deletions under exemption 1:

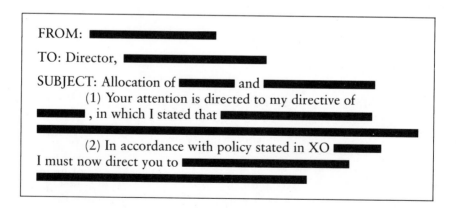

► **Internal personnel rules and practices of a federal agency.**
► **Material exempted by other statutes.** This covers a broad range of materials, such as Social Security, veterans' benefit, patent and

Census Bureau records. Contact with the FoI officer of a federal agency and bureau can provide more background on the nature of these exemptions.

▶ **Confidential trade and financial information.** The main thrust here is the government's attempt to protect the competitive position of businesses and to prevent serious financial harm that could arise from improper disclosure. However, criminal actions against these businesses generally are accessible.

▶ **Inter- or intra-agency material generally only available to parties in litigations with that agency.** Known as the "executive privilege exemption," in which records and documents related to an agency's decision-making process are withheld from public view, this exemption gives agencies a wide latitude—although media organizations have been successful in pressing their case that the public good outweighs a narrower need for protection of discussions that led to an agency action.

▶ **Personnel and medical files.** Obviously, this exemption attempts to protect the privacy of individuals who may have information on them in federal files. Agencies and courts must determine whether the release of this information would constitute an invasion of privacy not necessary for the public good.

▶ **Investigatory records compiled for law enforcement purposes.** This exemption and the national security exemption lead to the most serious erosion of the FoIA. However, this exemption does have validity when it is properly invoked—for example, to protect the safety of law enforcement personnel or to guarantee a fair trial for a criminal defendant. But like the corresponding state exemption, this proviso can be a too-convenient excuse not to release embarrassing information on agency actions and performance. In seeking this type of information, the information gatherer must get specifics on why the info request has been denied; "it's an ongoing investigation" is not a sufficient justification.

▶ **Information used in the supervision and regulation of financial institutions.** Before the savings and loan crisis of 1990, this exemption was used to protect financial institutions from the fallout over controversial financial reports submitted to and written by federal agencies. The multibillion-dollar scandal has proved that the media were not carefully tracking a rapidly deteriorating situation and were not pressing for greater details on the financial health of these institutions. Obviously, this is an exemption that will face greater resistance in the future.

► **Geological and geophysical information about wells, oil deposits and water resources.**

These exemptions are broader than those prescribed by many state public records laws. Journalist Carl Stern, himself an attorney, has observed what he terms a "10th exemption." He calls it an "I don't want to give it to you so I won't give it to you exemption." * And writing in a 1988 issue of the *Bulletin of the American Society of Newspaper Editors,* journalist James Derk contends that some federal officials abuse these exemptions; however, he says that persistence pays off: "I've used the act approximately 50 times and obtained information of page-one caliber several times. But it's more frustration than glory. And I can't help but think that there are some federal officials out there who know it."

Using the FoIA

Let's assume that you are researching federal investigations into and oversight of weight-loss products, and you are discovering a lack of documentation and reports about such investigations. What should you do? Here is a possible procedure:

1. Consult both the *U.S. Government Manual* and, with the help of a government documents librarian, the *Federal Register* to learn which agencies and boards deal with your issue and which reports must be filed by these groups.

2. Examine such publications as *Congressional Quarterly's Federal Regulatory Directory, CQ's Washington Information Directory* or the *Federal Staff Directory* to get names, addresses and phone numbers of FoI officers and public information officers for these agencies.

3. Draft your request to the agency's FoI officer. Be as specific as possible, and attach any information that will aid the search. Note that you may request a reduction and waiver of any search and copy fees.

---

* For a fascinating look at how bureaucrats have learned to stifle the FoIA see "Trashing the FoIA," *Columbia Journalism Review* (Jan.–Feb. 1985); 21–28.

4. If you do not receive a response within 10 days of the agency's receipt of your request, you should call the FoI officer to get his or her timeline for responding. (Agencies often will say they are severely backlogged.) If that is unsatisfactory, you should consider sending an appeal letter.

5. At this point you may be making some progress; if not, you should contact the 24-hour FoI hot line at 1-800-F-FOI-AID, sponsored by the Reporters' Committee for Freedom of the Press. If that group's suggestions don't work out, you may have to file suit in federal district court to force the agency's hand. If your (or your organization's) suit is successful, the law entitles you to collect reasonable attorney fees as well as other litigation costs.

It is hard to dispute that the FoIA is burdensome and frustrating. In truth, conducting inquiries and writing appeal letters to FoI officers can be an involved, time-consuming process. But consider where the media and the public would be without such legislation. Despite the various assaults on this act, the *presumption* of public access is a great victory—and we must build on it.

Federal open meetings legislation

Known as the 1976 Government in Sunshine Act, this is an extremely diluted version of the weakest state open meetings law. It applies to only 50 or so boards and agencies appointed by the president, and their compliance with the law is spotty at best. Suffice it to say that an open meeting in the federal bureaucracy is the exception rather than the rule.

When information gathering becomes harmful

The information gatherer bears a heavy responsibility in collecting information and disseminating it through the media. The following areas involve both law and ethics; they can inflict great damage on others—and be costly to the information gatherer as well: defamation, invasion of privacy, conversion and breaking of confidences.

Defamation

Defamation is a "tort" under our law—it harms because it injures one's good name and can be financially damaging to the individual. Although court decisions are constantly modifying the law of libel, the charge to the information gatherer is to ensure that the published material is true and that it is not being disseminated maliciously. In recent years, courts have placed the burden of proving the falsity of published information on the party initiating the lawsuit. However, many of these lawsuits are decided by juries, and judgments against media organizations often are measured in the millions, not thousands, of dollars. This is a high price to pay for sloppy or incomplete information gathering.

In addition to provable truth in the absence of malice, several other protections against a costly libel judgment exist:

- ▶ **Fair comment.** This generally ensures that statements of opinion will be protected; however, such statements must be on matters judged to be in the public interest and must not take on the assertion of fact. This protection makes it difficult for civil action to be taken against editorial commentary on, for example, a negative review of a public artistic performance.

- ▶ **Qualified privilege.** This complicated protection generally holds that material published in the course of reporting on public meetings and material that is part of the "official" record (such as a city council meeting or a criminal trial) are protected from libel judgments. When a city councilor alleges in an official meeting that a licensed garbage hauler is defrauding the public, a true report of what was said would not be held libelous. This doctrine allows the media great protection in freely discussing the public business—even to the point of publishing the embarrassing truth of a prominent citizen arrested for shoplifting, and even if it turns out that the charges are later dropped (which also should be reported, of course).

Invasion of privacy

Does the information you gather and publish deal with truthful but embarrassing or hurtful facts about someone—facts not seen to be in the public interest? Have you trespassed, intruded into a person's truly private moments or appropriated material that does not belong to you? If so, you may face an invasion of privacy lawsuit. Such cases are not as plentiful as libel actions, and that is in part due to the lack of clarity of and precedent in privacy law.

The weight of public interest, newsworthiness and private moments must be balanced in these cases. Two cases, 40 years apart, which illustrate this test, involve both writing and photography. The first case centered on a woman who was a voracious eater but who was still losing weight. Contrary to her wishes, a national magazine wrote about her medical condition and went so far as to send a photographer into her hospital room to take a rushed photo. In this case the magazine lost a privacy suit and had to pay a substantial financial settlement. In the second case a Florida newspaper carried a story and a photograph about an unclothed woman fleeing a motel room where her ex-husband had been holding her hostage. In this case the newspaper prevailed in court because the photograph was taken on public property and the incident, which was a public record because of the criminal act, obviously had high public interest value.

Conversion

Obtaining and using information that belongs to others without their permission can be not only an invasion of privacy but an illegal act as well, especially when it can be proved that the information gatherer knew the material was acquired illegally. While this is a matter of both common sense and morality, an argument certainly can be mounted that the use of purloined documents (as in the celebrated Pentagon Papers case of 1971) can be for a greater public good.

Breaking of confidences

A central tenet of information gathering is that sources sometimes will require—and should receive—anonymity. This creates the following problems: (1) If the information is not true, the information gatherer has only an unattributed source to offer to the public; (2) if the information gatherer cannot promise confidentiality, a valuable piece of information—perhaps an important key to a puzzle—will be lost; and (3) government is not usually sympathetic to the need for a confidential source, especially in a criminal action when a defendant's fair-trial rights conflict with the information gatherer's First Amendment rights.

In recent times the issue of confidences has been related to contract law. Two Minnesota newspaper reporters allegedly had offered a PR executive confidentiality for his information on the early arrest record of a political candidate (his client's opponent). However, the newspapers' editors overruled the reporters' pledges and published the name of the source on the grounds that this was an important public issue. When this information was published, the PR exec lost his job. He sued, alleging a breach of contract. The lower court upheld the exec's claim, but it was overturned on appeal. Nonetheless, it sent a message to the information gatherer that there may be some contract issues in force in matters of confidentiality.

Legal protections for the information gatherer

Do people who gather information as their profession have more rights than the average citizen? Do they have the right to protect confidential sources from disclosure? Can they be protected from the common law doctrine of "everyman's evidence," which compels every citizen to offer information that could help a criminal defendant's fair-trial rights? In other words, do information gatherers have a "shield of privilege" that protects them from court subpoenas, search warrants and contempt citations?

The answer is both complicated and controversial, although most observers would agree that the media professional has been granted greater rights than those guaranteed to the "average" citizen. For example, 28 states have given some form of statutory privilege to journalists.* Defenders of this privilege cite the media's watchdog function, saying that the information gatherer must be protected in order to expose wrongdoing and provide information helpful to the public. A 1990 Georgia law states that journalists are protected from being forced to reveal "any information, document or item prepared in the gathering or dissemination of news." However, most of these types of laws give only a "qualified privilege"—that is, they collapse when courts rule that disclo-

---

*As of 1990, the following states had some form of shield legislation: Alabama, Alaska, Arizona, Arkansas, California, Colorado, Delaware, Georgia, Illinois, Indiana, Kentucky, Louisiana, Maryland, Michigan, Minnesota, Montana, Nebraska, Nevada, New Jersey, New Mexico, New York, North Dakota, Ohio, Oklahoma, Oregon, Pennsylvania, Rhode Island and Tennessee.

sure is necessary because the information sought is not obtainable from any other available source. Some would argue that this really means that very little privilege exists; however, the various state laws have "educated" the courts into giving greater latitude to the media in the gathering and dissemination of information deemed helpful to the public. Such a qualified privilege has especially helped to limit courts' approval of search warrants that would examine materials gathered in the reporting process. It certainly has eliminated what the media have called prosecutorial fishing expeditions. Unfortunately, such privilege has traditionally been based on a narrow view of what constitutes a journalist or media professional. The Oregon Shield Law is a good model; it covers any "person connected with, employed by or engaged in any media of communication to the public . . ."

The information gatherer obviously appreciates the protections given to the media. However, such protection does not preclude a sense of professional responsibility. For example, is the use of a confidential and unattributed source a matter of laziness? Could the same information, properly attributed, have been obtained? Can the information that is being protected be corroborated? Ethics and professionalism must guide you here. If your position is correct—if you are providing information in the public interest and if you have not obtained this information illegally—you deserve protection from subpoena, search and seizure and compelled testimony. Fight for that right.

An issue of fairness

Our society does not legislate ethics. Beyond its broad statutory authority, our society does not enforce fairness. Such fairness is part of our educational models, peer pressure, market forces and professional standards. Some of our media industries have codes of ethics; groups such as the Society of Professional Journalists, National Association of Broadcasters and Public Relations Society of America have widely publicized codes of conduct. However, these codes are not enforced. This criticism reveals a basic irony about the U.S. media system: It is unconstitutional to license journalists, but the system is harassed because of its inability to control the conduct of its members.

Clearly, an ethical system must be in place in the media. Our gathering and dissemination of information have profound effects on people and institutions. We must *presume* a need to be fair, to have honest concern for our sources and for our audience. We must protect the integrity of our media institutions. As examples, we must question our motivations and actions in the following situations:

▶ Cooperating with the police by publishing a false story in order to help capture a criminal

▶ Knowingly appropriating private or stolen records in the information-gathering process

▶ Agreeing to provide confidentiality and to use unattributed sources because it makes the information-gathering task easier

▶ Caving in to advertiser pressure by not pursuing an in-depth story on, for example, the harmful effects of tobacco products

These examples are not hypothetical. In every case there are multiple episodes of these ethical breaches by the media. While these cases have not resulted in legal action, they have tainted the image of media professionals who bear a special responsibility to their public.

Being "fair" does not have to result in bland information gathering. Solid media work should be aggressive, but it doesn't have to be unnecessarily intrusive. Whatever your information search, you should be guided by the principle that an enlightened society is a progressive one; you should also never forget that our media must be responsible in order to be effective and respected.

Glossary of Sources

This is an alphabetized listing of key sources in information gathering. It is broken down into the following categories: one-stop basic references; general periodical indexes; specialty indexes—arts and humanities, biography, business and media, law and ethics, science and social sciences; government sources; and online databases. As you gain more experience with your researches, add to this glossary when you encounter other helpful, accessible sources.

ONE-STOP BASIC REFERENCES

Academic American Encyclopedia   An excellent recent encyclopedia, it features concise articles and bibliographies accessible through a good index in the final volume.

The Encyclopaedia Britannica World Atlas International   This authoritative work includes topographic and political maps, comparative tables and country-by-country summaries, as well as the usual maps.

Encyclopedia Americana   A useful general encyclopedia, it is noted for its articles on American places, even small ones, and on American organizations and institutions.

Facts on File   A weekly compilation of significant news events of the day, *Facts on File* records world events as reported in a number of metropolitan newspapers (from 1940 to present). The facts are recorded day by day but are quickly accessible through various cumulative indexes.

Information Please Almanac   A yearly compilation of facts and figures, this highly readable almanac includes numerous graphs and charts as well as special descriptive articles on the year's developments in selected fields.

The New Encyclopedia Britannica   This most famous and innovative of encyclopedias contains detailed scholarly articles with an international orientation. The index, a series of 10 volumes, serves not just as an index to the set but also as a quick reference for those looking for a simple fact.

Oxford English Dictionary   The language's most wonderful, most detailed guide, specializing in the derivation and history of words, is now out in its second edition. Also available on CD/ROM.

Rand McNally Commercial Atlas   Annually updated, it includes large, clear maps and is noted for its detailed treatment of the United States.

Statistical Abstract of the United States   A digest of data collected by the federal government's statistical agencies, this book is an information gold mine. Charts and tables concerning virtually every aspect of American life provide rich details (and citations to original documents).

The Times Atlas of the World   This famous five-volume set published by the *Times* of London is known for both the accuracy and the beauty of its maps.

Webster's Third New International Dictionary   This is one of the best unabridged dictionaries of the English language.

World Almanac and Book of Facts   This invaluable and justly famous reference is a yearly compendium of facts, figures, lists, charts and miscellany.

GENERAL PERIODICAL INDEXES

Magazine Index   Available in microform, CD/ROM and online versions, this is the best way to find articles published in consumer magazines. From familiar publications like *Time* to the more exotic *Archery World*, this tool indexes more than 400 popular magazines in a wide variety of fields. The only hitch: The index dates back only to 1977.

National Newspaper Index   Accessible on microfilm and online, it indexes articles, news reports and other editorial content from the *Chris-*

tian Science Monitor, *Wall Street Journal*, New York *Times*, Washington *Post* and Los Angeles *Times*.

Newsbank   This is a monthly service that both indexes (in book form) and provides (on microfiche) articles from more than 400 of the nation's larger daily newspapers. It is ideal for researching in libraries that do not have good newspaper holdings.

Newspapers, by Name   A variety of newspapers have their own indexes, the most ubiquitous of which are the *Washington Post Index*, *Index to the Christian Science Monitor*, *New York Times Index* and *The Times* (London) *Index*. Many other newspapers around the country, including the newspaper in your own community, may also be indexed, both formally and informally.

Poole's Index to Periodical Literature   This guide indexes periodicals published from 1802 through 1908.

Readers' Guide to Periodical Literature   The old standby for periodicals research, this guide has been eclipsed by the far more inclusive, easier-to-use *Magazine Index*. It is, however, necessary for periodicals research dating before 1977, when the *Magazine Index* picks up. *Readers' Guide* dates back to 1900 and indexes about 175 general-interest publications.

Specialty Indexes

ARTS AND HUMANITIES

Art Index   It indexes magazines, museum bulletins and annuals devoted to architecture, archeology, painting, sculpture, ceramics, graphic arts, photography and film.

Biographical Dictionary of Film   More encyclopedia than dictionary, this beautifully written reference book contains critical essays on 900 international film directors, producers and actors.

Cambridge History of American Literature   An authoritative history with index volume, this is a companion set to the British version, *The Cambridge History of English Literature*.

Dance Encyclopedia   A combination of brief articles and long, signed pieces, this encyclopedia covers dancers, dances and dancing with special attention to native folk dance.

Dictionary of Events   This is a handy reference for pinpointing historical events from 5000 B.C to 1936.

Encyclopedia of American History   One of the best single guides to the events of American history, this book is organized both chronologically and topically.

Encyclopedia of Philosophy   Almost 1,500 signed articles summarize and analyze the philosophies of every era in this comprehensive, multivolume set.

Encyclopedia of Religion and Ethics   A comprehensive work with extensive bibliographies, this multivolume set includes articles on all religions, ethical systems and movements, religious beliefs and customs, philosophical ideas and moral practices.

Encyclopedia of World Art   This 15-volume set includes more than 7,000 full-page plates and hundreds of essays on all of the visual arts.

Encyclopedia of World History   A one-volume reference to historical events anywhere in the world at any time in history, this handy work consists of a series of outlines from prehistoric times to 1964.

Encyclopedia of World Literature in the 20th Century   In addition to articles on individual authors, this three-volume set includes entries on movements, genres and national literatures.

Guide to Historical Literature   Covering the entire field of historical writing, this guide offers extensive bibliographies as well as brief histories of periods and biographies.

Guide to the Performing Arts   This is an index of articles on theater, television and dance.

Handbook of Denominations in the United States   A quick guide to the histories and doctrines of more than 200 religious denominations.

Music Index   This monthly subject index covers articles in more than 200 music-related periodicals published in the United States and abroad.

Oxford Companion to Music   A collection of more than 10,000 articles, this reference tool covers the history, composition, performance and performers of music.

Oxford Companion to the Theatre   This encyclopedia includes articles on actors, producers, dramatists, individual theatres and theatre history.

The Philosopher's Index   This is a quarterly index to almost 100 U.S., British and other foreign periodicals in the field.

Reader's Encyclopedia to American Literature   A single-volume reference tool, this includes articles on writers, writings, literary movements and groups, and fictional characters, both U.S. and Canadian.

Yearbook of American Churches   A quick guide to data on religious bodies, this includes information on church membership, organizations, agencies, theological seminaries, colleges and universities, and religious periodicals.

BIOGRAPHY

American Medical Directory   This register of U.S. physicians lists each doctor's name, address, medical school, specialty, type of practice and year of licensing.

American Men and Women of Science   This reference tool offers brief biographical summaries of the lives of notable physical, biological, social and behavioral scientists.

Biographical Dictionaries and Related Work   A comprehensive list of biographical reference works, this guide includes more than 5,000 listings.

Biography and Genealogy Master Index   This indexes more than 3 million biographical sketches in hundreds of biographical dictionaries. A supplement adds another million citations.

Biography Index   Published quarterly, it indexes biographical material found in current English-language books and 1,500 periodicals, for notables both alive and dead.

Contemporary Authors   Continually updated, this multivolume reference tool includes biographical sketches of both famous and obscure living authors. Personal information, education, jobs and publications are included.

Current Biography   A good, basic source for biographical information on anyone prominent in the news of the day, this reference tool is published annually. Photographs often accompany the entries.

Dictionary of American Biography   Accurate, concise entries profile prominent deceased Americans.

Directory of American Scholars   This guide includes biographical sketches of thousands of college and university professors.

The New York Times Obituary Index   This easy-to-use index pinpoints obituaries published in the *Times* through 1968, when the *Times* discontinued the service.

Who's Who in America   This biographical dictionary offers brief sketches of notable living Americans. It is a poor reference source for notable American women (see *Who's Who of American Women*).

Who's Who in American Politics   With more than 12,000 biographical sketches of political personalities, this reference work covers a wide range of current political figures, including local and minor officeholders and party officials.

Who's Who of American Women   To make up for the conspicuous lack of women in *Who's Who in America*, the same publisher offers this female-only volume with biographical sketches of notables in a variety of fields.

BUSINESS AND MEDIA

ABI-INFORM   A CD/ROM system, it indexes and gives abstracts for more than 800 business periodicals. Provides sources for a period of five years. Also available as an electronic database.

Bacon's Media Directories   This multivolume set (*Publicity Checker for Newspapers and Magazines*, *Media Alert* and *Radio/TV Directory*) is a bible for the public relations practitioner. Issued annually, with looseleaf updates during the year.

Broadcasting Yearbook   Annual listing of television and radio stations and cable organizations, with key staffers. Excellent updates on changes in telecommunications policy. Also provides a history of broadcasting and its regulation.

Business Index   This is a microfilm service that goes back only to 1979. It indexes more than 800 business periodicals. On a microform reader machine, it covers only the most recent three-year period.

Business Information Sources   Edited by business librarian Lorna Daniells, this is easily the most comprehensive and detailed narrative of its kind. Good breakdown by business category.

Business Periodicals Index   This is a print index that covers more than 300 business journals. Although it does not offer the breadth of coverage of *Business Periodicals Index*, it does provide citations that go back to 1958.

Corporate and Industry Research Reports (CIRR)   An annual microfiche set of approximately 25,000 research reports on businesses, written by analysts and economists at leading investment firms. Indexed by industry type, company name and investment firm.

Directory of Companies Required to File Annual Reports with the Securities and Exchange Commission This is an annual SEC report that shows the range of publicly held firms in the United States. All government depository libraries and many reference rooms carry this publication.

Directory of Corporate Affiliations A valuable annual publication of the National Register Company, it helps you discover the actual ownership of subsidiary companies. Indexed by company, states and standard industrial code. The *International Directory of Corporate Affiliations* helps you track firms owned by foreign companies.

Editor and Publisher International Yearbook This is an annual directory of daily and weekly newspapers published in the United States and Canada, with briefer listings for some European publications. Good listings of key staff and of production information.

Encyclopedia of Associations The best available listing of non-profit groups and associations in the United States. Gives names of key staffers and of the organization's publications.

Encyclopedia of Business Information Sources Edited by James Woy and published by Gale. Regularly revised, it lists reference sources, indexes and abstracts, databases, research centers and bibliographies on more than 1,100 business categories.

Gale Directory of Publications and Broadcast Media It replaces the *IMS* and *Ayer Directory of Publications*. This annual three-volume set covers a wide range of periodicals (except most newsletters), radio and TV.

McGraw-Hill Dictionary of Modern Economics This is a regularly updated compendium of business terms, presented in clear, concise language. An excellent first stop. Also recommended: *The MIT Dictionary of Modern Economics*.

Million Dollar Directory This five-volume service contains information on more than 160,000 publicly and privately held U.S. businesses that have a net worth of more than $500,000. It lists, among other things, directors, officers, divisions and sales volume.

National Trade and Professional Associations of the United States It provides a wide range of information on trade groups and labor unions. A much more specialized service than the *Encyclopedia of Associations*.

O'Dwyer's Directory of Corporate Communications   Lists almost 4,000 firms with sales, PR functions and PR budgets. Also helpful is *O'Dwyer's Directory of Public Relations Firms*, which lists 1,800 firms and their clients.

Predicasts F&S Index   Offers separate indexing for U.S., European and other international business publications. The U.S. index covers company, product and industry information from more than 750 business publications. The U.S. index goes back to 1960.

Q-Data   A St. Petersburg–based microfiche service that distributes most SEC reports on larger publicly held corporations. Records only go back to 1980. Has a print index.

Standard & Poor's Register of Corporations, Directors and Executives   This is a three-volume series that covers more than 50,000 U.S. companies. A more narrow service than the *Million Dollar Directory*. Has an *Ultimate Parent Index*, which covers subsidiaries, divisions and affiliates.

Standard Directory of Advertisers   Annual directory of major firms that advertise their products and services. Lists key corporate staff, including public affairs directors. Shows ad expenditures and ad agencies of record.

Standard Directory of Advertising Agencies   Alphabetical and geographical listing of major advertising agencies, their staffs, their accounts and ad expenditures by medium.

Standard Rate and Data Service   A multivolume set that provides production, audience, costs and personnel data on U.S. newspapers, magazines and broadcast media. It is heavily used by media buyers but is helpful to others in creating a more detailed picture of a medium's operations. Also see listing under "Social Sciences."

Thomas' Register of American Manufacturers   A well-indexed listing of products made by more than 100,000 U.S. businesses. Categories include business name, product type and brand name.

Wall Street Journal   Indexed regularly by both the *WSJ* and the *Newspaper Index*, this five-day daily business newspaper is clearly the best of the daily business publications. Issues are indexed back to 1950.

LAW AND ETHICS

Black's Law Dictionary   A classic, in-depth reference (regularly revised by West Publishing) that provides detailed definitions, relevant case citations and pronunciation guides. Directed to the legal professional, but enormously helpful.

Current Legal Index A recent (begun in 1980) but well-used monthly index to more than 700 legal periodicals. Effectively arranged by author and subject. Appears to have gained favor over the older and more traditional *Index to Legal Periodicals.*

Ethics in Action A periodic (approximately every three months) newsletter on ethical issues in the government, business and media, published by the Josephson Institute. JI also publishes a quarterly magazine, *Ethics: Easier Said Than Done.*

Federal Communication Law Journal Known as the *Federal Communication Bar Journal* before 1976, this thrice-yearly review is published by the UCLA Law School. It focuses on telecommunications and cable policy issues as well as on such diverse issues as copyright and reporter privilege.

Fineline A recent (begun in 1989) newsletter on journalism ethics, published 10 times annually by one of the former owners of the Louisville *Courier-Journal.*

Fundamentals of Legal Research A tremendously helpful compendium on the legal process, legal periodicals and the tracking of legal decisions. A must-read "encyclopedia" for anyone who needs to understand our legal machinery and its processes. (Note: Look for recent Jacobstein editions, not the earlier Pollack versions.)

Index to Legal Periodicals This monthly index of 500 or so periodicals reaches back to 1908, so it provides a good starting point for historical research. Some attempt has been made in recent years to be more competitive with the *Current Legal Index* in the choice of periodicals and subjects cited.

Legal Research Index A microfilm and electronic database form of *Current Legal Index.* No citations available prior to 1980.

LegalTrac The CD/ROM form of *Current Legal Index.* Updated monthly.

Lexis See the "Online Databases" section.

Media Law Reporter Published quarterly by The Reporters Committee for Freedom of the Press. Excellent review and analysis of FoI, confidentiality, copyright, libel and privacy issues. Also provides media alerts on access issues.

News Media and the Law A weekly looseleaf (and bound annually) reporting service on media law decisions by federal and state courts and by administrative agencies. Excellent topical index.

WESTLAW   See the "Online Databases" section.

West's Legal Desk Reference   Another "must" source. Among other things, it is a delightful plain-language dictionary of legal terms. Good bibliographic leads on research in legal topics as well as on laws of every state and of many countries. Good tips on legal search strategies.

SCIENCE

Applied Science and Technology Index   Published monthly, it indexes more than 200 of the top U.S. and British scientific and technical periodicals.

Asimov's Biographical Encyclopedia of Science and Technology   Compiled by prolific science and science fiction writer Isaac Asimov, this volume includes biographical sketches of more than 1,500 scientists from ancient times to the present.

Biological Abstracts   Offering both citations and summaries of research, this index covers biology, basic medical sciences, microbiology, immunology, public health and many other related subjects.

Chemical Abstracts   An efficient guide to research in the field, this index lists both citations and summaries.

Dictionary of Physics   This reference tool offers brief entries on a wide variety of applied and general physics topics.

Dorland's Illustrated Medical Dictionary   This standard reference contains almost 2,000 pages of medical terms.

Encyclopedia of Biological Sciences   A comprehensive guide to the broad field of biological sciences, this reference tool is designed for intelligent non-experts.

Encyclopedia of Physics   A detailed index guides you to specific information in this broad field. Many of the articles include bibliographies.

The Harper Encyclopedia of Science   An authoritative but readable reference, this book offers illustrations, tables and charts as well as entries written by experts.

Index Medicus   The most comprehensive guide in book form to journals in the medical sciences, this index is issued monthly and cumulates annually. (See *MEDLINE* in the "Online Databases" section.)

McGraw-Hill Encyclopedia of Science and Technology   A 15-volume set that includes more than 7,000 articles, this reference tool offers comprehensive coverage of the physical, natural and applied sciences.

Physicians' Desk Reference   Known as the *PDR*, this annually published volume lists more than 2,000 prescription drugs with information on dosage, effects and precautions.

Psychiatric Dictionary   Terms in psychiatry and allied fields are defined in brief articles.

Science and Engineering Reference Sources   A convenient guide to a variety of reference tools (indexes, periodicals, histories, handbooks, dictionaries), this book covers science in general and mathematics, physics, chemistry, astronomy, geology, biology, engineering and medicine.

Scientific and Technical Societies   A directory of societies, this volume contains information about the history, aims, membership, research funds, awards and publications of some 1,000 groups.

Van Nostrand's Scientific Encyclopedia   More than 16,000 science, engineering, mathematics and medical terms are explained.

SOCIAL SCIENCES

The American Political Dictionary   This reference work contains definitions and important information on general topics such as civil liberties, the legislative process and foreign policy.

American Universities and Colleges   A survey of U.S. higher education, this book contains a few broad articles on educational issues as well as an information-filled directory of universities and colleges.

Book of the States   Published biennially, this reference contains general articles on state government and many tables of statistical data on all the states.

Current Index to Journals in Education   More than 300 education and education-related journals are indexed monthly.

Dictionary of Anthropology   This reference tool defines terms and their origins and offers brief entries summarizing the field.

Dissertation Abstracts   Updated monthly, this is a guide to most all Ph.D. dissertations completed at U.S. colleges and universities. Full citation and a several-paragraph summary are included.

Education Index   Indexing books, pamphlets and some government publications as well as journal articles, this guide concentrates on material related to teaching, educational trends and administration.

Encyclopedia of Education   International in scope but primarily concerned with all levels of education in the United States, this multivolume reference work contains more than 1,000 signed articles.

Encyclopedia of Psychology   This book contains more than 5,000 entries written by authorities in their respective fields.

Encyclopedia of the Social Sciences   A comprehensive encyclopedia of the whole field, this multivolume work includes long, signed articles by specialists along with extensive bibliographies.

Encyclopedia of Social Work   Both an encyclopedia and a directory, it includes articles on social work and related topics, as well as biographies of those prominent in the field.

ERIC   This guide to reports on education research is available in CD/ROM and online forms. (See the "Online Databases" section.)

Handbook of Communication   Thirty researchers have contributed to this collection of review articles on the processes and effects of communication.

International Yearbook of Education   Published by UNESCO, this annual offers information on the condition of education in more than 80 countries.

The Literature of Political Science   This broad-based guide directs the researcher to periodical indexes, abstracts, book reviews, U.S. government and UN publications and other sources.

McGraw-Hill Dictionary of Modern Economics   More than a dictionary of terms, this reference work includes bibliographies of books and periodical articles.

A Modern Dictionary of Sociology   This work defines terms and concepts in sociology and other social sciences.

Political Handbook and Atlas of the World   Published annually, this tool gives information about the population, area, capital, government system, political leaders and press for every country.

Psychological Abstracts   Classified by subject, this reference tool indexes and abstracts books, journal articles, dissertations, monographs and reports.

Public Affairs Information Service Bulletin   Published weekly, *PAIS* is a subject guide to periodicals, pamphlets, documents and other material related to public administration, international affairs and social conditions.

Sociological Abstracts   This source indexes and abstracts a wide range of periodical literature dealing with sociological topics.

Sources of Information on the Social Sciences   An extensive guide to sources in sociology, psychology and other social sciences, this book offers detailed bibliographies and annotated lists of reference works.

Standard Education Almanac   A compilation of statistical data related to education, this annual offers material on enrollment, financing, degrees and other subjects.

Standard Rate and Data Service Publications   SRDS publishes more than a dozen prodigious collections of facts and figures about the mass media, including information about virtually all publications that accept advertising.

GOVERNMENT SOURCES

American Statistics Index   Published monthly by the Congressional Information Service, this index abstracts statistical publications from a wide variety of federal sources, including the Census Bureau. Its international version is *International Index of Statistics.*

"Blue Books"   The state equivalent of the *U.S. Government Manual.* Variously titled and almost always published by the state's secretary of state, these are wonderfully detailed manuals on state organization and functions. Good listing of key officials, with biographies.

Book of States   Published biennially by Council of State Governments. Good background articles and statistics on states and their government organization.

Congressional Directory   Issued every two years, this source provides biographical information on members of Congress, including their committee assignments. Some information on key aides also provided.

Congressional Index   This comprehensive index is a good record of all bills for a specific congressional session. An excellent source for tracking the history of a bill. Indexed by sponsor and subject over a two-year period.

Congressional Information Service Index (CIS/Index)   A highly reliable index and abstract to most congressional documents, including hearings and reports. Indexed monthly, with indexes cumulative up to five years.

Congressional Quarterly   This non-government publication gives excellent analysis of congressional action. Good for legislative history and background. CQ also publishes an annual almanac of congressional action on bills.

Congressional Record   Published every day that Congress is in session. Everything said on the floor of Congress (while in session) and everything that a member of Congress wants to insert finds its way into the *Record.*

Congressional Record Index Published daily while Congress is in session, it compiles all congressional action (except committee meetings and hearings) as well as material inserted out of session by senators and representatives. Indexed weekly by subject and member of Congress.

Congressional Staff Directory Detailed information (and phone numbers) for office and committee staffs.

County and City Data Book Published as a supplement to the Census Bureau's annual *Statistical Abstract of the United States*. Excellent statistical information on local government operations, including finances, labor, housing and health care.

CQ's Federal Regulatory Directory Published by *Congressional Quarterly*, this is a detailed source for experts and contacts in the 13 largest regulatory agencies. Offers briefer profiles for about 100 other agencies.

CQ's Washington Information Directory Nicely organized by subject area, this can put you in contact with 5,000 information sources in the legislative and executive branches of the federal government.

Federal Register Published every working day, this is a thick, if somewhat tedious, record of activity of federal regulatory agencies. Good listing of meetings and announcements of forthcoming regulations.

Federal Register Index Published by CIS, this is an indispensable source for tracking activities, programs, meetings and proposals of federal regulatory agencies. Indexed weekly.

Federal Staff Directory This lists key staffers of the executive branch, including cabinet-level departments and certain independent agencies. Also has biographies of top officials. Listings include job title, office address and phone number.

Federal Yellow Book Quarterly listing, by federal agency and department, of officials, staffers and their phone numbers. Does not provide information on staffers of legislative and judicial branches. Published by Washington Monitor.

Foreign Broadcast Information Service A compilation of political, military and economic information collected by the Central Intelligence Agency from both authorized and clandestine media. Organized in eight volumes by world region.

Government Reports, Announcements and Index (GRA&I) Offered in index and abstract form every two weeks, this source provides access to scientific and technical studies published by federal agencies and their contractors. An excellent source for tracking government-sponsored research.

Government Research Centers Directory   A broad-based guide to government and government-sponsored research in, among other things, the sciences, agriculture, business and education.

Guide to U.S. Government Publications   This energetic, annual source is helpful for a general overview of subjects and titles of publications in all three branches of government. Includes agency and title index.

Index to U.S. Government Periodicals   A helpful guide to material in approximately 200 federally published magazines and journals. Indexed quarterly by subject and author.

Monthly Catalog of U.S. Government Publications   Easily the most comprehensive source of federal publishing activity, this catalog is available in print, CD/ROM and electronic database form. Indexed monthly, with abstracts.

Monthly Checklist of State Publications   A well-indexed listing and abstract of all state publications received by the Library of Congress. (Note: All states maintain catalogs or directories of their publications as well.)

Municipal Yearbook   Published annually by the International City Managers Association. An excellent source for background and statistics on cities of all sizes. Key officials listed.

National Directory of State Agencies   Now published annually, this provides a good breakdown of agency function by states. Lists phone numbers of key officials.

The State and Local Government Political Dictionary   Last issued in 1988 by Jeffrey Elliott, this is an excellent "translation" of bureaucratic jargon. It is especially helpful in the area of economics and finance. Good discussion of organization of counties, towns and special districts.

State and Local Statistics Sources   An extensive annual listing of government and private data by the ubiquitous Gale Research Co.

United Nations Documents Indexes   Called *UNDOC* since 1979, and *UNDEX* from 1973 to 1978; unfortunately, indexing is very scattered prior to 1973. In general, a reliable source for all major UN documents. (UNESCO indexing is found in *UNESCO List of Documents and Publications.*)

Urban Affairs Abstracts   A weekly publication of the National League of Cities, this is a comprehensive abstract of more than 800 periodicals that deal with a wide variety of urban issues.

U.S. Government Manual   Broad information on activities and organization of all three branches of the federal government. An excellent starting point for some background briefing. Listing of key officials.

Want's Federal-State Court Directory Shows organization and jurisdiction of all federal and state courts. Provides names and phone numbers of key court administrators. Published annually.

The Yearbook of Education Law Published by the National Organization on Legal Problems of Education, this is a good analysis of current legal issues in education. Includes such topics as taxation, discipline, liability and teacher certification.

ASSOCIATIONS

American Association of School Administrators
1801 N. Moore Street
Arlington, VA 22209
(703) 528-7000
    —publishes *The School Administrator*

Council of State Governments
Iron Works Pike
P.O. Box 11910
Lexington, KY 40578
(606) 252-2291
    —publishes *The Book of States*

International City Management Association
777 N. Capitol, N.E.
Washington, DC 20002
(202) 289-4262
    —publishes *Public Management* (monthly) and the annual *Municipal Yearbook*, and offers an Urban Data Service

League of Women Voters of the U.S.
1730 M Street
Washington, DC 20036
(202) 429-1965
    —publishes the bimonthly *National Voter*

National Association of Counties
440 First Street, N.W.
Washington, DC 20001
(202) 393-6226
    —publishes the biweekly *County News*
(Note: Each state has a county association as well.)

National Conference of State Legislatures
1050 17th Street
Denver, CO 80265
(303) 623-7800
   —publishes *State Legislatures* (10 times a year)

National League of Cities
1301 Pennsylvania Avenue, N.W.
Washington, DC 20004
(202) 626-3000
   —publishes *Nation's Cities* (weekly)
(Note: Each state has a city association as well.)

National School Boards Association
1680 Duke Street
Alexandria, VA 22314
(703) 828-6722
   —publishes *American School Board Journal* (monthly)
(Note: Each state has a school board association as well.)

ONLINE DATABASES

ABI/INFORM A weekly updated database covering all phases of business management and administration, ABI includes citations and abstracts of articles in about 550 publications.

AGELINE This bibliographic database focuses on the social-psychological aspects of middle age and aging, including such issues as family relationships and demographic trends.

AGRIBUSINESS U.S.A. Updated every two weeks, this database provides informative abstracts from 300 trade journals and government publications.

AIDSDRUGS, AIDSLINE, AIDSTRIALS Produced by the National Library of Medicine, these databases effectively cover three important aspects of the AIDS crisis. AIDSDRUGS is a factual database that lists drugs currently being evaluated in the fight against the disease. AIDSLINE is a bibliographic database of journal articles, government reports, monographs, theses and other publications on the disease. AIDSTRIALS lists all clinical trials of substances being tested for use against AIDS and related complexes.

AP NEWS Updated daily and dating back to 1984, this database provides the full text of national, international and business news from the Associated Press (available 48 hours after it is originally transmitted).

BRS   A database vendor, BRS offers 150 different databases but specializes in information on medicine, pharmacology and life sciences.

BUSINESS DATELINE   This database includes the full text of articles from regional business publications from throughout the United States and Canada. Updated weekly, it covers trends as well as information about small companies, start-ups and family-owned or closely held firms.

BUSINESSWIRE   This continuously updated database contains the unedited text of news releases from more than 10,000 news sources, including companies, public relations firms, government agencies, political organizations, universities and research institutes.

CANCERLIT   A storehouse of information on research about the disease and its cures and experimental therapies, this database contains abstracts from a wide variety of journals.

CCRIS   This is a factual databank listing and describing substances that have been tested for their cancer-, tumor- or mutation-causing properties. The tests were published in a wide variety of scientific journals; test results were reviewed by cancer experts.

CHILD ABUSE AND NEGLECT   Provided by the National Center on Child Abuse and Neglect, this database includes bibliographic references as well as project and program descriptions related to the issue of child abuse and neglect.

CONSUMER DRUG INFORMATION   This full-text database contains in-depth descriptions of some 250 drugs, which make up more than 80 percent of all prescription drugs. Side effects, precautions, dosage and an explanation of how the drug works are part of each entry.

D&B—DUN'S ELECTRONIC YELLOW PAGES   This massive database contains addresses, phone numbers and descriptions of more than 8 million businesses and professionals throughout the United States.

Database, Database Searcher and Online   These three magazines, designed to serve the needs of online professionals, offer timely information about new and updated databases as well as insights into the online information industry.

DATATIMES   This is a full-text database of stories published in a variety of large and medium-sized daily newspapers.

DIALOG   The largest vendor of online databases, DIALOG gives its users access to more than 350 separate files, many of which are pertinent to the journalistic researcher.

Directory of Online Databases Published quarterly, this reference book keeps close tabs on the online industry, offering descriptions and updates of thousands of databases.

DISCLOSURE Based on information in reports filed with the Securities Exchange Commission, this database provides in-depth information on more than 12,500 publicly held companies.

DOE ENERGY The database of the U.S. Department of Energy, this is one of the world's largest sources of literature references for all aspects of energy, including solar, geothermal, nuclear, wind, fossil and tidal.

THE EDUCATIONAL DIRECTORY This database contains extensive economic and demographic information about public and private schools (kindergarten through graduate school), public school districts and public libraries.

ENERGYLINE Covering books, journals, congressional committee reports, conference proceedings, speeches and statistics from a wide variety of disciplines, this database specializes in energy issues and problems.

ENVIROLINE This database indexes and abstracts more than 5,000 international publications reporting on all aspects of the environment. Updated monthly, it covers periodicals, government documents, industry reports, meeting proceedings, newspaper stories, films and monographs.

ERIC With records dating back to 1966, this database covers significant education research reports and indexes more than 700 periodicals pertaining to all aspects of education.

FAMILY RESOURCES This database provides bibliographic and biographical coverage of research in a variety of fields (psychology, sociology, education, medicine) as it relates to the family. With references to articles from more than 1,200 journals, books, government publications and newsletters, this file covers issues such as marriage, divorce, family trends and relationships, sexual attitudes and behavior, and therapy.

HEALTH PERIODICALS DATABASE Updated weekly, this database provides indexing and full text of journals covering a broad range of health subjects and issues.

LEGI-SLATE This database covers all bills and resolutions introduced into the U.S. Congress from 1978 to the present and all federal agency regulations since 1981. It also contains the status of every bill pending in Congress, voting records of each member of Congress on every bill and schedules of committee hearings and lists of witnesses.

LEXIS Equivalent to a moderate-sized law library, this massive database provides full-text coverage of federal court cases and case law for all 50 states, along with selected statutes and regulations.

MAGAZINE ASAP Updated weekly, this database provides indexing and full text for 120 publications chosen from the almost 500 publications indexed by *Magazine Index* (also available online).

MEAD DATA An online vendor specializing in full-text databases such as LEXIS and NEXIS.

MEDLINE With more than 6 million records, MEDLINE covers virtually every subject in the broad field of biomedicine. This database indexes articles from more than 3,000 international journals, including not just the myriad of medical specialties but dentistry and nursing as well.

MOODY'S CORPORATE NEWS This database offers current, comprehensive coverage of business news and financial information on 13,000 publicly held U.S. corporations. Updated weekly, it includes financial data like earnings reports and balance sheets.

NEWSEARCH Good for the current month only, this database is a daily index of more than 2,000 stories, articles and reviews from 1,700 top U.S. newspapers, magazines and periodicals. It also includes indexing and abstracts from more than 100 local and regional business publications as well as the complete text of PR Newswire.

NEXIS This database contains the full text of more than 125 newspapers, magazines, newsletters, wire services and broadcast transcripts.

OCCUPATIONAL SAFETY AND HEALTH Covering all aspects of occupational safety and health including hazardous agents and unsafe work environments, this database includes citations to more than 400 journal articles.

POPLINE Offering bibliographic citations to journal articles, monographs and technical reports, this database covers issues related to populations, demographics and family planning.

PR NEWSWIRE Continuously updated, this database contains the complete text to news releases prepared by companies, public relations firms, trade associations and government agencies at all levels. Almost three-quarters of the records are business/financial in nature.

PTS MARKETING AND ADVERTISING REFERENCE SERVICE This daily updated database contains information about the marketing and advertising of consumer goods and services. Information about what agencies are in charge of which campaigns, what media are used and what strategies are employed is abstracted from advertising industry journals and newsletters, trade and business journals and major newspaper columns.

SCISEARCH This is a multidisciplinary index to the considerable literature of science (pure and applied) and technology, containing all the records published in *Science Citation Index* plus additional sources.

TRAC An acronym for Transactional Records Access Clearinghouse, this is a computer service that taps into the massive data stores of federal enforcement agencies, analyzes the information using sophisticated software and distributes it in understandable and graphic form to members of the news media.

TRADE AND INDUSTRY INDEX Updated weekly, this huge database provides comprehensive coverage of business journals relating to trade, industry and commerce. It includes citations and selective abstracts to material in more than 300 trade and industry journals as well as 1,200 additional publications.

UPI NEWS This database contains full-text news stories carried on the United Press International wire. Stories are fed in daily, 48 hours after they have been transmitted on the wire.

VU/TEXT Produced by the Knight-Ridder company, this full-text database includes all Knight-Ridder newspapers plus a variety of other dailies.

WASHINGTON PRESSTEXT Updated daily, this database provides the complete text of White House and State Department news releases, policy statements and background information. Also included are in-depth historical and economic profiles of more than 170 nations.

WESTLAW The chief competitor to LEXIS, this database focuses more deeply on case law in all 50 states.

WILSONLINE This is the online version of a variety of important indexes produced by the H. W. Wilson Company, including *Readers' Guide to Periodical Literature, Education Index, Business Periodicals Index, Applied Science and Technology Index* and *Book Review Digest*.

Index